FERPA Clear and Simple

FERPA
Clear and Simple

The College Professional's

Guide to Compliance

Clifford A. Ramirez

JOSSEY-BASS
A Wiley Imprint
www.josseybass.com

Published by Jossey-Bass
A Wiley Imprint
989 Market Street, San Francisco, CA 94103-1741—www.josseybass.com

Jossey-Bass books and products are available through most bookstores. To contact Jossey-Bass directly call our Customer Care Department within the U.S. at 800-956-7739, outside the U.S. at 317-572-3986, or fax 317-572-4002.

Jossey-Bass also publishes its books in a variety of electronic formats. Some content that appears in print may not be available in electronic books.

Library of Congress Cataloging-in-Publication Data

Ramirez, Clifford A., 1952-
  FERPA clear and simple : the college professional's guide to compliance / Clifford A. Ramirez.
      p. cm.
  Includes bibliographical references and index.
  ISBN 978-0-470-49877-4 (pbk.)
  1. United States. Family Educational Rights and Privacy Act. 2. Student records--Law and legislation--United States. 3. Privacy, Right of--United States. 4. College administrators--United States--Handbooks, manuals, etc. I. Title.
  KF4156.5.A3281974A2 2009
  342.7308'58--dc22
                                        2009023239

Printed in the United States of America
PB Printing

10 9 8 7 6 5 4 3 2 1   FIRST EDITION

The Jossey-Bass
Higher and Adult Education Series

Contents

Visual Aids and Sidebars

CHAPTER FOUR

for
DAN GEPHART

Preface

A New Approach and Perspective on FERPA

WHENEVER I CONDUCT training on the federal Family Educational Rights and Privacy Act (FERPA), I find it especially beneficial for participants to include the three basic components I identified in "Managing the Privacy of Student Records," my very first FERPA workshop for UCLA.

First of all, since the goal of FERPA training is to educate ourselves on the federal regulations to ensure our policies and practices are in compliance, we need to establish a common ground for our language and terms. Even the structure of the regulations themselves acknowledges this important point, providing an extensive introductory section (34 CFR §99.3) to define terms used within the regulatory text. Many of us in education are familiar with terms such as *student, attendance*, and *academic record*. Not all of our definitions agree, however, prompting the need to be specific about our terms before we can go on to talk about legal requirements that incorporate and depend upon the specific meanings of those terms.

The second portion of FERPA training is the exposition of the requirements and parameters of FERPA—what we, as education officials, are required to do to remain in compliance with the regulations. I used the word

---

ELEMENTS OF SUCCESSFUL FERPA TRAINING

- Review of definitions and language
- Understanding and application of FERPA
- Developing FERPA decision-making abilities

parameters here because FERPA, like other regulations, is not composed exclusively of mandates—those unequivocal, binding requirements that dictate compliance. Recognizing the differences and traditions that exist among institutions and educational communities, FERPA includes areas in which only general guidance on establishing policy and practice is given. These are the permissions within FERPA—those actions that are *permitted, but not required* of education officials.

While it is important to understand the language, intent, and requirements of the regulations, it is also important for education officials to develop their own decision-making abilities. To be effective in carrying out their academic or student services functions, administrators need to develop an expertise in using FERPA to make decisions in their everyday transactions at the school, college, university, or other educational setting. The use of examples or scenarios for developing such expertise is extremely helpful in this regard.

Having provided FERPA training since 2000, I have become aware of yet another area that has become increasingly important and vital to include in our educational initiatives about FERPA: context. And by context, I mean that education officials—especially those who develop policy or make public relations decisions about student information—need to recognize and maintain a big picture appreciation of the economic, political, and philosophical dialogue in which—and from which—FERPA arises.

For many of our frontline staff, it is probably sufficient for them to be cognizant of the federal regulations and the institutional policies that impact how they perform their work. With adequate training and ongoing professional development, our people become empowered to take initiative in making decisions that ensure efficient and effective student services. But for managers and policy makers, a broader and deeper understanding of FERPA and privacy is required. Managers may be confronted with situations for which there are no clear directions, either in office policy or in FERPA. Policy makers, who essentially set the standards for institutional practice, cannot successfully create procedure or provide direction without some understanding and appreciation for the broader context of privacy from which FERPA emerges.

Participants in my FERPA workshops have included admissions and recruiting professionals, information technology technicians and programmers, financial services accountants, and customer services staff. Some of these individuals do not have responsibilities that explicitly involve the disclosure of information from education records. Yet, the perception exists, and rightfully so, that FERPA touches all aspects of education records, and there is a hunger for knowledge and guidance on records management concerns such as records creation, access, disclosure, retention, and destruction. While FERPA may not address these issues directly, the privacy concerns and the political dialogue from which FERPA arose give considerable and reliable guidance on many of these areas.

In this book, I have endeavored to provide a new, more comprehensive approach to FERPA for education officials throughout our colleges, universities, and other educational organizations. Education officials from the K–12 environment will also find much of the information in this book helpful, although the guidance offered in the application of the regulations is given with a focus on higher education.

With the incorporation of the extensive amendments proposed and incorporated into FERPA in December 2008, this book presents FERPA from the vantage point of a quote that has been a part of my own education and has often been ascribed to the great 13th-century thinker, St. Thomas Aquinas: "Intelligence is the ability to see implication."

In the pages that follow, I have attempted to summarize the thrust of the dialogue on privacy for education officials, highlighting some of the primary concerns and events that led to the codification of American legislation on privacy. This is not a legal history of privacy but rather an overview with a definite slant toward the concerns of privacy in education. Within that context, and prompted by the same predisposition for identifying implications, FERPA, infused by the extensive amendments of 2008, is explored in its language and terms, as well as in its application and guidance.

This book is not necessarily intended to be read cover to cover, although the chapters and unfolding of this presentation have been arranged with a definite intent and direction. For those readers interested in a specific aspect of FERPA or seeking guidance regarding the implications and requirements of the regulations, there are sufficient guideposts throughout the book for you to begin from any perspective or interest.

To assist in this exploration of FERPA, I will use three types of information summaries throughout this text.

- FERPA citations
- Visual aids
- Sidebars

The first instructional aid is the FERPA citation, direct quotes from the regulations themselves, including the specific regulatory reference. The FERPA citations, enclosed with a dotted-line border (as illustrated below), are presented because "legalese," or the language of the law, is often subject to interpretation. And interpretation may differ between individuals, attorneys, and even the courts. Providing you with the exact FERPA citation under discussion allows you to make your own assessment of the interpretations and guidance provided in this volume.

> The purpose of this part is to set out requirements for the protection of privacy of parents and students under section 444 of the General Education Provisions Act, as amended.
>
> §99.2

As an additional benefit, the complete text of the FERPA legislation is provided in Appendix I of this book.

Visual aids are meant to organize information in such a way as to facilitate your understanding or grasp of the material. If this were an in-person presentation, most of the visual aids would be PowerPoint slides accompanying the verbal presentation of this material.

In some cases, the visual aids are tables of information, organized for ease in understanding and contrast. But there are also other kinds of visual aids that are included throughout this volume, such as samples of disclosure language, excerpts from forms, and sample procedures. For consistency, visual aids are presented in boxes that are bound by a single, continuous line. An example of a visual aid is the one at the beginning of this Preface entitled "Elements of Successful FERPA Training."

The last type of instructional aid is the Sidebar. These summaries offer additional information regarding initiatives, organizations, entities, or individuals that are mentioned in the text. While not critical to understanding the information in the primary flow of the text, the sidebars are intended to elaborate on content and so encourage a deeper exploration or appreciation of the subject, people, or events depicted in these short reports. Sidebars are bound with a double-border. An example of a sidebar is the one entitled "FERPA Legislation" below.

Now, some readers may think all of this information too overwhelming and perhaps ultimately irrelevant. After all, I have been confronted in some of my workshops with the attitude that invariably cries, "Just tell me what I have to know. That's all! Just tell me what I have to know to get my job done and be in compliance." Indeed, my goal is to accomplish this mission—but, it is also more.

One of my primary values as an educator or trainer is to help participants develop the ability to make their own decisions, to become confident and

---

FERPA Legislation

In the canon of U.S. Law, FERPA is codified at 20 USC §1232g and assigned to 34 CFR §99.

The "USC" in the first citation refers to the U.S. Code. FERPA is cataloged at Title 20, Chapter 31, Subchapter III, Part 4, §1232g of the U.S. Code. The U.S. Code establishes the policy from which the regulations flow in the CFR.

CFR refers to the Code of Federal Regulations, the catalog of legislative literature approved and passed into law by the federal government. §99, or Part 99, is the particular section of the 34th index or volume that is specifically FERPA. Whenever text in the regulatory language refers to FERPA as a whole, it means 34 CFR §99 and may use the phrase "this part."

References to paragraphs or regulatory citations from sections of the CFR are often prefaced with the legal section icon: §. Once context within a particular CFR is established, as with 34 CFR §99, specific citations to language within the regulations may be indicated as simply §99 and the specific citation. Throughout this publication, direct quotes from the FERPA regulations are so listed.

---

empowered in performing their daily job responsibilities. That is the reason for this broader, more multifaceted approach to training about FERPA.

When I was facilitating Franklin Covey workshops, one of the quotes we often referenced came from the ancient Chinese philosopher Lao Tzu. He said this:

Give a man a fish and you feed him for a day;

Teach him how to fish and you feed him for a lifetime.

My goal is not just to tell you what you need to know right now to do a job and be in compliance with FERPA. My goal is to help you develop your own expertise about FERPA, to empower you with the knowledge and confidence to perform your academic and student services functions with assurance and confidence. Aware of the implications of both our actions and our decisions, we ensure that how we comply with FERPA echoes the spirit and the unique values and missions of our individual institutions.

Therein lies the excitement and joy of education and continuing professional development!

Clifford A. Ramirez

Cliff Ramirez & Associates

Cliffordramirez@aol.com

(909) 208–1452

Acknowledgments

NUMEROUS AUTHORITIES AND resources were consulted for the composition and compilation of content for this book. Some are resources that I have used consistently in my training and in the writing of my previous books. Most are listed in the Bibliography and Resources section of this book. However, there are a few that have been my primary sources for information and for inspiration in the development of this book.

Official legislative material from the U.S. National Archives and Records Administration, including the *Federal Register*, were the primary sources for the text of the regulations and of their amendments.

Other government websites, including those of the White House, Congress, and the U.S. Senate, were consulted for information regarding legislation, enforcement, and the historical background of legislative sponsorship. For the chronology of privacy legislation and initiatives, the Electronic Privacy Information Center (EPIC) and the Privacy Rights Clearinghouse yielded a wealth of practical information and further additional resources.

The U.S. Department of Education, specifically its website and the training efforts of LeRoy Rooker, former director of the Family Policy Compliance Office (FPCO), have been the primary foundation for information and resources on FERPA. Notably, it is the Department of Education which has jurisdiction for the interpretation and enforcement of FERPA.

Publications and the website literature of the American Association of Collegiate Registrars and Admissions Officers (AACRAO) and the Council on Law in Higher Education (CLHE) were consulted in the interpretation and application of FERPA.

Lastly, the questions and comments of colleagues at my training programs and through other consultations contributed to the development and expansion of the practical tools and guides for the application of FERPA.

About the Author

CLIFFORD A. RAMIREZ has worked in higher education for almost 20 years and is the founder and president of his own training and consulting company, Cliff Ramirez & Associates (www.pdrenterprises.net). The company, founded in 2004, offers higher education consulting in the areas of FERPA, registrar and student services, leadership and organizational development, and records management.

Working primarily in registrar operations, Cliff spent 14 years at UCLA. For two of his years at UCLA, Cliff assumed an additional part-time appointment as a staff welfare coordinator, becoming certified as a Franklin Covey facilitator and laboring in the areas of professional development, organizational climate, and staff representation. Cliff has also worked in the registrar's offices of both Pomona College and Antioch University Los Angeles. In addition, he was interim director of Admissions and Financial Aid at Antioch University Los Angeles.

Cliff has been active and visible in organizations such as the Pacific Association of Collegiate Registrars and Admissions Officers (PACRAO), the American Association of Collegiate Registrars and Admissions Officers (AACRAO), the Council on Law in Higher Education (CLHE), and the UCLA Administrators and Supervisors Association (ASA). He served as the 2003 president of PACRAO and was elected to multiple terms as ASA president. Cliff has been a member of numerous committees and editorial boards, most recently for CLHE's newsletter the *Regulatory Advisor*. Cliff has also served on the advisory board for LRP Publications' *The Successful Registrar*. Cliff is the founder of three prestigious institutes: the PACRAO Emerging Professionals Institute (EPI) in 2003, the ASA Leadership Development Institute in 1997, and the UC Management and Leadership (UCML) Conference in 1995.

In the year 2000, Cliff assumed the post of manager for Training and Communication Services in the Registrar's Office at UCLA. Charged with FERPA training responsibilities, Cliff created a four-hour workshop entitled "Managing the Privacy of Student Records" and went on to publish his textbook and the facilitator's guide for this workshop through LRP Publications. He has written two other books—*The FERPA Transition: Helping Parents Adjust to Higher Education Records Laws* (2004) and *Records Management in Higher Education* (2006), the latter in collaboration with colleague Linda Arquieta-Herrera. Most recently, he worked with attorney Aileen Gelpi on updates to *The FERPA Answer Book for Higher Education Professionals*.

Cliff is a regular presenter on FERPA at workshops, conferences, and other professional development events. Cliff has been featured in numerous national audio conferences, as well as in webinars and a training video.

A native of Southern California, Cliff attended the University of Notre Dame, from which he graduated cum laude with a B.A. in English. Cliff attended the Jesuit School of Theology at the Graduate Theological Union in Berkeley, California, while studying for the Roman Catholic priesthood. He worked in the banking industry for 12 years, in both Northern and Southern California, before coming to higher education.

Currently, Cliff is the FERPA expert for College Parents of America and on the advisory board for Docufide, Inc. He is a member of the Registrars and Enrollment Services Consulting for Colleges and Universities (RESCCU) team and is affiliated with Painted Dreams Ranch (PDR) Enterprises, the records management and customer services consulting company of colleague Linda Arquieta-Herrera.

FERPA Clear and Simple

Chapter 1

FERPA and the Regulatory Universe of Privacy

WHEN THE FEDERAL Family Educational Rights and Privacy Act (FERPA) was germinating in the legislative consciousness of Washington, the nation— and, indeed, the entire world—was immersed in an intense dialogue and heated debate about how to manage the explosion of information and data in every facet of government, business, and industry.

Who was keeping information about private individuals? How were they storing, maintaining, and releasing that information? What rights allowed them to do so? And what rights did private citizens have in this escalating inundation of unsupervised and unregulated data and information?

> *No one shall be subject to arbitrary interference with his privacy, family, home, or correspondence, nor to attacks upon his honor and reputation. Everyone has the right to protection of the law against such interference or attacks.*
> —UNIVERSAL DECLARATION OF HUMAN RIGHTS,
> *United Nations, 1948*

From the global and national discourse on privacy, legislation emerged in the United States that, however different in format from its European counterparts, sought to establish and ensure universal tenets for information and records management that would impact every sector of our society.

For the higher education community, FERPA has had the dominant impact. But as American society and campus operations have become increasingly complex, other legislation has affected institutional policy and procedure so that a thorough understanding and appreciation of the privacy debate is necessary to ensure comprehensiveness and compliance in our daily practice and work responsibilities.

Toward the Codification of Privacy Rights

The Constitution of the United States recognizes the privacy of United States citizens as an inalienable right, both explicitly and implicitly. The Fourth Amendment codifies the right of individuals "to be secure in their persons,

---

Wheaton v. Peters

Wheaton v. Peters, in 1834, is considered the first ruling by the U.S. Supreme Court on copyright. The case involved two reporters of the courts in Pennsylvania—Henry Wheaton and his successor, Richard Peters. Wheaton had compiled court rulings, arguments, and summations in a set of 24 volumes for use by attorneys. When Peters took over, he continued to provide the same service but streamlined the content of Wheaton's earlier work. Reduced to just six volumes of materials, Peters' less expensive work quickly became more popular than Wheaton's.

After Wheaton sued Peters in the Pennsylvania courts and lost, he appealed his case to the Supreme Court. The Supreme Court, however, upheld the lower court's ruling and, in essence, created legislation regarding copyright that set written work apart from patents for inventions and other creations. The Court upheld the property of writers but also held that individuals could not hold copyrights on the decisions and rulings of the court system.

---

houses, papers, and effects, against unreasonable searches and seizures" and goes on to set limits and specifications for such searches and seizures. Privacy advocates have also used the First Amendment right to free assembly and provisions in both the Ninth and Fourteenth Amendments to further base legal challenges supporting the privacy of individuals.

In 1890, attorneys Samuel Warren and Louis Brandeis, founders of the distinguished Boston law firm Nutter, McClennan, & Fish, published an article in the *Harvard Law Review* entitled "The Right to Privacy." In addition to coining the expression "the right to privacy," the article is considered the first publication to argue for individual privacy and to advocate for legislation that would provide legal protections and remedies against the invasion of privacy. Warren and Brandeis incorporated the phrase "the right to be let alone" in their text, quoting the 1834 Supreme Court case of *Wheaton v. Peters* and *A Treatise on the Law of Torts,* a 1888 textbook by T. M. Cooley. In these initial platforms on privacy, the contention was generally viewed as one between the private individual and government.

In fact, the dialogue on privacy has frequently focused on the relationship between government and private citizens. Historians often summarize the immigration to the New World as an escape from a European system that was attempting to fetter the private citizen and deprive him of personal and public freedoms. Against the prospect of such tyranny and control, the American Revolution was waged and a new nation forged.

As American society evolved, the fledgling nation would experience and be forced to deal with many of the same challenges that have faced governments since the dawn of civilization. With advances in industry, technology, and business practice, the privacy debate would arise again in a new context.

In the years following World War II, distrust and suspicion swelled across America in response to widespread government initiatives to conduct national census activities. The compilation of a massive database about private citizens raised fear and anxiety about the potential misuse of such data. European immigrants, in the shadow of the Holocaust and the attempted extinction of the Jews, were wary of government interest in ethnicity and religious affiliation. In truth, memories were still all too recent regarding the branding, stamping, and tattooing practices inflicted upon prisoners in the Auschwitz concentration camp complex. The post-World War II population of the United States included many, citizen and refugee alike, who had witnessed or escaped the crimes of Nazi Germany.

The introduction and use of any type of national identification system in the United States was an understandable cause for concern. After all, even in the United States, ethnic identification efforts had already been used to locate Japanese immigrants for relocation and internment during the Pacific conflict.

In the wake of World War II, Europe had quickly organized efforts to protect the privacy of citizens against big government. In 1970, the German centralization of computer records regarding citizens spawned the first privacy laws. Sweden passed the first national data protection law in 1973 and initiated a process to issue national identity (ID) cards. A similar initiative was launched in Great Britain as England centralized the issuance of national drivers' licenses.

As country after country embarked upon its own privacy legislation, it became apparent to the Europeans that national initiatives would soon impact international economic trade. A British company that had applied to produce magnetic stripes for Sweden's ID cards was denied the contract because in Sweden's evaluation, British law did not provide sufficient protections for the privacy of information about Swedish citizens. To facilitate trade and commerce among the European nations, an initiative was launched to establish international agreements on privacy, trade, and communication.

On January 28, 1981, the Council on European Convention for the Protection of Individuals with Regard to the Automatic Processing of Personal Data came together in Strasbourg, France, setting into motion the events that would lead to the first international law on data protection. The Data Protection Act was ratified and enacted on October 1, 1985, in France, Germany, Norway, Spain, and Sweden. Other Europeans countries would

---

Council of Europe

The Council of Europe was founded in 1949 with the objective of promoting and facilitating unity among the nations of Europe. The council's specific goal is developing throughout Europe "common and democratic principles based on the European Convention on Human Rights."

Headquartered in Strasbourg, France, the council comprises 47 member countries. The council also claims five observer countries: the Holy See, the United States, Canada, Japan, and Mexico.

The council's website is www.coe.int.

---

subsequently follow. Then, in 1995, the European Union's Data Protection Directive was adopted.

Despite the national and international legislative developments, however, it soon became apparent, through assessments and surveys conducted throughout Europe, that individual citizens remained unaware of their personal rights and protections. This was a tremendous concern for the Council of Europe, which had incorporated public education into its mission.

On January 28, 2007, the first Data Protection Day was held throughout Europe. Organized by the Council of Europe, the intent of the celebration was to commemorate the beginning of dialogue on privacy and individual protections and to educate citizens throughout the continent about their rights. Individual member nations were encouraged to determine, budget for, and sponsor educational and social events for their citizens. The council's website was used as an organizational base to compile a listing of events throughout Europe and to promote unity for the multinational initiative.

The Adoption of Fair Information Practices

With the exception of some European influences, the story of privacy in America took a somewhat different course.

It was a long time before the work of Warren and Brandeis would significantly impact legal thought in America. Despite foundations in the U.S. Constitution, privacy was essentially left to state and local courts, leading to inconsistencies across court jurisdictions. In many views, privacy was understood as a personal right, one that ends with the death of an individual and one that only generated legal action when an invasion of privacy was determined to have occurred. Because privacy was viewed as

---

Louis Dembitz Brandeis

Born in 1856 in Louisville, Kentucky, Louis Dembitz Brandeis was an attorney, Supreme Court Justice, and prominent advocate for free speech, privacy, women's rights, trade unions, and the minimum wage.

Attending schools in Louisville and Dresden, Germany, Brandeis graduated from Harvard University. He practiced law in Boston before being appointed to the U.S. Supreme Court by President Woodrow Wilson in 1916. He was the first Jewish Supreme Court Justice in U.S. history and was the leader of the American Zionist movement. In addition to influencing Wilson's New Freedom economic doctrine, Brandeis published two important works in 1914: *Other People's Money and How the Bankers Use It* and *Business–A Profession.*

Upon his death in 1941, Brandeis was cremated and his remains were transported to the Louis D. Brandeis Law School at the University of Louisville, where many of his personal files are archived. In 1948, Brandeis University was founded in Waltham, Massachusetts, and named in his honor.

---

a personal right, corporations and partnerships were judged to possess no particular right to privacy.

These premises would be challenged over the years through cases that would be heard by courts at every level. It was not until *Olmstead v. United States* that Brandeis would once again incorporate the phrase "the right to be left alone" in his legal arguments. From those 1928 proceedings, the first wiretapping case heard by the U.S. Supreme Court, concerns about privacy exploded, eventually expanding beyond mere protection against government inquiry.

In 1965, a Special Inquiry on Invasion of Privacy was convened by the U.S. House of Representatives. The House Committee on Government Operations examined a diverse variety of activities where the privacy of citizens could potentially be invaded and violated. The areas probed focused upon operations within the federal government, including the psychological testing of employees and applicants, the use of data from farm census questionnaires, and the confidentiality of federal investigations, employee files, and income tax returns. The committee's scrutiny extended to an examination of surveillance practices at government facilities, including electronic eavesdropping, mail deceptions, prying into private trash, and even to the existence of strategic peepholes.

Underlying those discussions in the mid-1960s was the emerging realization that, with the advent of computers and technology, the stage was being set for the formation of a national database on U.S. citizens. With personally identifiable information (PII) about individuals being systematically collected by a number of federal agencies, it would not be difficult or inconceivable to compile, collate, and index data to create extensive and comprehensive profiles about private citizens.

> *The real danger is the gradual erosion of individual liberties*
> *through automation, integration, and interconnection of many*
> *small, separate record-keeping systems, each of which alone may*
> *seem innocuous, even benevolent, and wholly justifiable.*
> —US PRIVACY STUDY COMMISSION (1977)

Agencies were already using social security numbers (SSN) as an index. Establishing the SSN as a "standard universal identifier" (SUI) would facilitate the creation of a national database and its speedy population

Social Security Numbers

The social security number (SSN) was established in 1936, when the New Deal Social Security Program was enacted through the Social Security Act (42 USC §405(c)(2)). Initially established as a means to track individual accounts within the Social Security Program, the number has since become a national identification (ID) number, beginning with its usage by the U.S. Army and the Air Force in 1969.

Initially, individuals did not need an SSN until the age of 14 or when an individual could first participate in the work force and file federal income taxes. By 1986, the minimum age was lowered to 5, since dependent children could be claimed on federal income tax forms. By 1990, age 1, or as soon as possible after birth, became the norm for procuring an SSN.

The nine-digit structure of the SSN is delineated AAA-GG-SSSS. The AAA, or area number, refers to a geographical region, not necessarily a state. By 1973, area numbers were based upon zip codes. The group number (GG) is used to provide natural breaks in blocks of allocated numbers. The SSSS is the serial number assigned to specific individuals. There are some number structures that are not used in the SSN. These include all zeroes in any one of the numbers groupings, numbers beginning with 666, and certain number sequences that have been set aside for advertisement purposes.

Social security accounts were established to provide for the economic welfare of citizens. The first laws for public welfare date back to the English Poor Law of 1601, which the colonists brought with them to the New World. In his last pamphlet, *Agrarian Justice,* Thomas Paine, in 1795, argued for the establishment of a public system to provide economic security for citizens. But the first systematic program was not devised until 1862 when legislation established the Civil War Pension Program, designed to care for soldiers after the war and for the widows and children of disabled soldiers. Despite numerous amendments through the early 1900s, the program was never extended to the general public.

As far back as 1862, company pension programs sought to address economic security for workers. The Alfred Dolge Company, a producer of pianos and organs, was one of the first to establish such a program. As late as 1932, however, less than 15% of the work force was covered by any type of pension program.

The Social Security Program began making its first payments in 1937, initially in single, lump sums to the beneficiary. In 1939, an amendment to the Social Security Act established the monthly payment system, which has been in use since 1940.

with vital and confidential information. No one could be sure about how much data sharing was occurring between agencies of the federal government. And given the fact that the government was comprised of numerous agencies, who would challenge the appropriateness of such information sharing, especially since it was all supposed to be one government?

The availability of information, questions about the transmission and access of data, and the security of information were issues that cried out for answers and raised concerns for many citizens. But in the early and mid-1960s, an organized platform for dialogue and activism was essentially nonexistent in the United States. A model would soon emerge from Europe, however, where international commerce would drive the discussion and compel the first privacy laws regarding personal information.

Concerns about privacy, databases, and information access continued into the next decade. As already mentioned, privacy became a global concern that expressed itself in different ways and in a variety of arenas—in medical, financial, commercial, and communications.

In Europe, Sweden took the lead with strategies and dialogue that evolved into the adoption of what became known as the Fair Information Practices. Privacy Commissioners were soon designated in a number of European countries, as well as in Canada, Australia, New Zealand, Japan, and Hong Kong.

The Fair Information Practices would strongly influence the development of privacy legislation in the United States. Among the privacy discussions taking place in the early 1970s was one that focused on the privacy of medical records in the wake of mounting computerization. A task force was convened under the direction of the U.S. Department of Health, Education, and Welfare (HEW) and, in 1973, it issued a report entitled "Records, Computers, and the Rights of Citizens."

The HEW report is significant in the development of and its influence on privacy legislation in the United States. Its achievements included the following.

- *Code of Fair Information Practices.* The report established a Code of Information Practices, based upon practices developed and established in Europe. This code set the standards and defined benchmarks for best practices in privacy legislation and records and information management.

- *Privacy Legislation.* The report recommended that Congress pass legislation to adopt the code for all organizations maintaining automated personal data systems. The recommendations included not only requirements for the documented specification of protections and safeguards but a mandate for annual disclosures of policy and practice to the public.

- *Restrictions on Using the Social Security Number.* Concerned with the potential of using the SSN to establish a standard universal identifier (SUI), the report recommended that the SSN should be used only where absolutely necessary or where existing legislation already required the use of the SSN. Further, the report stipulated that no citizen should be compelled to provide an SSN unless required by Congressional ruling.

All of these provisions directly influenced the passage of the Privacy Act of 1974, as well as the numerous privacy regulations that followed. Of prime importance was the codification of the Fair Information Practices, not only as a precursor to subsequent privacy legislation and records management initiatives but as a qualification of the United States' participation in the global economy.

The U.S. Code of Fair Information Practices

The 1973 HEW task force identified five key components in its Code of Fair Information Practices. A generation after their adoption, these practices may seem logical and self-evident. However, one must remember that the political, economic, and technological climate of the early 1970s was a very different landscape from that of our 21st century. The code not only influenced subsequent privacy legislation but provided a solid foundation for best practice and for determining policy and procedure in records and information management in nearly every U.S. industry.

A brief examination of the Code of Fair Information Practices will contribute to a deeper understanding of FERPA as well as provide some guidance for policy development strategies in all areas of college and university administration.

The first two Fair Information Practices are a prohibition against secrecy and a mandate to disclose the existence of a database and its contents to the population about whom the database is compiling information. Any entity that collects and maintains personally identifiable information about individuals must disclose to its clients and to the public the fact that information is being collected. Recordkeeping systems cannot remain secret or private. Individuals have a right to know that information is being kept about them—and, moreover, to know *what* information is being collected and how that information is being used.

The third tenet is designed to prevent secondary or "further disclosure" of collected information. Further disclosure refers to the release of information beyond the recordkeeper, beyond those authorized to access the

CODE OF FAIR INFORMATION PRACTICES

- *Database Existence.* A recordkeeping system that compiles and stores personally identifiable information about individuals must not be kept secret.

- *Primary Usage.* Individuals whose personally identifiable information is being collected and stored have a right to know what information is being kept and how it is being used.

- *Secondary Usage.* Individuals must be able to prevent recordkeepers from disclosing personally identifiable information about themselves without their consent.

- *Amendments.* Individuals must be able to correct or amend personally identifiable information that is being stored about them.

- *Security Protections.* Organizations that collect and store personally identifiable information about individuals must ensure that data will only be available for internal use and must take precautions to prevent the misuse of that data.

data, including the individual identified by the data. Entities that gather or receive data cannot use the information for anything other than for the purpose that was initially disclosed to the subjects of the data. In order to disclose information for any other purpose, the recordkeeper must first obtain the consent of the individual or individuals identified by the data.

Because nothing is perfect, and because inaccurate or incorrect data can easily make its way into any information system, individuals have a right to seek to amend the information that is being kept about them. This fourth practice implies that individuals must have some access to inspect the information that is being collected about them. Otherwise, how would individuals become aware of inaccuracies? More to the point, the code advocates distinct processes that allow individuals to request amendments to the content of records that are being maintained.

Lastly, recordkeepers have a responsibility to provide security protections for the data they keep. They must ensure that the information collected will only be used for the purposes disclosed. Further, they must take the necessary precautions to prevent the misuse, misappropriation, and unauthorized access of data. Initially, these security concerns focused on physical access. By the end of the 20th century, however, electronic access would create the need for technological and virtual protections as well.

All of these practices are represented in the Privacy Act of 1974 and are evident in subsequent U.S. privacy legislation, such as the Fair Credit Reporting Act and FERPA.

The Privacy Act of 1974

On the heels of the HEW report and the country's adoption of the Code of Fair Information Practices, both the U.S. House of Representatives and the U.S. Senate entertained separate and distinct legislative debates on privacy. Both were narrowly focused on the privacy of information that was being collected and maintained by agencies of the federal government. And both produced two somewhat different proposals for privacy in America.

HR 16373 was the proposal initiated in the House of Representatives, while S 3418 represented the Senate's effort. While the Senate bill was viewed as the more rigorous in its requirements, the House bill was criticized as harsher in its application of consequences or penalties. The House bill required that damages or penalties could only be assessed against the government if a violation was demonstrated as "willful, arbitrary, or capricious." But the House bill also proposed the creation of a Privacy Protection Commission to oversee the implementation and enforcement of its legislation.

> *The privacy and dignity of our citizens [are] being whittled away*
> *by sometimes imperceptible steps. Taken individually, each step*
> *may be of little consequence. But when viewed as a whole, there*
> *begins to emerge a society quite unlike any we have seen—a*
> *society in which government may intrude into the secret regions of*
> *a [person's] life.*
> —ASSOCIATE JUSTICE WILLIAM ORVILLE DOUGLAS

The bill that President Gerald Ford signed in December 1974, and which passed into law the following year, was a compromise between the proposals of the House and the Senate. The Senate passed the amended legislation, known as the Privacy Act of 1974, on December 17. It was ratified the next day by the House of Representatives.

The Privacy Protection Commission, originally proposed by the House bill, was reduced to a Privacy Protection Study Commission, with only advisory responsibilities. It had neither oversight nor enforcement authorities. In 1977, however, the commission published its "Personal Privacy in an Information Society" report, detailing its concerns regarding inadequacies of the Privacy Act of 1974. Among these was the definition of "system of records," which limited application of the act to systems in which data retrieval was accessed by name, SSN, or some other personal identifier. Further, public disclosure in the act was tied to publication in the government's *Federal Register,* which the commission judged too limited in its circulation and accessibility.

Features of the Privacy Act of 1974 included the following.

Application. The act applied only to certain agencies of the federal government and had no impact on state and local governments. Curiously enough, although the Office of the President was covered by the act, the act applied to neither the House nor the Senate.

Appeals for Amendment. Assuring individuals that they can seek to amend records, the act stipulated that if a request for amendment is refused, the recordkeeper must advise the individual of an appeal process and allow 30 days for an appeal to be submitted. Individuals may also provide a statement to the recordkeeper detailing their objections to any record and that statement must be retained and disclosed by the recordkeeper whenever the disputed record is disclosed.

Disclosures without Consent. The act detailed exceptions to its requirement of prior consent for further disclosure of information beyond the purpose for which the data was initially collected. Among the exceptions is one for "routine use" by government agencies, which critics claim has been abused over the years.

Retention Requirements. To ensure an audit trail, records of disclosures must be retained for a period of five years. With the exception of records detailing disclosures for law enforcement purposes, these records of disclosure must be made available for inspection whenever requested by the individual identified in the records.

Data Minimization. Agencies must maintain only those records that are "relevant and necessary" to accomplish their purposes. The intent was to prohibit the collection and maintenance of information for which the agency had no right or privilege to maintain.

Data Sharing Limitations. Agencies that share data must do so by written agreement, detailing purposes, legal authority, data matching practices, and other information relevant to the exchange of information. The agreement must be renewed every 18 months and must be made available to the public, the Committee on Government Affairs of the Senate, and the Committee on Government Operations in the House.

Right to Sue. Individuals can sue to have their records amended and can recover reasonable attorney fees and litigation costs from the United States government. Courts can also rule against agencies for any violation of other parts of the Privacy Act if the violation is determined to be "intentional or willful." In addition to reasonable attorney fees and costs, the act specified that individuals could recover no less than $1,000.

Section 1983: Right to Sue

Section 1983 of Title 42 of the U.S. Code has its beginnings in the Ku Klux Klan Act of 1871 and the Civil Rights Act of 1872. Requested of Congress by President Ulysses S. Grant, the legislation was enacted as an emergency measure against the growing racial violence and social unrest that struck the Southern states following the end of the Civil War.

More than a century later, Section 1983 continues to serve as the basis by which citizens enforce their Constitutional rights.

> Every person who, under color of any statute, ordinance, regulation, custom, or usage of any State or Territory or the District of Columbia, subjects, or causes to be subjected, any citizen of the United States or other person within the jurisdiction thereof to the deprivation of any rights, privileges, or immunities secured by the Constitution and laws, shall be liable to the party injured in an action at law, suit in equity, or other proper proceeding for redress.

Criminal Penalties. A number of criminal actions and penalties are defined. Government employees who knowingly and willfully disclose personally identifiable information may be found guilty of a misdemeanor and be fined up to a maximum of $5,000. Agencies may be fined up to the same maximum amount for failure to disclose the existence of their systems of records. In addition, the act provided that anyone who requests records under false pretenses may be found guilty of a misdemeanor and fined a maximum of $5,000.

Use of the SSN. No federal, state, or local agency can require anyone to provide a social security number, unless such disclosure is required by federal statute. Agencies that require individuals to provide an SSN must disclose by what legal authority the requirement is being made.

Oversight. The director of the Office of Management and Budget (OMB) was designated to have oversight authority for the implementation and enforcement of the Privacy Act of 1974.

U.S. Office of Management and Budget

The United States Office of Management and Budget (OMB) is the largest office within the Executive Office of the President of the United States (EOP) and is a cabinet-level office. It performs administrative responsibilities for the White House by overseeing the activities of the many federal agencies. The OMB gathers data for the President's annual budget as well as communicates with the agencies.

The OMB is run by six managers, all of whom are appointed by the President and approved by the Senate. Among the directors are the administrators of the Office of Information and Regulatory Affairs, the Office of Federal Procurement Policy, and the Office of Federal Financial Management.

The OMB's website is www.whitehouse.gov/omb.

Sector Approach to Privacy

Except for the adoption of the Code of Fair Information Practices, the United States embarked upon an approach to privacy that differed significantly from the European approach. Whereas European strategy consisted of comprehensive legislation and the national designation of privacy secretaries or ministers, the U.S. undertook what has been called a *sector approach* to privacy. That is, the development and enforcement of privacy standards in the United States is achieved through a mixture of federal, state, and local legislation as well as through self-regulation within the various sectors of business and industry.

Examples of Privacy Initiatives in the United States

Year	Legislation/Action	Focus
1968	Wiretap Act	Written, oral, and, later, electronic communications
1970	Fair Credit Reporting Act (FCRA)	Accuracy, fairness, and privacy of consumer credit information
1974	Privacy Act of 1974	Personally identifiable information collected and maintained by government agencies
1974	Family Educational Rights and Privacy Act (FERPA)	Privacy of student education records
1996	Health Insurance Portability and Accountability Act (HIPAA)	Portability of health insurance coverage and standards for communication of medical records
1996	Economic Espionage Act	Protection of trade secrets
1999	Gramm-Leach-Bliley Act, or Financial Modernization Act	Protection of consumer information held by financial institutions
2000	Safe Harbor Program	Framework of privacy standards for information exchange proposed to avoid interruptions in business between the U.S. and Europe
2001	Uniting and Strengthening America by Providing Appropriate Tools Required to Intercept and Obstruct Terrorism (USA PATRIOT) Act	Increased government authority to investigate and deter terrorism
2002	Homeland Security Information Sharing Act	Sharing of Homeland Security information with state and local entities
2002	Sarbanes-Oxley Act	Corporate financial reporting and accounting fraud
2003	Fair and Accurate Credit Transactions (FACT) Act	Amendments and enhancements to Fair Credit Reporting Act
2004	Identity Theft Penalty Enhancement Act	Aggravated identity theft established as a federal crime

Each facet of American enterprise has developed its own legislation to address specific issues within its unique operations. Federal regulations were established where economic and informational transactions involved either government recordkeepers or national and international business endeavors. State and local governments developed geographically specific policies and rules that, while limited to a defined jurisdiction, have also contributed to broader debates and inspired adaptations in arenas beyond their original applicability.

California was the first state to establish an Office of Information Security and Privacy Protection, a state agency charged with promoting and protecting the privacy of individual consumers. In 2003, the California Senate passed Senate Bill 1386 (SB 1386), called the California Security Breach Information Act or California Information Practice Act. SB 1386 is directed at all individuals and businesses that conduct operations in the state of California and who collect and manage personally identifiable information about consumers. The bill requires these entities to notify affected individuals whenever there is a breach of their information systems that compromises the personally identifiable information they maintain. Since the enactment of SB 1386 in California, other states have passed similar legislation protecting their own residents.

Another aspect of this sector approach to privacy regulation has been the development of professional associations and organizations to establish standards within their theater of operations and to provide collegial guidance for the promulgation of best practices and ongoing professional development. The American Medical Association (AMA), the American Dental Association (ADA), and the American Bar Association (ABA) are prominent examples of such profession-specific organizations. In some

---

California Office of Information Security and Privacy Protection

California Senate Bill (SB) 90 created the Office of Information Security and Privacy Protection (www.oispp.ca.gov/) in 2000. The office opened for business in 2001, with two distinct offices, each with a specific purpose.

- The Office of Privacy Protection was created to focus on consumer protections and to monitor consumer privacy.

- The Office of Information Security, which existed as part of the State Department of Finance, focuses on the privacy of data gathered and maintained by state government agencies.

Both divisions encourage adherence to fair information practices.

American Association of Collegiate Registrars and Admissions Officers

The American Association of Collegiate Registrars and Admissions Officers (AACRAO) is an international, nonprofit organization representing professionals in higher education admissions and registration offices. Founded in 1910 as the American Association of Collegiate Registrars (AACR), the association has grown swiftly from its initial group of only 24 higher education professionals.

AACR changed its name to AACRAO in 1949. By 2008, the association boasted 10,000 members from some 2,500 institutions in 30 countries. Across the United States, state and regional associations focus efforts in specific geographical areas.

AACRAO serves its membership in a variety of ways, providing professional development programs, annual conferences, and other events. Business activities also include publications and newsletters, consulting, and legislative interpretation and guidance.

AACRAO has also become a respected source for information on foreign education and evaluations. What began as a cooperative agreement with the U.S. Agency for International Development in 1964 eventually evolved into the creation of an AACRAO-AID Office and finally the Office of International Education Services.

AACRAO is headquartered in Washington DC. The Association's website can be found at www.aacrao.org.

fields, strategy-specific groups have arisen such as the American Society for Training and Development (ASTD) and the Association of Records Management Administrators (ARMA), now ARMA International. The list goes on and on.

Higher education has benefited from the work and contributions of such organizations as the National Education Association (NEA), the American Association of Collegiate Registrars and Admissions Officers (AACRAO) and its regional chapters, the National Association of College and University Business Officers (NACUBO), and the Council on Law in Higher Education (CLHE).

Common threads throughout the development of privacy legislation in the United States have evidenced the widespread impact and influence of the HEW's adoption of the Code of Fair Information Practices and the implementation of standards established for government recordkeeping through the Privacy Act of 1974. In many cases, their influences are direct and immediately apparent, utilizing language and practice that merely translates the original guidance to industry-specific protocols.

It is legislation, records management strategies, and basics of student services administration that finally come together in a national approach for the education sector in the Family Educational Rights and Privacy Act (FERPA).

Council on Law in Higher Education

The Council on Law in Higher Education (CLHE) is a nonprofit organization that provides a variety of resources to higher education leaders in the areas of government legislation, interpretation, and guidance. Founded in 1998 by attorney Daren Bakst, CLHE has published newsletters such as *The Regulatory Advisor* and, in 2004, a collaborative compendium entitled *Privacy in the 21st Century.*

CLHE's website can be found at www.clhe.org. The website includes links to various government branches and legislative bodies as well as extensive search tools for both federal and state government agencies and legislation.

Regulations for Student Records Privacy

In 1974, within the regular proceedings of the U.S. Senate, Senator James Buckley of New York proposed an amendment to the General Education Provisions Act (GEPA). The new section, sometimes referred to as the Buckley Amendment, was formally entitled "Protection of the Rights and Privacy of Parents and Students" and focused on safeguarding the privacy of education records. On August 21, 1974, President Gerald Ford signed into law the federal Family Educational Rights and Privacy Act (FERPA) or the Education Amendments of 1974.

In the canon of U.S. Law, FERPA is codified at 20 USC §1232g and assigned to 34 CFR §99.

The "USC" in the first citation refers to the U.S. Code. FERPA is cataloged at Title 20, Chapter 31, Subchapter III, Part 4, §1232g of the U.S. Code. The U.S. Code establishes the policy from which the regulations flow in the CFR.

"CFR" refers to the Code of Federal Regulations, the catalog of legislative literature approved and passed into law by the federal government. §99, or Part 99, is the particular section of the 34th index or volume that

---

James Lane Buckley

A one-time hopeful for the Republican presidential nomination, James Lane Buckley hails from New York City, where he was born in 1923. A Yale graduate, Buckley served in the Navy and later worked as a corporate director and vice president. In 1971, as a candidate of the Conservative Party of New York, he was elected senator and served until 1977. Senator Jesse Helms led a group of Republicans who encouraged Buckley to run for president, but the nomination that year went to Gerald Ford.

In 1982, Buckley was named President of Radio Free Europe and held the post until 1985, when President Ronald Reagan appointed him to the U.S. Court of Appeals for the District of Columbia. Buckley served as a federal judge until 2000.

In 1975, Buckley published *If Men Were Angels: A View from the Senate.*

is specifically FERPA. Whenever text in the regulatory language refers to FERPA as a whole, it means 34 CFR §99 and may use the phrase "this part" when referring to itself in its legislative entirety.

References to paragraphs or regulatory citations in sections of the CFR are often prefaced with the legal icon for paragraph or section: §. Once context within a particular CFR is established, as with 34 CFR §99, specific citations to language within the regulations may be indicated as simply §99 and the specific paragraph or line. For example, §99.2 was the citation quoted in the Preface. Throughout this publication, direct quotes from the FERPA regulations are so listed.

Once it was signed by President Ford, FERPA was set to go into effect on November 19, 1974. The new act, however, contained so many ambiguities that numerous questions and concerns about its implications and enforcement were raised—not only by the education community but by the bill's sponsors as well. Taking into account issues raised by institutions, students, and parents, Senator Buckley and his colleague, Senator Claiborne Pell, collaborated on and presented a "Joint Statement in Explanation of the Buckley/Pell Amendment." Passed on December 13, 1974, the Joint Statement amended the original Buckley Amendment and was made retroactive to FERPA's effective date.

As a privacy regulation, FERPA was designed to apply to both K–12 and postsecondary education. The language of the regulations reflects this applicability. But discussion continued about the application of privacy to the K–12 environment, identifying a need for even greater protections since the subjects of K–12 schools were minors. In 1978, the Protection of Pupil Rights Amendment (PPRA), or the Hatch Amendment, was proposed and

Claiborne de Borda Pell

Senator Claiborne Pell is best known to the education community for his efforts in the creation of the Basic Educational Opportunity Grants, or Pell Grants, which he proposed in 1973. A native of New York, where he was born in 1918, he served as its Democratic senator between 1961 and 1997.

A graduate of Princeton and Columbia, Pell went on to serve in the U.S. Coast Guard and the Coast Guard Reserve. For a time, he worked in the U.S. Department of State, serving in Czechoslovakia, Italy, and Washington, D.C. Upon retiring from the Senate, he was appointed as a delegate to the United Nations.

Pell was a strong supporter of education and was the primary force behind the bills that created the National Endowment for the Arts and the National Endowment for the Humanities. He was also an advocate of mass transportation, recognized by the renaming of Newport Bridge to the Claiborne Pell Bridge.

The Pell Center of International Relations at Salve Regina University is named in Senator Pell's honor. He passed away on New Year's Day, 2009.

Protection of Pupil Rights Amendment

The Protection of Pupil Rights Amendment (PPRA) is the privacy legislation at 34 CFR §98 and applies to the K–12 segment of education that receives funding from the federal government. Passed in 1978 and amended in 2002, the statute is, like FERPA, administered by the Family Policy Compliance Office (FPCO).

PPRA guarantees parental rights to involvement in the decision and policy-making process where surveys and nonemergency physical examinations of students are concerned. Local educational agencies (LEA) are required to notify parents of their policies on an annual basis at the beginning of the school year, disclosing their policies in regard to surveys, educational materials, and physical examinations. Notification within a reasonable time period must also be made whenever there are any changes in policies.

Parents are guaranteed rights under PPRA, including the right to inspect and review educational materials and surveys as well as the right to opt out of or remove their children from participation in any survey. The No Child Left Behind (NCLB) legislation amended PPRA to require parental consent before the administration of surveys that include questions about the student or the student's family in eight specific areas:

- Political affiliations and beliefs
- Religious practices or beliefs
- Mental and psychological problems
- Sexual behavior and attitudes
- Behavior that is illegal, antisocial, self-incriminating, or demeaning
- Critical appraisals of individuals with whom there are close familial relationships
- Privileged relationships—ministers, physicians, lawyers, etc.
- Income

The PPRA is sometimes referred to as the Hatch Amendment.

passed to address the additional concerns in the primary and secondary school environment.

At the same time, the Family Policy Compliance Office (FPCO) was established in the U.S. Department of Education and given responsibility for the administration, interpretation, and enforcement of both FERPA and the PPRA.

Since its passage, FERPA has needed clarifications, amendments, and updates to stay current with the national education scene. For a number of years, little change was made to the FERPA regulations. But then in the 1990s, a series of ameliorations addressed issues of the decade and FERPA concerns in a changing business and social landscape. Some of these changes were focused on specific incidents that drew national attention and affected both FERPA and higher education—such as the dorm hall murder of co-ed

Jeanne Clery, the escalation of alcohol and drug usage on campus, 9/11, and increased incidents of violence in the schools. In addition, other changes arose as legislation in other sectors of American society imposed their own amendments on FERPA and on how institutions conduct the business of education.

Amendments to FERPA over the Years		
1974	December 31	Buckley/Pell Amendment
1979	August 6	Education Amendments of 1978
1979	October 17	Department of Education established
1990	November 8	Campus Security Act
1992	July 23	Higher Education Amendments of 1992
1994	October 20	Improving America's Schools Act
1998	October 7	Higher Education Amendments of 1998
2000	October 28	Campus Sex Crimes Prevention Act
2001	October 26	USA PATRIOT Act of 2001
2008	December 9	Amendments of 2008

The most recent set of amendments was proposed in the March 24, 2008, edition of the *Federal Register*. The amendments were surprisingly from the perspective of the sheer volume of changes proposed. In many ways, however, these extensive amendments held little that was new. The majority of the amendments signified an incorporation of interpretation and guidance made by the Department of Education (ED) over the years. Some of the amendments incorporated much-needed updates; after all, records management practice in 2008 had evolved and experienced vast changes in application and policy since FERPA was first proposed in 1974. And still other changes were incorporations of the impact of recent federal legislation to amend FERPA.

In the December 9, 2008, edition of the *Federal Register*, the final FERPA regulations were issued. In essence, all of the proposed amendments were adopted, with relatively few changes made to the final text of the proposed changes. Throughout this book, references to the March 24 and December 9 editions of the *Federal Register* are quoted, with citations to the applicable page numbers in each of the publications.

FERPA continues to be amended as needed, as the changing cultural environment and operational needs of our educational institutions warrant.

Evolution of the U.S. Department of Education

Originally proposed by President Warren Harding in 1923, the Department of Health, Education, and Welfare (HEW) did not come into existence until 30 years later in 1953. President Dwight D. Eisenhower, using his reorganizational authority, created the department as a cabinet-level department, under a Secretary of Health, Education, and Welfare. HEW was the only such department to ever be created by presidential authority.

In 1979, the HEW was reorganized by the Department of Education Organization Act, signed by President Jimmy Carter. The act separated the department into two distinct entities—the Department of Education (ED) and the Department of Health and Human Services (HHS).

The ED opened its doors on May 4, 1980. It is the smallest of the cabinet departments, employing less than 5,000 people.

Enforcement of FERPA

When it was passed in 1974, the enforcement of FERPA was initially assigned to the Department of Health, Education, and Welfare (HEW). But in 1979, the HEW was reorganized. The Department of Education (ED) was born in 1980. Jurisdiction for the interpretation, adjudication, and enforcement of FERPA became the responsibility of the Family Policy Compliance Office (FPCO).

Part of the ED in Washington, D.C., the FPCO is responsible for administering both FERPA and the PPRA. LeRoy Rooker, the office's longest-serving director, managed the FPCO from 1988 until early 2009.

CONTACTING THE FAMILY POLICY COMPLIANCE OFFICE (FPCO)

The Family Policy Compliance Office (FPCO) may be contacted directly by school administrators, students, parents, and the general public by writing to:

Family Policy Compliance Office
U.S. Department of Education
400 Maryland Avenue SW
Washington DC 20202–5920
(202) 260–3887 or FAX (202) 260–9001

Education officials *only* may send electronic inquiries to *FERPA@ed.gov*.
www.ed.gov/policy/gen/guid/fpco/index.html

The FPCO regularly works with a myriad of constituencies—institutions, students, parents, state and local departments of education, government agencies, public and private organizations, and other citizens. Its scope of responsibility covers kindergarten, along with elementary, middle, junior, and high school (K–12), as well as higher education and other postsecondary institutions. Since FERPA applies to education agencies, the office also deals with providers of different services related to educational research and records management for the education community.

Inquiries to the FPCO are welcome; however, since the office services the entire nation and deals with legislative interpretation and guidance, questions are best submitted in writing. Parents, students, and other citizens should submit written correspondence by U.S. mail or fax. Education officials should check with the registrar of their individual institutions regarding local policy and practice prior to inquiring with the FPCO.

All communications, regardless of the delivery method, should include a few basic information items that affect the FPCO's response. These items include the following:

- Composer's name and contact information (address, telephone number)

- Full name of the school in question

- Location of the school in question—complete address, city and state, and school district (if applicable)

It is important to provide location information since state and local law may sometimes have critical or intervening implications in regard to how an institution administers the federal regulations.

The FPCO maintains extensive information on the Department of Education website and posts valuable and timely communications for parents, students, and institutional administrators. In addition to news and legislative updates, the website houses a library of reference information on FERPA and other legislation affecting education in general. A collection of "Dear Colleague" letters share official responses to inquiries and complaints that provide official interpretation, guidance, and instruction on issues arising from the administration of FERPA.

As the primary interpreter, adjudicator, and enforcer of FERPA, the FPCO has the responsibility and authority to respond to complaints about alleged violations of FERPA. This is, in fact, one of the four guarantees that the regulations make: the right to file a complaint when FERPA rights are violated or thought to have been violated by institutions or educational agencies. The FPCO investigates, thoroughly examining the issue of the complainant, reviewing the processes and practices of the institution, and mediating a response that ensures compliance with FERPA.

Further discussion regarding the submission of complaints is provided in Chapter Three.

Applicability of FERPA and Penalties for Noncompliance

FERPA is referred to as a spending clause or spending statute, a definition that focuses the applicability of the regulations and identifies the area of potential penalty. Indeed, both application and penalties are financial, or financially based.

> Except as otherwise noted, in Section 99.10, this part applies to an educational agency or instituti nds have been made available under any program administered by the Secretary. . .
>
> *§99.1(a)*

The first section of the regulations addresses the issue of their applicability, noting specifically that if an institution receives monies or funding from the federal government, that institution is required to comply with FERPA. Funding includes financial aid programs, and the regulations go on to mention specifically Pell Grants and the Guaranteed Student Loan Program. But funding can also include other government or agency grants, cooperative agreements, contracts, subgrants, and subcontracts with the federal government.

In its statement of applicability, the regulations go on, in §99.1(d), to clarify that not only is the institution as a whole required to comply with the regulations but that compliance is also expected from each and every component of the institution. In other words, the regulations do not merely govern operations in the records unit but apply to every department and office throughout the institution.

> If an educational agency or institution receives funds under one or more of the programs covered by this section, the regulations in this part apply to the recipient as a whole, including each of its components (such as a department within a university).
>
> *§99.1(d)*

a. The Office reviews a complaint, if any, information submitted by the educational agency or institution, and any other relevant information. The Office may permit the parties to submit further written or oral arguments or information.

b. Following the investigation, the Office provides to the complainant, if any, and the educational agency or institution a written notice of its findings and the basis for its findings.

§99.66

If the statement of applicability is to institutions that receive funding from the federal government, then the penalty for noncompliance is a loss of that federal funding. Noncompliance can be identified in *any* area of an institution, but the consequence—a loss of federal funding—would impact the *entire* institution. It is a daunting realization that an institution could lose its eligibility to participate in federal funding based upon a violation that could occur in any one segment of its operational areas!

According to §99.66, when an investigation is undertaken and a determination of a violation has been made, the FPCO issues a formal notice of its findings. It then allows the institution a reasonable amount of time to rectify the situation that created the violation. The "reasonable amount of time" is determined by the nature of the complaint and the seriousness of the violation.

During this period, the FPCO works with the institution to bring the institution back into compliance with FERPA.

If the Office finds that an educational agency or institution has not complied with a provision of the Act or this part, it may also find that the failure to comply was based on a policy or practice of the agency or institution. A notice of the findings issued under paragraph (b) of this section to an educational agency or institution that has not complied with a provision of the Act or this part—

1. Includes a statement of the specific steps that the agency or institution must take to comply; and

2. Provides a reasonable period of time, given all the circumstances of the case, during which the educational agency or institution may comply voluntarily.

§99.66(c)

The situation that initiated the complaint may have been a misguided policy or procedure or a departmental practice developed under erroneous information. It might also involve misunderstanding on the part of an employee with regard to an institutional policy or procedure. Whatever the cause, once identified, the institution must make the appropriate changes to bring itself into compliance with FERPA. If it does not, then the FPCO can utilize any number of actions—including the withholding of federal funding—to bring the institution into compliance.

> If an educational agency or institution does not comply during the period of time set under §99.66(c), the Secretary may take any legally available enforcement action, including, but not limited to, the following enforcement actions available in accordance with part E of the General Education Provisions Act—
>
> *§99.67(a)*

In the more than 35 years since its enactment, no institution has lost its federal funding. In investigating complaints of alleged violations of FERPA rights, the FPCO has always worked with institutions to bring their policy and practice into compliance. This is not to say, however, that the threat may not become justified by some future infraction.

One of the questions often voiced by staff in discussions about the penalties under FERPA focuses upon whether a student has the right to sue under these regulations—and especially whether an individual recordkeeper at an institution can be sued under FERPA. Although the Privacy Act of 1974 included a Section 1983 right to sue, that right was never carried over into the final language of the FERPA regulations. This does not mean that individuals and institutions cannot be sued under other privacy and ethics regulations and statutes. Depending upon the circumstances and upon the applicability of other state and local laws, legal suits may still be possible.

The issue of Section 1983 rights—the right to sue—has been raised numerous times over the years and evidenced quite dramatically in the case of *Gonzaga University v. Doe.* In this case, John Doe sued Gonzaga University not only on the basis of a violation of his privacy rights but also for defamation of character, a breach of his educational contract, and other complaints. In 1997, the Spokane County Superior Court ruled in the student's favor,

---

Gonzaga University v. Doe

In 1993, John Doe was an undergraduate student enrolled in the School of Education at Gonzaga University in Spokane, Washington. John planned to work in a Washington elementary school but would first have to graduate and obtain an affidavit of good moral character from his school. Roberta League was the teacher certification specialist at Gonzaga, working with Dr. Susan Kyle, director of Field Experience, Janet Burcalow, chair of the Education Department, and Dr. Corrine McGuigan, dean of the school.

In October 1993, League overheard a conversation between students accusing John of date rape and other aberrant sexual behavior. League took the news to Kyle, and the two began an investigation that included interviewing the alleged victim, Jane Doe. Despite conflicting reports and Jane's request to Burcalow not to pursue the matter, McGuigan concluded that there was sufficient evidence to preclude her issuing an affidavit of good moral character on John's behalf. John learned of this decision on March 4, 1994, after having submitted his final tuition payment.

John filed a suit against Gonzaga and League. Jane was initially included in the suit and she countersued. Later, however, John and Jane dropped their charges against each other, and Jane testified via videotape and deposition that John had not sexually assaulted her.

In 1997, the Spokane County Superior Court decided in John's favor, awarding damages that totaled $1.15 million. The damages included $100,000 for invasion of privacy, $500,000 for defamation, $55,000 for breach of educational contract, $50,000 for negligence, and $450,000 in punitive damages and for violation of FERPA rights.

The case went to the Washington Court of Appeals and then to the U.S. Supreme Court, which, in 2002, endorsed the award on John Doe's behalf except for the damages claimed under FERPA. In its decision, the Supreme Court concluded that FERPA's nondisclosure provisions did not confer a private or individual right to sue. The only penalties defined in the FERPA regulations are the withholding of federal funds from institutions, which is an action administered solely by the Department of Education.

---

awarding a sizeable monetary settlement. But the university appealed and the case was eventually heard by the U.S. Supreme Court. While most of the student's award was preserved, the Supreme Court ruled that FERPA did not provide a basis for an individual's right to sue. The Supreme Court reversed the portion of the previous court's award that had been based upon FERPA.

Although the Supreme Court ruling on *Gonzaga University v. Doe* explicitly determined that individuals have no right to sue under FERPA, the issue continues to be raised from time to time.

Moreover, the bases for the monetary awards in *Gonzaga University v. Doe* serve to illustrate the kinds of complaints that can be used as a basis for legal action against an institution. In other words, FERPA does not cover everything in regards to the wider implications of privacy and educational rights. FERPA cannot be used as a basis for legal redress, but other legislation may very well provide those platforms.

Further, the case of *Gonzaga University v. Doe* illustrates quite clearly that education officials—not just their institutions—can be cited for complaints and violations that escalate privacy rights beyond FERPA. FERPA trainers would do well to include ethics and moral responsibility as additional topics in their FERPA training curriculum.

Chapter 2

Understanding FERPA Basics

WHETHER OR NOT an institution has ever lost its federal funding as a result of a FERPA violation is essentially irrelevant. With the potential of losing government funding and grants as an ever-present, operational threat, it behooves institutions and their administrators to become intimately familiar with FERPA—its definitions, its provisions, and its scope of liability for making determinations in both extenuating and day-to-day circumstances.

In an increasingly litigious world, it is important to understand the intent and spirit of FERPA to fully understand the regulations. Chapter One of this book dealt with the regulatory environment out of which FERPA arises. As one of the many articulations of regulation and legislation that make up the exhausting body of legal literature for the United States, FERPA is not an isolated expression. It must function in concert with other federal regulations and take into account where state and local jurisdiction may have implications.

While FERPA has application to the elementary through secondary school environment—what we call "K through 12" (K–12)—as well as to the post-secondary environment, this publication focuses on the latter. And it is here where the tension with other laws and regulations is often most heartily felt.

In the college and university setting, FERPA assigns its privacy rights to students, nearly all of whom are 18 years or older. If these individuals were not in school, they would most likely be part of the working world, responsible for complying with the same laws and regulations that apply to other adult citizens. Hence, the FERPA regulations must co-exist and take into account the provisions of other national legislation, such as the Privacy Act of 1974, the Fair Credit Reporting Act, and the Code of the Internal Revenue Service (IRS).

Understanding all of the intricacies and implications of regulatory language is daunting to many individuals who are not accustomed to such stringent rhetoric. However, as familiar as college and university administrators may be with extensive policy and procedure, it is often a surprise—and sometimes a befuddlement—to learn that while FERPA compels certain requirements, it also permits institutions to make individual determinations in other instances. The regulations are not without their own consideration and appreciation for educational practice, unique pedagogy, and institutional history.

As it declares in §99.2, the purpose of FERPA is to protect the privacy of education records. Recognizing that these education records relate to individuals, FERPA assigns rights consistent with other regulations and in the spirit of the Code of Fair Information Practices. Finally, FERPA seeks to define, interpret, and make decisions about the application and implications of those privacy rights in the education environment.

> The purpose of this part is to set out requirements for the protection of privacy of parents and student…
>
> *§99.2*

Terms such as student, record, attendance, and alumni are familiar to postsecondary administrators. While these terms vary slightly in interpretation from institution to institution, they are universally understood terminology. Into this mix of nomenclature, however, FERPA introduces expressions such as eligible student, personally identifiable information, directory and nondirectory information, sole possession records, education official, prior written consent, further disclosure, and third party.

To understand what the regulations mean, it is important to begin with an agreement about definitions. In the regulations, most of these definitions are contained in an introductory section, §99.3.

Student and Eligible Student

Since FERPA applies to both K–12 and the postsecondary environment, the phrase "parents and eligible students" appears throughout the regulations. In the K–12 environment, of course, students are minors and, therefore, privacy rights are assigned to parents and guardians. This is not the case in postsecondary education. Most, if not all, students in the postsecondary

---

Minors

The definition of a minor comes from civil law. It specifies that a minor is an infant or a person who is under the age of legal competence. Generally, an individual ceases to be a minor when he reaches the age of either 18 or 21. The demarcation between a minor and an adult is that the adult is not prohibited from certain acts and behaviors, such as drinking or purchasing liquor. Further, minors require an adult custodian, who becomes responsible not only for the nurturing but for the behavior—and the consequences of behavior—of the minor child.

environment are 18 years or older. And in higher education, the applicability of privacy rights is strictly to the eligible student.

FERPA defines a *student* as an individual who meets the following characteristics.

- One who is or who has been in attendance at an institution
- One about whom the institution maintains education records

> Student, except as otherwise specifically provided in this part, means an individual who is or has been in attendance at an educational agency or institution and regarding whom the agency or institution maintains education records.
>
> *§99.3*

There are two important parts to this definition that need elaboration.

First of all, the term *in attendance* is not given a comprehensive definition in §99.3. In attendance generally means participating in the educational programs of the educational agency or institution. Immediately, classes or classroom activity come to mind. The regulations specifically mention participation in work-study programs and attendance by correspondence, but there are an increasing number of new pedagogical methods that have become popular in the early 21st century. The 2008 Amendments to FERPA expand the definition of attendance to include other types of participation, such as videoconferencing or education in other electronic format delivery systems.

> Attendance includes, but is not limited to—
>
> a. Attendance in person, or by paper correspondence, videoconference, satellite, Internet, or other electronic information and telecommunications technologies for students who are not physically present in the classroom; and
>
> b. The period during which a person is working under a work-study program.
>
> *§99.3*

The question not answered by the regulations is the temporal one about *when* student status begins. Is an individual a student from the first day of classes, from the point that a favorable admissions letter is issued or acknowledged, or when the individual first shows up on campus for orientation or other new student activities?

Determination of the response to this important question is left to the institution—and it is one that should be made and incorporated into institutional policy and procedure. FERPA assigns privacy rights to eligible students, but institutions determine when those rights begin for their new and incoming students. Furthermore, from a records management perspective, the answer to the question of student status establishes a foundation for enacting policy and practice regarding records maintenance and, more importantly, access to records.

The only guideline evident from the definition of student is that student status cannot begin any later than the first day of classes. Because the academic record is the single most important record maintained by an educational agency or institution, recordkeeping begins at the moment that classes begin and a student begins to participate in classes.

Thereupon, the regulations go on to define a more specific term—and, indeed, the more critical one for higher education. It is, after all, to the eligible student that privacy rights in FERPA are guaranteed.

> Eligible student means a student who has reached 18 years of age or is attending a postsecondary institution.
>
> *§99.3*

The definition of eligible student is made up of two parts, each exclusive of the other. An eligible student is a student who meets one of the following conditions.

- An individual who has reached the age of 18
- An individual who attends a postsecondary institution

This means that for a student to be an eligible student, only one portion of this definition need apply. Reference to the age of 18 is made because most laws and regulations define 18 as the age at which an individual ceases to be a minor. This is the voting age and, in some states, the legal drinking age. For all intents and purposes, once an individual reaches the age of 18, he is an adult and responsible for conducting himself as a responsible citizen.

The second part of the definition, however, is the more important and relevant one for colleges and universities because it identifies *all* postsecondary students as eligible students, regardless of age. If an individual is in attendance at a postsecondary institution, she is an eligible student and, therefore, guaranteed all rights under FERPA. Operationally, higher education faculty and administrators do not need to determine the age of a student to ascertain whether the individual has rights under FERPA. As long as the individual is in attendance at the postsecondary institution, those FERPA rights are guaranteed.

The regulations go on to underscore the rights of eligible students and state specifically and unequivocally that when a student becomes an eligible student, privacy rights transfer from the parent to the student.

When a student becomes an eligible student, the rights accorded to, and consent required of, parents under this part transfer from the parents to the students.

§99.5

Acknowledging this transference of rights is critical because it streamlines for education administrators the task of determining the applicability of FERPA rights. In the postsecondary arena, one does not need to be concerned about whether a student is 18 or not in order to ensure that rights are guaranteed the student. FERPA unequivocally declares that the student attending a postsecondary agency or institution is an eligible student and, therefore, assured of all rights under the regulations. The implication, of course, is that even if a student is under the age of 18, as long as that student is attending a postsecondary institution, that student is guaranteed rights under FERPA.

Included in this set of eligible students are those students who are not yet 18 but who are attending advanced classes or other educational programs at the college or university. To encourage students to pursue higher education degrees, many institutions conduct classes and programs that welcome the participation of high school students. Regardless of their ages, these students attending programs at the postsecondary institution are eligible students under FERPA. Privacy rights belong to the student.

The concern, of course, arises regarding what kind of access parents have to information about their minor children who are attending courses at a postsecondary institution.

Generally, postsecondary institutions have already established arrangements and agreements with the local high schools from which the students come. These agreements usually include some reciprocal reporting functions, based upon legitimate educational interest, between education officials at the college or university and the high school. Information from the college or university would certainly be helpful to high school teachers and counselors in guiding the students toward a postsecondary education. So, the postsecondary institution can share information with the high school, based upon legitimate educational interest, but it may not do so with the parents of the high school students enrolled at the college or university. Where does that leave the parent?

Because the parent has privacy rights at the high school, the parent can still approach high school teachers and counselors about their students' progress in postsecondary education courses. And the high school would be the appropriate venue in which this kind of information disclosure would take place. College and university staff who are approached by parents of high school students should refer the parents back to the high school for any and all information.

Records and Education Records

It is impossible to conduct business and industry without records and some system of recordkeeping. And just about everything we work with, react to, file, or issue is a record.

> Records means any information recorded in any way, including, but not limited to, handwriting, print, computer media, video or audio tape, film, microfilm, and microfiche.
>
> *§99.3*

Records exist in many forms, created by any number of recordkeepers and service providers. Where once records were thought of solely as paper files stored in office cabinets or locked away in vaults, records now exist in an endless array of manifestations. Records include information in databases and data that is visible on computer monitors. Various media recordings in image, sound, graphic representation, or other computer language are records as well. In fact, the word *recording* includes and is derived from the word *record*.

Records—In Many Forms	
Paper or print	Biometric records
Computer media	DNA
Video	Fingerprints or thumb prints
Audiotape	Ocular identification
Film, microfilm, and microfiche	Voice print recognition

Personally Identifiable Information

Privacy becomes important when records point to or document information about individual private citizens. The term *personally identifiable information* (PII) refers to the kind of information or data from which the identity of a specific person can be determined.

There is no way to realistically list every single item of data that can be personally identifiable information. But FERPA does provide some examples of personally identifiable information in §99.3, including the name of a student, the name of a student's parent(s), addresses, and personal identifiers such as the social security number (SSN) and student ID (SID) number. Essentially, any record that contains information from which you can deduce the identity of a particular student is said to contain personally identifiable information.

Personally identifiable information.
The term includes, but is not limited to—

a. The student's name;

b. The name of the student's parent or other family members;

c. The address of the student or student's family;

d. A personal identifier, such as the student's social security number, student number, or biometric record;

e. Other indirect identifiers, such as the student's date of birth, place of birth, and mother's maiden name;

f. Other information that, alone or in combination, is linked or linkable to a specific student that would allow a reasonable person in the school community, who does not have personal knowledge of the relevant circumstances, to identify the student with reasonable certainty; or

g. Information requested by a person who the educational agency or institution reasonably believes has direct, personal knowledge of the identity of the student to whom the education record directly relates.

§99.3

The 2008 Amendments added biometric records to FERPA's list of examples of personally identifiable information. The addition was ignited by the post-9/11 environment and the federal investigations that were initiated following the national tragedy. Among the educational facilities of interest to investigators were research laboratories, many of which use high-tech identification methods that employ biometric records of individual human beings. FERPA includes a definition of biometric records in §99.3 that focuses on "measurable biological or behavioral characteristics" of an individual and provides some examples.

> Biometric record, as used in the definition of personally identifiable information, means a record of one or more measurable biological or behavioral characteristics that can be used for automated recognition of an individual. Examples include fingerprints; retina and iris patterns; voiceprints; DNA sequence; facial characteristics; and handwriting.
>
> *§99.3*

Records that contain personally identifiable information have been the reason for privacy laws and legislation. Recall that it was the concern about personally identifiable information in government and private business records that provided the genesis for the dialogue that led to establishing the Code of Fair Information Practices and the subsequent passage of the Privacy Act of 1974.

Personally identifiable information in FERPA also includes indirect identifiers and information that may be the subject of "targeted" inquiries.

Indirect identifiers are more general than personally identifiable information but can, in certain situations, be used to identify an individual. A student's date of birth, birthplace, or mother's maiden name can certainly be used for identification purposes, particularly when the information is known within a community. Descriptions, either physical or the result of situational involvement, may be indirect identifiers if the identity of specific individuals can be deciphered from the descriptions or data provided.

Lastly, the 2008 Amendments added provisions to assist and prevent institutions from releasing information that may be the subject of a "targeted" request. These are expressed in subparagraphs (f) and (g) of this definition of personally identifiable information. Institutions know that personally identifiable information can be released if the information has been *de-identified*. That is, if you strip a record of personally identifiable information, if you *redact* the record, you can usually release that record without any type of prior authorization.

A problem arises, however, when that redacted information is so unique to a particular student or group of students that, even if redacted, the record can directly identify a student or several students. Inquiries for this kind of information are *targeted*, because they seek private information that would not ordinarily be released in response to a direct request. By asking for de-identified or redacted records, the requesting party is attempting to utilize and subvert a process that normally protects personal identification. Most likely, the inquiring party already knows the identity of the student involved when requesting de-identified records. Ultimately, the request is an attempt to dupe the recordkeeper into making an unwitting, albeit otherwise authorized, disclosure.

Under FERPA, recordkeepers in higher education are not required to disclose information to anyone but the individual whom the education record concerns. Targeted requests should most definitely be denied.

Education Records

Campuses create all kinds of records, many of which include personally identifiable information about students. The focus of concern for FERPA is the education record.

Education records. (a) The term means those records that are:

1. Directly related to a student; and

2. Maintained by an educational agency or institution or by a party acting for the agency or institution.
   §99.3

In FERPA, the term *education record* refers to those records that are directly related to a student *and* that are maintained by the educational institution. Both parts of this definition are essential to classifying a record as an education record.

Records that contain personally identifiable information about a student are "directly related" to the student. Enrollment records, transcripts,

EXCEPTIONS TO EDUCATION RECORDS

- Sole possession records
- Law enforcement records
- Employment records
- Medical records
- Alumni records
- Grades on peer-graded papers before they are collected and recorded

declarations and petitions, and other items related to the individual student's matriculation at the institution are directly related to the student and maintained by the institution. This last part of the definition includes not only the institution but all education officials and representatives of the institution. Faculty, staff, and administrators who create and keep documentation related to particular students are maintaining education records. And whenever we refer to education records, we mean records that are governed by the privacy rights in FERPA.

But not all records with personally identifiable information about students, maintained in the custody of a postsecondary institution or its representatives, are education records. A number of exclusions, or exceptions, are delineated in §99.3 of the regulations. In fact, there are six.

Sole Possession Records

The first exception to the definition of education records is the one for sole possession records, or records that are kept in someone's sole possession. Sole possession means that an individual creates and uses these records for his own purpose and never reveals or shares those records with anyone else. Student services administrators may create records when tracking or attending to specific issues for a particular student. These records may be temporary, but the distinguishing characteristic about these records is that they are not shared. They remain in an individual's sole possession.

The most evident example of a sole possession record is that of the faculty member who creates records about her students so that she can assign a grade or make an evaluation at the end of the term. If she never shows those records to anyone, they remain sole possession records and a student would not have rights under FERPA to inspect and review those records.

> Records that are kept in the sole possession of the maker, are used only as a personal memory aid, and are not accessible or revealed to any other person except a temporary substitute for the maker of the record.
>
> *§99.3*

FERPA has made some allowances in the matter of the faculty member's sole possession records. These provisions have to do with the sharing of those records with alternate faculty, substitute teachers, and teaching assistants. These records remain sole possession records as long as they "are not accessible or revealed to any other person except as a temporary substitute for the maker of the record" (§99.3). In other words, FERPA considers the temporary substitute teacher or the teaching assistant as an extension of the faculty member. With that understanding, these sole possession records remain sole possession because they have not been shared beyond the individual faculty function.

Obviously, the critical distinction here is in the availability of records to other education officials and, therefore, to the student. The faculty member who submits sole possession records for consideration to a committee in a disciplinary hearing surrenders the sole possession status of those records. At that point, the records become education records, and rights are now assigned as provided under FERPA.

A similar situation arises when faculty in a department store their sole possession records in a common file so that other faculty members can access their assessments and evaluations of students. In creating a file that is available to other education officials, the department creates education records, and these records are subject to the provisions under FERPA.

In determining whether or not records qualify as sole possession records, recordkeepers need to identify the availability of the record to other education officials and may also need to assess the intent of the record's creation. The 1991 case of the *Parents Against Abuse in Schools v. Williamsport Area School District* raises issues that focus on the intent for which records are made and the extent to which that intent or purpose has been evident to others.

Law Enforcement, Employment, and Medical Records

Law enforcement, employment, and medical records are records that are created by specific individuals in a professional capacity and used only for

---

Parents Against Abuse in Schools v. Williamsport Area School District

The Commonwealth Court of Pennsylvania heard the case of *Parents Against Abuse in Schools v Williamsport Area School District* (594 A 2nd 796) in 1991. The case involved fourth-grade students who had been emotionally and physically abused by a fourth-grade teacher. The school district retained a psychologist to interview the affected students as part of the investigation. Parental consent was given on condition that the psychologist's evaluations would be released to the parents in the event that later treatment for the children might be warranted.

The interviews of the children were conducted, but no formal report was ever made to the school district. The psychologist remained in possession of the interview notes. Although demanded by the children's parents, the psychologist claimed that the interview records were sole possession records that he kept in a personal file at his home. On that basis, he claimed that the records were not education records and, therefore, not subject to FERPA.

The court ruled in favor of the parents, determining that, based upon the earlier agreement with the school district and the parents, the psychologist's notes were, from the beginning, intended to be shared. Even though kept in a personal file at home, the psychologist had no right to claim sole possession.

---

the purpose of that professional activity. These records become education records under FERPA only when they are introduced into an education record or student file—such as when a psychological assessment is introduced into a student record by the dean of students to make a determination about impediments to academic progress in a particular term.

Obviously, the directive is to prevent such records from becoming a permanent part of an education record. A medical record can be verified and a notation made within a student file, but recordkeepers should not retain the original record in the education record. If retained in that education file, the student has a right to inspect and review those records because they are now education records.

For security reasons, some schools maintain videotapes from surveillance cameras in dormitories, libraries, and student centers. These records, if created and maintained by a law enforcement unit, such as a campus police or security department, are law enforcement records. These records would not be subject to FERPA. But the same tapes kept in a dean of students office or a campus facilities office are education records and are, therefore, subject to FERPA.

An exception is made in the case of employment records. If a contingency of employment is that the individual be a student at the institution, then the employment records would be education records subject to FERPA. Such contingencies exist in the case of work-study students, tutors, teaching and research assistants, and for other student employment opportunities. The qualifier in this case is that the position *requires* that the employee be a student in attendance at the institution. If the position specifies no such qualification, then the employment record would not be a student record, even if the person filling the position is also a student at the institution.

i. Records relating to an individual who is employed by an educational agency or institution that:

    A. Are made and maintained in the normal course of business;

    B. Relate exclusively to the individual in the individual's capacity as an employee; and

    C. Are not available for use for any other purpose.

ii. Records relating to an individual in attendance at the agency or institution who is employed as a result of his or her status as a student are education records and not excepted under paragraph (b)(3)(i) of this definition.

    §99.3

In the case of medical records, there is often confusion about whether FERPA or the Health Insurance Portability and Accountability Act (HIPAA) governs with respect to privacy and disclosures of student health records. In November 2008, the Family Policy Compliance Office (FPCO) and the Department of Health and Human Services released an 11-page *Joint Guidance on the Application of FERPA and HIPAA to Student Health Records*. HIPAA, of course, administers privacy for "protected health information" that is maintained by a covered entity. Covered entities include health plans, health care clearinghouses, and health care providers who transmit health information in an electronic format.

According to the *Joint Guidance*, the health information records maintained by educational institutions are education records covered by FERPA. Even though these records may relate to the medical or psychological health of a student, the records are not maintained by a covered entity that would otherwise be guided by HIPAA. Therefore, FERPA supersedes.

Health Insurance Portability and Accountability Act

Passed in 1996 and codified at 45 CFR §160, §162, and §164, the Health Insurance Portability and Accountability Act (HIPAA) sets standards on electronic health care information to protect the privacy of personally identifiable health information. HIPAA, also known as the Administrative Simplification Provisions, applies to covered entities, defined as health plans, health care clearinghouses, and health care providers who electronically transmit health care information. The administration of HIPAA is the domain of the Department of Health and Human Services.

Like FERPA, HIPAA has been amended since its enactment. The Privacy and Security Rules were added in 2003. These recent rules address the communication of protected health information (PHI), detailing compliance provisions in three areas—administrative, physical, and technical.

In 2006, an Enforcement Rule was added to specify civil money penalties for HIPAA violations. The amendment also established procedures for investigations and hearings regarding HIPAA violations.

The issue of treatment records is addressed in the *Joint Guidance* as follows:

> *At postsecondary institutions, medical and psychological treatment records of eligible students are excluded from the definition of "education records" if they are made, maintained, and used only in connection with treatment of the student and disclosed only to individuals providing the treatment… These records are commonly called "treatment records." An eligible student's treatment records may be disclosed for purposes other than the student's treatment, provided the records are disclosed under one of the exceptions to written consent under 34 CFR §99.31(a) or with the student's written consent under 34 CFR §99.30. If a school discloses an eligible student's treatment records for purposes other than treatment, the records are no longer excluded from the definition of "education records" and are subject to all other FERPA requirements. [Joint Guidance, p. 2.]*

Treatment records are the kind of medical and psychological records that are typically excluded from education records under FERPA. These records may be maintained by a university psychologist or student health center. If treatment records are disclosed by the institution to any party for any purpose other than treatment, these records become education records and, consequently, are subject to provisions in FERPA.

Treatment records might be disclosed, for example, to a school in which an individual seeks to enroll (§99.31(a)(2)), if there is "an articulable and significant threat" (§99.36) to the safety of the student or others in the education community. Once disclosed, those records become education records and all of the FERPA provisions and protections now apply.

There is one exception to this conversion of treatment records into education records. When the treatments records are disclosed to a HIPAA-covered entity, they are covered by HIPAA because that entity—a hospital, clinic, or otherwise—would be required to comply with HIPAA but not be required to comply with FERPA. The *Joint Guidance* document states this provision as follows.

> *...if the treatment records are disclosed to a third-party health care provider that is a HIPAA-covered entity, the records would become subject to the HIPAA Privacy Rule. The records at the educational institution continue to be treatment records under FERPA...* [Joint Guidance, p. 8.]

There are some instances where HIPAA may apply to records maintained by a component of the institution. The *Joint Guidance* document gives the example of a clinic which offers psychological services to students as well as to other, nonstudent members of the local community. In such a situation, the records of those patients who are eligible students are covered by FERPA. The records of the nonstudents are covered by HIPAA.

Alumni Records

Records created or received by an educational agency or institution after an individual is no longer a student in attendance and that are not directly related to the individual's attendance as a student.

§99.3

Alumni records are records that are created and maintained about students after they are no longer students. These kinds of records are usually maintained by alumni associations, development offices, and other such public relations offices. Typically, alumni records include current contact information, graduation information, employment information, salary data, and celebrity status, public service commitments, or other high-profile information. The purpose of maintaining such records involves public relations, donations and institutional advancement, and the generation of other development income.

The 2008 Amendments further clarified the creation of alumni records to exclude those records that may be created *after* the individual is no longer a student but that relate to the individual when he *was* a student. Records that relate to the individual while he was in attendance, even if created after he has ceased to be a student, are education records and covered by FERPA.

It should be noted that, for the institution, education records are always education records. Even after the individual has left the institution, those records created while the individual was in attendance will always be education records and subject to FERPA.

Peer-Graded Papers

The 2008 Amendments added a sixth exception to education records, although this exception rarely, if ever, applies to higher education. Grades on peer-graded papers are not considered education records. Grades become education records when they have been recorded by the teacher and are being maintained by the education institution.

Peer grading is a practice commonly used in the K–12 environment, wherein students exchange papers to correct the content during class. Teachers use this process as a pedagogical tool to immediately review material with students and to more fully engage them in the test process. Once the papers are scored or graded, teachers typically run down their class rosters, calling out the individual names of students. In response, the individual who corrected that student's paper would call out the grade or score achieved. Because this is done in class, all of the students present hear each other's grades.

> Grades on peer-graded papers before they are collected and recorded by a teacher.
>
> *§99.3*

On the surface, the practice of publicly attaching student names to grades seems a FERPA violation, however instructive the pedagogical method may be. The inclusion of this exception is a direct result of the 2002 U.S. Supreme Court decision in the case of *Owasso Independent School District v. Falvo.*

In that suit, the mother of an elementary school student claimed that her child's privacy rights were being violated because the child's grades on tests were being announced in class whenever students exchanged papers to correct or grade them. The case, which had a number of extenuating circumstances, was heard in the Oklahoma courts and was eventually appealed to the U.S. Supreme Court.

In its deliberations, the Supreme Court had to determine at what point a record becomes an education record and so, subject to the protections

---

Owasso Independent School District v. Falvo

Elementary schools commonly employ a practice known as "peer grading" to quickly correct and score student papers. Students exchange papers in class and are directed on how to score answers. At the end of the process, the teacher asks for scores on each student, with the grades being called aloud by the individual who corrected that student's paper.

In 1997, Kristja J. Falvo objected to the practice when one of her children, who suffers from a mild learning disability, was ridiculed when a failing score was called out in class. The child was called "dummy" by classmates when the grade was announced.

Ms. Falvo fought with the Owasso Independent School District in Oklahoma, pleading with the district to abandon or change its practice. Unsuccessful, she filed suit and the case made its way to the U.S. Supreme Court.

In 2002, the Court handed down a unanimous decision, affirming that peer grades were not education records because they had not yet been recorded by a teacher and were not yet maintained by the education institution.

---

of FERPA. The Supreme Court ruled that peer-graded scores were not education records because they were not, at the time of disclosure, being maintained by the education institution. Since the grades were not education records at the time the students were vocalizing them in class, there was no violation under FERPA.

Directory and Non-Directory Information

The FERPA regulations distinguish and classify the information in education records as being either directory or non-directory information.

> Directory information means information contained in an education record that would not generally be considered harmful or an invasion of privacy if disclosed.
>
> *§99.3*

The first category is directory, or public, information—although the term "public information" is no longer used, to avoid confusion with public and open records laws.

Directory information is information that is not generally considered harmful or an invasion of privacy if it is released. This is not to say that such information might not be used with harmful intent, but it is generally not considered harmful for an institution to make this kind of information available. In our local communities, after all, certain information is determined necessary to be made public in order for a community to exist and operate. Phone directories are published with names, addresses, and telephone numbers. Education institutions are given the same option of determining what information should be made publicly available in order for the campus community to thrive.

Whatever an institution determines to be directory information should be published in its annual notification (see Chapter Three). This is because directory information, by definition, does not require the prior consent of the student for release. And the institution should notify students what information it is making available to the public.

What Directory Information May Include

Name	Enrollment status
Address	Dates of attendance
Telephone listing	Degrees, honors, and awards received
Electronic mail address	Most recent educational agency or institution attended
Student user ID that alone cannot be used to gain access to education records	Participation in officially recognized activities and sports
Photograph	Weight and height of members of athletic teams
Date and place of birth	
Major field of study	
Grade level	

While institutions determine what they will designate as directory information for their individual campuses, the regulations do identify a number of data elements that can be designated directory information. These are listed in the Directory Information table. Some clarification is required in defining these terms.

- Grade level refers to the classification level of the student: first-year (formerly, freshman), sophomore, junior, or senior.
- Enrollment status refers to undergraduate or graduate, as well as to full-time, half-time, or part-time. The specific number of units or credits in which the student is enrolled is not included in this definition.
- Dates of attendance refer to term listings or the official, published dates assigned to those terms. For instance, you can disclose that a student was enrolled during the Fall 2009 term (quarter or semester),

or you can provide the official beginning and ending dates of that term. If the student ceased to attend during the term, however, you cannot disclose the exact date that the student stopped attending. Daily attendance records would not be considered directory information, as challenged in the case of *F.A.T v. the State of Florida*.

Dates of attendance.

a. The term means the period of time during which a student attends or attended an educational agency or institution. Examples of dates of attendance include an academic year, a spring semester, or a first quarter.

b. The term does not include specific daily records of a student's attendance at an educational agency or institution.

§99.3

- Most recent educational agency or institution attended is limited to the previous school in which the student was enrolled.
- Participation in officially recognized activities and sports refers to activities recognized as official by the educational agency or institution.
- Weight and height of athletic team members refers to these two items of information that are typically published about athletes.

There are some categories here that can be broken down further, such as address and telephone. Campuses have raised questions about including cell phone numbers, dorm room telephone numbers, mailing address, permanent address, and campus (dormitory or residence hall) addresses in directory information. FERPA does not make any further clarification in regard to these items, once again leaving a final determination to the individual institution.

When making a determination of what constitutes directory information, an institution should be cognizant of the kinds of information that are necessary to facilitate official and campus activities. While disclosures to the campus may not easily be withheld from the outside public, the general guide is to ensure the safe and smooth functioning of campus life.

One item that is often overlooked in designating directory information is photographs. Schools that publish student annuals or

---

F.A.T. v. State of Florida

Just how "dates of attendance" is interpreted was the subject of *F.A.T. v. the State of Florida* (690 So. 2d 1347), a Florida District Court case in which a group of students, determined to be delinquent students, took issue with their school's disclosure to officials about their truancy.

The students in this case had been assigned to Florida's Truancy Arbitration Program, which required the students to attend school on a regular basis. When the students failed to do so, the school reported their lack of attendance, basing its disclosure on the protection of disclosing directory information. But the students contested the disclosure after being charged with criminal contempt for not complying with the agreements of the Truancy Arbitration Program.

In the adjudication of the case, the court looked at how other directory information elements are used in FERPA. Recognizing a broad characterization of elements such as "field of study," the court determined that "dates of attendance" should refer to time periods defined in official publications such as class directories, school yearbooks, and academic calendars. Focusing on such an annual or yearly account, the court could find no basis for including day-to-day attendance records in the definition of "dates of attendance."

In fact, the court determined that daily attendance records were similar to other "reports and records" in a student's education record. As such, daily attendance records could not be considered or treated as directory information. Disclosure of these kinds of reports would, as with other non-directory information, require the prior written consent of the parent or eligible student.

---

yearbooks and regularly include images of student activities in catalogs and campus newspapers should include photographs as a directory information item. Without that inclusion, the prior written consent of the individual students whose identities can be determined from photographs and images that may be published or released should be obtained prior to publication.

Because students can initiate restrictions on directory and non-directory information at any time, it is a good practice for institutions to obtain individual student consent whenever major publications or publicity that involves student names and images are released. Such instances include not only annuals and student directories but also websites in which individual students and student work is featured. A simple disclosure could be added to the authorization protocol and a signature required from students participating in the particular venture.

Over the years, the FERPA regulators have entertained the addition of other data elements to the list of potential directory information items. At one time, there was strong support for including class schedule in this list. Most institutions, however, felt that releasing such information provided too much location information and created a serious potential for disruptions to class meetings.

SAMPLE AUTHORIZATION LANGUAGE

I certify that the information provided above is correct and agree to be included in [the project]. I understand that by agreeing to inclusion in [this project], my name, photograph, and other student information will be published in [name] and available to the public [and/or recipients of this project].

_____

Signature and Date

The 2008 Amendments included a new addition to the items that can potentially be designated as directory information. "Student user ID" was proposed as the latest addition to the list, along with certain caveats.

> Directory information includes a student ID number, user ID, or other unique personal identifier used by the student for purposes of accessing or communicating in electronic systems, but only if the identifier cannot be used to gain access to education records except when used in conjunction with one or more factors that authenticate the user's identity, such as a personal identification number (PIN), password, or other factor known or possessed only by the authorized user.
>
> §99.3

By student user ID, the regulators meant an identifier used by the student to access or to communicate within the institution's computer systems. Campuses may assign logon IDs or user IDs as part of an e-mail account or for access to the school's computer system. The ID may even be a student ID number. Often these identifiers are not easily kept confidential, appearing in an e-mail address or other type of student directory disclosure.

The caveats on use of the student user ID as directory information are these:

- The student user ID cannot be used alone to access non-directory information.
- The student user ID cannot be used alone to authorize transactions that would otherwise require a signature or signed, written consent.

If the student user ID is used to access personally identifiable information or to provide signatory authorization, a "two-factor authentication" protocol should be used. That is, an additional authentication device, such as a password or personal identification number (PIN), must be required in addition to the user ID or logon ID in order to access non-directory information. If the student user ID can be used alone to access non-directory information or to provide an electronic signature, then it cannot be designated directory information.

Discussion about designating the student user ID as directory information is often confused, particularly when the "student user ID" is also the "student ID." The FPCO advises against designating a student ID as directory information, so what is the distinction that the regulations are attempting to make with this amendment and the singling out of student user ID or, simply, user ID?

The problem is illustrated by the experience of the University of Wisconsin-River Falls. At this institution, prospective applicants are issued a "student account ID," an identifier that follows the individual into directory listings after the applicant is admitted to the institution. Because of

---

Student User or Account ID

In May 2004, the University of Wisconsin-River Falls wrote to the Family Policy Compliance Office (FPCO), requesting guidance on whether it could designate "student account ID" as directory information.

At the time of admission, incoming students at UW-River Falls are issued an account ID number to access the university's electronic student information system (eSIS). The account number consists of the letter W and a seven-digit, randomly assigned, computer-generated number. The number has no relationship to the student's social security number (SSN), which is not used as a student ID number. When first accessing the system, students use their birth date and the last four digits of their SSN, after which they are prompted to select another password and to establish a security question.

The problem arose in that eSIS uses the student's account ID in order to provide information about the student. While non-directory information is protected through use of the password, directory information, if not suppressed by the student, appears in the student electronic directory with the account ID number. The university could find no way to suppress display of that account ID number.

In his "Dear Colleague Letter" of November 5, 2004, FPCO Director LeRoy Rooker found no violation where the disclosure of the account ID was involved, as long as the information would not be disclosed if the student requests that the university not disclose it. Like e-mail address, account ID, user ID, logon ID, or any other personal identifier could be designated directory information because these identifiers cannot be used alone to access non-directory information and could not be used as an electronic signature, the requirements for which are set forth in §99.30(d).

the way the university's system operates, the student account ID cannot be concealed and is easily and readily made available on screens that display that student's information.

Responding to the concerns of the UW-River Falls, the FPCO decided that the revelation of the student account ID does not violate FERPA because the ID alone cannot be used to access personally identifiable information about the student from education records. Further, the ID alone cannot be used as an electronic signature to authorize transactions. For students to obtain information such as grades and class schedules from the UW computer system, a unique password, individually created by the student, must also be entered. Because non-directory information and personal identity is protected in this manner, the FPCO saw no problem with the release or designation of the student account ID as directory information.

What Directory information May *Not* Include	
Student ID number	Race
Social security number	Ethnicity
	Nationality
	Gender

Again, it is the prerogative of the institution to determine what, if anything, it will consider directory information. And some institutions neither designate nor release any directory information about their students. There is no requirement to do so.

If the institution does designate directory information, however, the Department of Education has cautioned against designating certain items as directory information. The prohibition on two of these items—student ID number and social security number (SSN)—was codified with the changes proposed by the 2008 Amendments.

Directory information does not include a student's—

1. Social security number; or

2. Student identification (ID) number, except as provided in paragraph (c) of this section.

   §99.3

The restriction on student ID takes into account the earlier discussion regarding the student user ID. What the regulations are attempting to prevent is the disclosure of data that may provide unprotected access to personally identifiable information about a student. If the student user ID allows such access, it cannot be designated as directory information. But if a secondary key, such as a PIN or password, is required to access non-directory information, then the student ID can be designated directory information. (See the discussion of disclosures and the SSN in Chapter Three.)

Dispositions on Directory and Non-Directory Information

DATA ELEMENT	DIRECTORY INFO	NON-DIRECTORY INFO
Social security number (SSN)	Never	Always
Student ID number (SID)	Permitted, if used as a student user ID	Recommended
Student user ID	Permitted if alone, the data element does not provide access to non-directory information	Recommended

Over the years, the FPCO has advised against designating certain other items as directory information, primarily due to changing social conditions in the United States. Among such data elements are race, ethnicity, nationality, and gender, which have been used as the basis for prejudice, discrimination, violence, and hate crimes.

Religious affiliation, although neither mentioned in the regulations nor in the 2008 Amendments, is another category that is often included in nondiscrimination statements and which the FPCO advises should not be included in the designation of directory information. Certainly, the potential for discrimination, violence, and hate crimes continues to be high where religious affiliation and practice are concerned.

Information that is not directory information is non-directory information. And non-directory information is comprised of everything else that is contained in student records, including grades, transcripts, declarations, correspondence, reports, and other documentation.

Disclosure of non-directory information almost always requires the prior written consent of the student.

Prior Written Consent

When in doubt, think prior written consent.

—LEROY ROOKER, *former director of the*
Family Policy Compliance Office

If ever there is doubt about whether or not to disclose *any* information about a student, obtain a prior written consent. The prior written consent is the student's authorization for the recordkeeper—the institution or the education official—to disclose personally identifiable information from education records.

In §99.30(b), the regulations detail the three required components of the prior written consent.

a. The parent or eligible student shall provide a signed and dated written consent before an educational agency or institution discloses personally identifiable information from the student's education records, except as provided in §99.31.

b. The written consent must:

   1. Specify the records that may be disclosed;

   2. State the purpose of the disclosure; and

   3. Identify the party or class of parties to whom the disclosure may be made.

   §99.30

First, the consent must specifically identify what records are to be released. In response to requests for "all records," recordkeepers have a right to ask the requesting party to specify the particular record or records being sought. Even subpoenas detail specific records demanded by a court or attempt to refine the focus of the kind of information under investigation. The prior written consent must state the purpose of the disclosure and identify the entities to whom disclosure is to be made. The receiving party may only use the records for the purpose stated herein; further disclosure is not permitted. When the receiving party no longer has a need of the records, the records should be destroyed or returned to the institution that disclosed the records in the first place. From a records management perspective, institutions would do well to advise the receiving party to destroy the records when the purpose for which they were requested has concluded. Institutions will not want to get into the practice of requesting that records be returned because of the tracking and additional monitoring that may be involved. While these provisions are not recorded here specifically, the regulations do outline extensive requirements in §99.31(a)(6), when discussing the disclosure of information for the purposes of educational studies.

The prior written consent must identify the entities to whom disclosure is to be made. And institutions are only authorized to release such

ELEMENTS OF THE PRIOR WRITTEN CONSENT

- Specify the records to be disclosed
- State the purpose for the disclosure
- Identify to whom records are to be disclosed
- Date
- Authorized signature

information to the entities identified therein. It is this party or class of parties that will be held accountable for preventing further disclosure of the records being released.

Finally, the prior written consent must be dated and must include a signature of the eligible student whose records are to be released. For a long time, only the handwritten signature of the student could be accepted and was required in disclosures of non-directory information to third parties. Advancements in technology, however, have had their impact on the acceptance and legality of contractual signatures that are provided in an electronic format.

Business and industry were quick to implement the use of electronic and digital signatures at the end of the 20th century. On the commercial and financial front, wide acceptance of automated teller machines (ATM) and electronic data interchange (EDI), including electronic funds transfers (EFT), revolutionized global strategies for business transactions in banking and finance, health care, and government. Then in 2000, the United States ESign Act adopted standards for electronic commerce.

In higher education, EDI was immediately attractive as a communication protocol between institutions that could effectively eliminate the potential for fraudulent transcripts. As envisioned in the late 1990s, however, EDI proved a difficult and massive undertaking that would require the development of extensive datasets for participating institutions—not only for the transmission of data but for the interpretation of data received. A well-organized effort required buy-in and voluntary transformation of records into datasets defined from a common lexicon. As a national initiative, EDI never really gained steam. But states such as Arizona, North Carolina, and Texas have successfully adopted strategies and statewide policies that have facilitated the implementation of EDI within the state.

EDI protocols included several important elements:

- The formal establishment of agreements to communicate between and among institutions in a common language or dataset

- Protocols for the tracking of origination requests and of exchange acknowledgments
- Utilization of a secure network for the transmission of all data exchanges

Security was enhanced through the incorporation of public key infrastructure (PKI) systems that utilized encryption and digital signatures. These EDI protocols, founded upon strategies in American business and industry, set the standards for what would eventually develop into web-based, information access systems or portals for students, faculty, and other education administrators.

Utilizing a closed or secure system that incorporates authentication and validation procedures, institutions can be relatively sure—at least for the purposes of transacting internal business—of the identity of individuals requesting information and the disclosure of personally identifiable information. Login IDs, accompanied by personal identification numbers (PIN) or passwords, provide the assurance of authentication and validated rights of access and transaction.

Recognizing the rapidly developing technology surrounding electronic signatures and their acceptance in financial and in other government applications, Volume 68, Number 44, of the *Federal Register*, in July 2003, proposed to amend FERPA and allow institutions to accept electronic signatures for student-initiated transactions.

Stressing that FERPA was essentially "technology neutral," the proposed amendment to the regulations focused on setting standards for

Electronic Signatures

The history of the use and acceptance of electronic signatures can be traced back to before the American Civil War, with the implementation of Morse Code as a method of communication and accepted performance contracts. Then, the 1980s witnessed a rise in the utilization of fax as a speedy method of communicating facsimile documentation.

In 1999, the National Conference of Commissioners on Uniform State Laws (NCCUSL) released a definition of electronic signatures that was adopted by the Uniform Electronic Transactions Act. The conference defined an electronic signature as "an electronic sound, symbol, or process attached to or logically associated with a record and executed or adopted by a person with the intent to sign the record." One year later, the process was adopted at the federal level through the Electronic Signatures in Global and National Commerce Act, or the U.S. ESign Act.

Electronic signature is often confused with the term "digital signature." Although the terms have been used interchangeably, digital signature more appropriately refers to a signature protocol that uses cryptographic techniques. Electronic signatures utilize digital signature technology to detect alterations. Further, electronic signatures incorporate authentication tools, such as the use of digital certificates, smart cards, biometric identification, and other measures.

the implementation of the acceptance of electronic signatures, rather than designation of a technology product to accomplish the task.

Initially, four qualifications were identified in the standards specified in §99.30(d), beginning with the requirement of establishing the identity of the individual submitting the request for records and adequately determining the authenticity of that identification. Electronic and digital signatures provide their own authentication protocol, but institutions needed a method that could be implemented easily and still stand up to verification scrutiny.

> "Signed and dated written consent" under this part may include a record and signature in electronic form provided the educational agency or institution follows a process to—
>
> 1. Identify the individual and authenticate the identity of the individual requesting disclosure of education records;
>
> 2. Attribute the signature to the consent;
>
> 3. Secure and verify the integrity of the consent in transmission and upon receipt; and
>
> 4. Document and record the signed message.
>
>   *Proposed §99.30(d)*

The language of what was proposed as the amendment to §99.30(d) seemed to take its inspiration from the EDI protocols. But institutions objected to the requirements as too specific and restrictive. The final regulation that was adopted in 2004 simplified the requirements, essentially leaving the authentication protocols to the institution adopting the use of electronic signatures.

> "Signed and dated written consent" under this part may include a record and signature in electronic form that—
>
> 1. Identifies and authenticates a particular person as the source of the electronic consent; and
>
> 2. Indicates such person's approval of the information contained in the electronic consent.
>
>   *§99.30(d)*

On this basis, many institutions now accept electronic requests for the disclosure of information from student records as long as the electronic request originates within the institution's secure network or student access system (SAS). Requests that originate via external e-mail systems or by telephone are still not accepted and are not authorized under FERPA.

Once a secured network or SAS is established, the institution must disclose to users the purpose of the network, indicating that use of that network by any user constitutes acknowledgment and consent to the implications of transactions within the system. Verification protocols for requests, acknowledgment of completed transactions, and recordkeeping of the particulars of each transaction follow from records management practices and standards already in place in banking and the financial industry and commerce.

Institutions may use other terms for the SAS, but the SAS should not be confused with the student information system (SIS) that is often the

Student Access Systems

Many government agencies along with financial and medical institutions make information available to their constituents over the Internet. In higher education, these systems go by various names but are most commonly known as student portals or student access systems (SAS). These kinds of systems facilitate two important processes for institutions—the authentication of user identity and the acceptance of authorizations for customer service transactions.

SAS transactions began with web registration for many colleges and universities, but the unlimited aptitude, flexibility, and reliability of the Internet has resulted in an explosion of possibilities for student transactions. In addition to electronic enrollment, students can pay fees, verify progress toward their degrees, change majors, declare nonattendance for a term, and complete financial aid processes. Ordering verifications and transcripts, changing addresses, electing privacy options, and updating emergency contact information are also possible. Many systems even give students one-stop-shop access to health care information and appointment-making abilities at student health centers. In addition, access to employment databases at the campus career center often provides another valuable link.

Because many student transactions would otherwise require proper identification of the student or former student if performed in person, the authentication ability of an SAS is particularly attractive for institutional business. The SAS requires a logon or user ID along with a personal identification number (PIN) or password to access the system. These are the same two-factor authentication devices used for automated teller machines (ATM) and other information-sensitive websites.

Access to an SAS may be made available to individuals from the moment an electronic application for admission is submitted. Institutions such as the University of California Los Angeles (UCLA) make their systems available to former students for as long as access activity is logged or up to 10 years after the student has left the institution.

institution's primary database of student information. Direct access to the SIS is restricted to the registrar, student services staff, and other education officials on the campus. An SAS usually reads data on the SIS, but the two are very different systems. Transactions initiated on the SAS may update the SIS, but may not always be performed in real time.

Since May 2004, institutions have been authorized to accept electronic signatures as tantamount to prior written consent for the disclosure of non-directory information from education records. The impact of that singular decision has amounted to unleashing a universal transformation in student services and educational records management.

Education Officials and Legitimate Educational Interest

Curiously, while FERPA uses the term *school official* throughout its regulatory language, no definition of the term is ever given. Instead, the U.S. Department of Education offers guidance in a draft or model version of an annual notification that is published on its website. Here, the department provides a working definition of an education official.

Education officials—or, *school* officials, as it is termed in the regulations—are employed by the institution. These individuals access records in the custody of the institution and act in the stewardship of or service to the institution. But the term *education official* is narrowly defined and does not include all employees of an institution.

Education official refers to employees charged by the institution with specific responsibilities—those of administration, supervision, academic or research interaction, or other supporting roles. Employees in these functions

---

EDUCATION (SCHOOL) OFFICIAL

- A person employed by the educational agency or institution in an administrative, supervisory, academic or research, or other support staff position, including law enforcement and health staff

- A person serving on an institution governing body

- A person or entity employed by, or under contract to, the institution to perform a special task or to act as its agent in providing a service, such as an attorney or auditor

- A student serving on an official committee, such as a disciplinary or grievance committee, or assisting another school official in performing his or her tasks

include teachers and faculty, deans and academic program chairs, student services providers and administrators, financial aid and accounting staff, academic advisors and auditors, information technology professionals, and certain campus clerical staff. In effect, any employee who has responsibilities for the creation, maintenance, and disclosure of information from education records is an education official.

Simply because an individual is an education official, however, does not mean that the individual has carte blanche access to all student records. It should be pointed out that the access authorized for education officials is couched in the regulations amidst other exceptions to the requirement of a prior written consent. The implication is that access to education records is by exception and only under conditions that the regulations go on to outline.

In §99.31(a)(1), the regulations purposely limit access to education records by education officials, specifying that a "legitimate educational interest" must exist in order for the education official to gain access to education records. There must be a need to know information from those records to complete a function of the institution or to accomplish a task on behalf of the student.

Under what conditions is prior consent not required to disclose information?

The disclosure is to other school officials, including teachers, within the agency or institution whom the agency or institution has determined to have legitimate educational interests.

§99.31(a)(1)

The trouble with the regulations, however, is that they do not provide a specific definition for the term *legitimate educational interest*. Because each institution has established its own methods and mode of operation, the regulations leave definition of the term to the prerogative of the institution. Nevertheless, a definition is required as a component of the annual notification.

In developing a definition of legitimate educational interest, institutions should focus on the need to know information, specifically, non-directory information from education records. What drives that need to know or need to access such information is the particular responsibility of the employee in accomplishing the individual's job or assigned function. And because the

LEGITIMATE EDUCATIONAL INTEREST

Education officials have a legitimate educational interest when, in the exercise or completion of their responsibilities on behalf of the institution, they incur the need to know and utilize specific information from education records.

Department of Education has already provided a definition of education official, the kind of employee with legitimate educational interest can be identified with similar specificity. Accordingly, Cliff Ramirez & Associates has compiled and uses the following text as a working definition of *legitimate educational interest.*

> *Education officials have a legitimate educational interest when, in the exercise or completion of their administrative, supervisory, academic, research, or other administrative support responsibilities on behalf of the educational agency or institution, they incur the need to know, access, or utilize specific information from education records.*

There are education officials whose responsibilities involve the need to access education records on a daily basis, but there are also those whose need may only arise on an ad hoc basis. To facilitate access by these education officials, FERPA does not require the prior written consent of the student where legitimate educational interest exists.

It should be noted that legitimate educational interest is specific to a particular need and limited by that need. Only information relevant to that particular and expressed need should be disclosed to the education official. In other words, legitimate educational interest does not provide access to all of a student's records but only to those records for which the specific need to know exists.

The case of *Krebs v. Rutgers* is evidence that legitimate education interest should not be generally applied but made relevant to the specific need for information.

Members of an institution's governing body are included in the definition of *education official.* Charged with responsibility for the integrity and maintenance of the institution's academic programs, members of a board of regents, a board of trustees, or other system of guardianship may need to access education records in their monitoring, auditing, and management responsibilities for the institution. That right of access is provided under the definition of *education official.*

Krebs v. Rutgers

In 1992, the New Jersey case of *Krebs v. Rutgers* (797 F. Supp. 1246) drew attention to a number of FERPA-related issues including the use of the social security number (SSN), legitimate educational interest, and the applicability of FERPA itself.

Keith Krebs and six other students filed a class action suit under Section 1983 alleging that Rutgers University was abusing their privacy rights in requiring the disclosure of SSNs for campus services, from dining hall to mail privileges. Further, student SSNs were printed on student identification cards and on class lists that were distributed widely to campus offices. Rutgers claimed that the use of the SSN for campus services was covered by legitimate educational interest. Further, the school insisted that it was not, as a semi-private institution, obliged to comply with FERPA.

The court ruled in favor of the students in regard to the use of the SSN, ruling that the SSN is an education record and defined *legitimate educational interest* as specific to the interests of the student, not the institution. Further, the court found that Rutgers, as a recipient of federal funding programs, was, indeed, obliged to comply with the FERPA regulations.

The definition of education official goes on to include other third-party entities that may also have access to education records without the need for prior written consent. These third-party entities are individuals, groups, organizations, or other bodies that are neither the student nor the institution.

The definition specifies individuals and entities who may receive information from the institution's education records on an ad hoc or on a continuing basis. Ad hoc examples include attorneys and auditors, for whom access to education records is necessary to perform contracted work. The most recognizable example of contracted officials on a continuing basis is the National Student Clearinghouse, which performs a variety of records-related and reporting services on behalf of colleges and universities nationwide. In the performance of its contracted work, the National Student Clearinghouse requires ongoing access to the education records of the institution and maintains its own database of information from which to execute its responsibilities.

The outsourcing of institutional functions has never been prevented by FERPA. Higher education service providers assist colleges and universities in a variety of tasks, including enrollment and degree verification, payments and collections, development and fundraising, technology services, alumni relationship management, institutional advancement and reporting, legal services, student health and psychological services, and police and security services.

In an effort to codify practice as outsourcing strategies expand, the 2008 Amendments propose an expansion of the definition of education official by including contractors, consultants, volunteers, and any entities working for and on behalf of an educational agency or institution.

> Under what conditions is prior consent not required to disclose information?
>
> A contractor, consultant, volunteer, or other party to whom an agency or institution has outsourced institutional services or functions may be considered a school official under this paragraph provided that the outside party—
>
> 1. Performs an institutional service or function for which the agency or institution would otherwise use employees;
> 2. Is under the direct control of the agency or institution with respect to the use and maintenance of education records; and
> 3. Is subject to the requirements of §99.33(a) governing the use and redisclosure of personally identifiable information from education records.
>
> *§99.31(a)(1)(i)(B)*

In this inclusion, the regulators are cautious to insist on the contractor's continuing relationship with the institution. For the protection of the institution, such relationships should be bound by written agreements in which specific reference is made to FERPA and to operational compliance with the regulations. Strict adherence to the provisions of the regulations is an unconditional basis for the continuity of the contract.

To underscore the precautions, Volume 73, No. 57 of the *Federal Register*, the edition which proposed the 2008 Amendments, states the following:

The outside party who obtains access to education records without consent must be under the direct control of the agency or institution and subject to the same conditions governing the use and redisclosure of education records that apply to other school officials under §99.33(a) of the regulations. [FR 15578]

Essentially, outsourced entities who function as education officials for an institution must comply with FERPA to the same degree that other education officials on the campus must adhere to the regulations. As if to stress the point further, the *Federal Register* goes on to make the following declaration in regard to further disclosure:

Educational agencies and institutions are responsible for their outside service providers' failure to comply with applicable FERPA requirements. The agency or institution must ensure that the outside party does not use

or allow anyone to obtain access to personally identifiable information from education records except in strict accordance with the requirements established by the agency or institution that discloses the information.
[FR 15579]

As frightening as the statement may come across to institutional management, the directive to institutions is that written agreements with outsourced service providers must be comprehensive in communicating the parameters of the service providers' use of information from education records. Any breach of contract must be reported immediately to the FPCO. And the consequence, as given in §99.33(e), could very well be that the institution may not disclose education records to that third party for a period of not less than five years.

If this Office determines that a third party outside the educational agency or institution improperly rediscloses personally identifiable information from education records in violation of this section, or fails to provide the notification required under paragraph (b)(2) of this section, the educational agency or institution may not allow the third party access to personally identifiable information from education records for at least five years.

§99.33(e)

Lastly, students may themselves be considered education officials if they serve on official committees that involve access to or require the utilization of information from education records. Many campuses seek to involve students in various leadership and management initiatives that not only include disciplinary hearings but committees on academic procedures, policy development, and strategic planning. In some cases, access to information from education records is critical to effectively executing the responsibilities of the assigned position.

Students in such roles should only have access to the specific records from which they have a need to know information. As with student workers functioning in various areas of the campus, these students should be thoroughly apprised of their responsibilities for confidentiality about the records and the knowledge to which the student may be exposed. A written acknowledgment from the student at the time of delegation to such committee work would not be out of order. Such an acknowledgment should disclose disciplinary consequences for failure to comply with the privacy requirements of the position.

Chapter 3

Understanding the Privacy Rights under FERPA

FROM A NARRATIVE perspective, the FERPA regulations are curiously constructed in that the rights guaranteed under 34 CFR §99 are announced indirectly when they appear in the legislation.

The title of §99.5 presents the question "What are the rights of students?" Yet, the section deals more with the application of rights rather than with an identification or explanation of those rights. In an immediate answer to its query, the regulations declare that FERPA rights transfer from the parents to the student when the student becomes an eligible student (§99.5(a)).

> When a student becomes an eligible student, the rights accorded to, and consent required of, parents under this part transfer from the parents to the student.
>
> *§99.5(a)*

Then, after patently insisting upon this transfer of rights, the regulations address the expansion of those rights, even before the basic rights are ever discussed. In §99.5(b), the regulations propose themselves as the minimum requirements for the privacy of education records. Institutions and other entities may assign more rights than those that are detailed in the FERPA regulations, but no less.

> The Act and this part do not prevent educational agencies or institutions from giving students rights in addition to those given to parents.
>
> *§99.5(b)*

Situated as it is, following the clause about the transfer of rights, this assertion about giving more student rights than the regulations afford recognizes the eligible student as an adult under the law, with rights and privileges that may exceed those prescribed under FERPA. In other words, while the regulations identify basic privacy rights, institutions have the responsibility and the prerogative of applying those rights within the individual regulatory context of their states and local communities. In some of those instances, the rights at the individual institution may be more than what FERPA requires.

Annual Notification: Rights under FERPA

There are, in fact, four basic rights under FERPA. But when these rights are presented in §99.7 of the regulations, they are presented as part of the content that should make up the annual notification of rights under the regulations. The annual notification seizes the spotlight as the first requirement of institutions in FERPA. In the shadow of the Code of Fair Information Practices, this requirement may even be seen as the first right under FERPA: the right to disclosure of policy and practice on an annual basis.

Annual Notification Requirement

Like other federal legislation that deals with citizen rights, FERPA follows the guidance of the Code of Fair Information Practices, beginning with a requirement that no database should be kept secret. In §99.7(a)(1), FERPA, therefore, requires a disclosure of rights to the individuals affected and requires that such disclosure be made on an annual basis.

> Each educational agency or institution shall annually notify parents of students currently in attendance, or eligible students currently in attendance, of their rights under the Act and this part.
>
> *§99.7(a)(1)*

The phrase "currently in attendance," of course, refers to students who are enrolled, those who are currently attending classes or maintaining a student status at the institution. Under this definition, the institution need not attempt to notify others about FERPA rights, including both former and prospective students. Only the current population of students in attendance needs to be advised of their rights under the regulations.

Methods of Annual Notification

Notification does not need to be direct to each individual student. That is, unlike the Truth In Lending provision that requires notifications to individual financial account holders, FERPA merely insists that the annual notification be easily accessible to all students in attendance. The notification should be made in a manner that will reasonably reach or be available to all students in attendance.

Most institutions publish their annual notification as a policy statement regarding how information from education records is maintained and disclosed. This statement is often published in annual or more frequently distributed publications, such as the catalog, the schedule of classes, a student handbook, or as an insert into student newspapers. At the very least, the notification must be made on an annual basis.

The regulations go on to make specific disclosure requirements in regard to the disabled and those whose first or primary language is not English.

An educational agency may provide this notice by any means that are reasonably likely to inform the parents or eligible students of their rights.

1. An educational agency or institution shall effectively notify parents or eligible students who are disabled.

2. An agency or institution of elementary or secondary education shall effectively notify parents who have a primary or home language other than English.

   §99.7(b)

The first provision flows from the Americans with Disabilities Act (ADA), which requires public entities to make reasonable accommodations for those with cognitive and physical disabilities. This is to say that the annual notification should be available to those with disabilities in a format that makes the information accessible to them. A number of web text and other publication tools assist institutions in adapting written or published disclosures so as to reach individuals with specific challenges.

Americans with Disabilities Act

The Americans with Disabilities Act (ADA) was passed in 1990 and codified at 42 USC §12101. The act prohibits discrimination against persons with disabilities and provides protections that were subsequently expanded by the ADA Amendments Act of 2008 (ADAAA), which detailed a list of impairments to major life activities.

The act requires reasonable accommodation on the part of institutions and employers in the provision of services, living or working conditions, and accessibility to information.

The second provision is a result of the No Child Left Behind (NCLB) Act and is specific to the K–12 community. The NCLB had already drawn attention to increasing populations of non-English speaking citizens throughout the United States and focused institutional outreach efforts on the unique educational needs of the school districts' local communities. FERPA takes up the banner with this stipulation regarding the annual notification. Schools that have large populations of children whose parents or guardians do not speak English as a primary language must ensure that these individuals are made aware of their rights under the regulations. This requirement, however, has no impact in the postsecondary arena since the students themselves possess privacy rights in postsecondary education.

No Child Left Behind Act

The No Child Left Behind (NCLB) Act, sometimes pronounced "nicklebee" because of its initials, was established in 2001 as an initiative to improve the performance of primary and secondary schools, as well as to contribute to the academic development of students enrolled in those schools. Federal programs were identified to address issues in K–12 education, including testing, teacher preparation, and a commitment to quality on the part of schools and parents. Because of an ever-growing minority population, the act included outreach to students and their parents whose first language was not English.

The NCLB initiative, last amended in 2008, is extensive and reaches into every area of K–12, with implications for higher education as well. Embedded in the legislation is a provision for the disclosure to military recruiters of name, address, and home telephone numbers for all students enrolled in secondary schools—provided the student or the student's parent has not opted out of directory information disclosure.

The February 2009 issue of *Legal Update for Teachers*, the newsletter of the Center for Education and Employment Law, reported on a November 2008 survey of 147 educators conducted by Edweek.org. The survey asked educators to rank the critical education issues that should be addressed by newly elected President Barack Obama once he takes office. Fifty-eight percent of those surveyed said that the new President's top priority should be major reforms to NCLB.

Disclosure of privacy rights in K–12 is very different from the annual notification that is made in the postsecondary environment. In K–12, privacy rights are directed to the parents since the students in primary and secondary education are minors. In the postsecondary environment, the students are adults under the law, and privacy rights belong completely and solely to the student.

Regardless of these differences, it is the requirement of disclosure that is significant and vital to K–12 and postsecondary compliance with this first mandate of the regulations.

Disclosure of FERPA Rights

It is in the context of requiring an annual notification that FERPA specifies its guaranteed rights. In fact, the fundamental content of the annual notification is that the notice identify what rights are guaranteed under the regulations and disclose how the individual may exercise those rights.

The notice must inform parents or eligible students that they have the right to—

i. Inspect and review the student's education records;

ii. Seek amendment of the student's education records that the parent or eligible student believes to be inaccurate, misleading, or otherwise in violation of the student's privacy rights;

iii. Consent to disclosures of personally identifiable information contained in the student's education records, except to the extent that the Act and Sections 99.31 authorize disclosure without consent; and

iv. File with the Department a complaint under Sections 99.63 and 99.64 concerning alleged failures by the educational agency or institution to comply with the requirements of the Act and this part.

§99.7(a)(2)

Fundamentally, the four rights of eligible students are summarized as follows:

- The right to inspect and review their education records
- The right to seek to amend their education records

- The right to have some control over the disclosure of information from their education records
- The right to file a compliant with the Department of Education for the alleged violation of FERPA rights

Each of these rights is examined individually and in detail in the pages that follow. For the purposes of the annual notification, however, the regulations go on, in §99.7(a)(3), to make some specific provisions in regard to the disclosure of these rights.

The notice must include all of the following.

i. The procedure for exercising the right to inspect and review education records.

ii. The procedure for requesting amendment of records under §99.20.

iii. If the educational agency or institution has a policy of disclosing education records under §99.31(a)(1), a specification of criteria for determining who constitutes a school official and what constitutes a legitimate educational interest.

§99.7(a)(3)

The first two provisions merely require institutions to provide guidance to students on how their FERPA rights are to be exercised. It is important to emphasize that implicit in these directions is not merely the establishment of practice but the need to codify policy and procedure that can be produced for students, parents, the public, and the courts as proof of compliance with the regulations. If challenged regarding an alleged violation of FERPA rights, it is policy and procedure that will be required by the FPCO to demonstrate the institution's adherence and compliance with the regulations.

The third provision adds two components to the structure of the annual notification: an identification of school officials and a definition for legitimate educational interest.

Other Components of the Annual Notification

The specification of education officials in §99.7(a)(3)(iii) is of critical importance at institutions where information is shared among or made available to faculty, staff, and others. Indeed, such practices sound like common operating procedure since it would be essential that certain information be made available to those conducting the business of the institution. But there is an important distinction here that refers back to the Code of Fair Information Practices.

Recall that the generation of the Code of Fair Information Practices occurred in the midst of growing apprehension about the increasing amount of information being collected by government agencies. The sharing of that information between agencies suggested a potential for establishing a very powerful and comprehensive database about private citizens—one that was initially seen as a serious invasion of privacy. In the distillation of the Code of Fair Information Practices, provisions were made for how information in databases of personally identifiable information would be used. Even within specific entities, legislation was careful to stipulate that information would only be used for the purposes for which it was collected. Recordkeepers were charged with guarding against the misuse and the potential misuse of the data they collected.

FERPA	Code of Fair Information Practices
Right to inspect and review education records	No recordkeeping system can remain secret. Individuals have a right to know what is being maintained about them.
Right to seek to amend education records	Individuals must be able to correct information that is being stored about them.
Right to have some control over the disclosure of information from education records	Individuals must be able to prevent disclosures of information without their consent.
Right to file a complaint for an alleged violation of FERPA rights	Organizations must ensure appropriate use of data and take precautions against potential misuse.

Institutions of higher education, therefore, must disclose their practices of sharing and utilizing information both within and outside the organization. Disclosure in the annual notification must include institutional definitions of education (or school) official as well as criteria for legitimate educational interest, the basis upon which information is shared within the educational institution. Further, if the institution has a practice of regularly providing or releasing information to the parents of dependent children or to schools in which the student may be intending to transfer, these practices must also be disclosed in the annual notification.

Why go into so much detail? Note that the privacy rights are made specifically to the eligible student in higher education. It is the eligible student alone who has the right to inspect and review, to seek to amend, and to consent to disclosures. Availability of information about the eligible student beyond the student himself needs to be disclosed so that the student is aware of the extent to which his personally identifiable information is being made accessible.

In this last provision, the regulatory language refers to instances and situations identified in §99.31, which is the section that identifies exceptions to the requirement of prior written consent. The sharing of education records with education officials, the parents of dependent children, and other third parties are contained in this section, making such disclosures *exceptions* to the regulations and not daily business or common practice. Therefore, if an institution regularly makes such disclosures, the institution must disclose those practices in its annual notification.

> *A society that will trade a little liberty for a little order will lose both, and deserve neither.*
>
> —THOMAS JEFFERSON

The influence of the Code of Fair Information Practices and the Privacy Act of 1974 becomes readily apparent. Beyond the basic rights defined by FERPA are considerations that arise as corollary or implied by the wider context of privacy rights in general. As legislative regulation, FERPA does not stand alone but rather in the context of other privacy provisions and general legislation.

Understanding the implications of the Code of Fair Information Practices becomes important not merely in determining resolutions to individual situations wherein FERPA has implication but in guiding deliberation along fair and consistent strategy for the establishment of sound institutional policy and procedure.

Right to Inspect and Review

The first precept of the Code of Fair Information Practices states that no recordkeeping system can remain secret. Individuals have a right to know that a recordkeeping system exists and that an entity is compiling information about them. Further, citizens have a right to know what kind of information is being stored in this database.

Therefore, the first guarantee that FERPA makes to parents and eligible students is the right to inspect and review education records. Students have a right to know that information is being collected and maintained about them *and* to be able to inspect and review that information.

FERPA guarantees eligible students the following rights.

- **The right to inspect and review education records**
- The right to seek to amend education records
- The right to have some control over the disclosure of information from education records
- The right to file a complaint for an alleged violation of their FERPA rights

The Registrar and Other Recordkeepers

In the past, education records about students were fundamentally centralized in the custody of one of the highest ranking officials of the school. This recordkeeper—or registrar—was guardian of the primary business record of the institution: that of the education records of its students. The registrar served, and still serves, as steward over these education records, charged with maintaining accurate and complete records about student achievement in the student's academic pursuits at the institution. Moreover, it is the registrar who issues official verification and documentation of student academic achievement at the institution.

As schools grew, and especially with advancements in technology, business necessity mandated that records be created and maintained at various levels and in different locations throughout the institution. Academic departments, tracking specific information about students in their majors, found it necessary to keep their own records, apart from the official record maintained in the registrar's office. Faculty had always maintained their own private systems for monitoring and evaluating student performance in individual classes. And as programs developed within departments or combined the efforts of multiple disciplines, new and expanding databases of student records began to emerge across campus.

For all intents and purposes, the registrar has continued to be regarded as the official custodian of student records. It is the registrar who generally evaluates and nominates candidates for degrees from the institution. The registrar issues official transcripts, which are regarded as the unequivocal proof of student academic achievement, as well as certifies student information and issues diplomas. When law enforcement is investigating a student, it is to the registrar that initial inquiries are directed. And when the Department of Education approaches institutions regarding student data, the singular focus is on the registrar's office.

The Registrar

From the legal perspective, the term *registrar* is used to identify the official keeper of records. The word comes from a shortening of the medieval Latin word *registrarius* and was once used in its longer variation *registrary*.

Registrars exist in many kinds of businesses. Hospital administrators who admit patients are called registrars. In banking, the term is used to identify the keeper of official documents for clients and business entities. The registrar of voters oversees the voting process. And in some cultures, the Justice of the Peace or civil commissioner authorized to record birth, deaths, and to perform marriages is called the registrar.

In the academic arena, the registrar is the official custodian of student records. Charged with maintaining academic records, the registrar has been an important position throughout the history of educational institutions. In the United Kingdom, the registrar is often the head of the university's administration.

It is the registrar, as the primary and official institutional recordkeeper, who assumes and is charged with responsibility for compliance with FERPA. Over the years, this responsibility has expanded to include the training of campus officials and to serve as a resource or sort of "FERPA police" for the institution.

> If an educational agency or institution receives funds under one or more of the programs covered by this section, the regulations in this part apply to the recipient as a whole, including each of its components (such as a department within a university).
>
> *§99.1(d)*

Recognizing the multiplicity of recordkeepers across the campus, FERPA emphatically states its application to *all* areas of the institution (§99.1(d)). This means that compliance with FERPA, at an institution that receives funds from the federal government, applies to each and every custodian of education records throughout the campus.

If recordkeepers are scattered throughout the campus, then education records are also spread throughout the campus. Wherever education records are maintained, these regulations apply. The responsibility for privacy belongs to the local recordkeeper in whose charge the records are kept; nevertheless, the total liability for compliance with the FERPA regulations is to the institution as a whole.

Access to Education Records

Issues that arise with access to and the disclosure of information from education records always revolve around non-directory information. While directory information can be released, as long as the student has not restricted such disclosure, the disclosure of non-directory information almost always requires prior written consent. To facilitate the business of education, FERPA does make some exceptions, detailed in §99.31, but even these exceptions require careful scrutiny and evaluation.

> The educational agency or institution, or SEA (state educational agency) or its component, shall comply with a request for access to records within a reasonable period of time, but not more than 45 days after it has received the request.
>
> *§99.10(b)*

Once authorized access is established, the recordkeeper must permit inspection and review of those records within "a reasonable period of time" (§99.10(b)). The vague and subjective nature of the phrasing is intentional and not altogether a hindrance for the institution.

In the first place, the regulatory language acknowledges the jurisdiction of public information laws and court procedures within the various states. Courts have local authority to set their own specifications in regard to requirements for the production of evidence in compliance with a court order or subpoena. This is the standard that dictates time frames for the production of records in other arenas. Institutions and their recordkeepers must comply with the regulations and guidelines that have been established for the state in which the institution is located.

The time frame set by local regulation is the guiding rule, so long as that time frame does not exceed 45 days. For the purposes of FERPA, compliance with a request for the inspection and review of records must occur within 45 days of receipt of that request.

FERPA sets this 45-day limit not to confuse recordkeepers but to indicate when complaints regarding noncompliance with inspection and review may be referred to the Family Policy Compliance Office (FPCO). An individual state may require recordkeepers to comply with documentary disclosure and surrender on a court-ordered subpoena within a 10-day period. If an institution in that state fails to comply with a request within 20 days, the requesting party may have grounds to initiate legal action within the local courts, but the Department of Education will not entertain a complaint on a FERPA violation for another 25 days since its limit is the longer period of time—45 days.

Complaints about the Availability of Records		
	Time Period	**Where to Complain**
State/local regulation	Established per state/local legislation	State/local courts
FERPA	45 days	Family Policy Compliance Office

A secondary condition in regard to "a reasonable period of time" is deference on the part of the regulations to policy and procedure established by the institution. Institutions must define how compliance with inspection and review is to be guaranteed to students. This definition is in the form of policy and procedure—written documentation that applies officewide or campuswide. Of course, such policy and procedure must comply with state and local regulations as well as with FERPA. And moreover, employees across the campus must be obliged to follow those regulations in the course of conducting business on behalf of the institution.

For example, although technology facilitates the creation or duplication of records almost instantaneously, some campuses may not wish or be able to produce records for students on such short order. An institution may require students to make appointments to inspect and review records.

RECORDS MANAGEMENT CONCERNS: CONTENTS

- Students have a right to inspect and review the contents of their education records, wherever they exist on the campus.
- Do files include records to which the student should not have access or that are not appropriate for the education record?
- What is the procedure for inspecting and reviewing education records at your campus?
- Once a request is made, how long before a student can inspect and review education records?
- What time period is specified for the production of records in your individual state?

Appointments are generally made within three business days of the initial request. The important point here is that the request is immediately acknowledged, and the availability of records is scheduled for a specific date and time. As long as that date is not "unreasonable," such a response would be in compliance with the regulations.

An important clarification is necessary at this point. When this book refers to policy and procedure, written documentation is always a contingency of its definition. Often, campus departments become so immersed in operations that they fail to document their practice in a written and easily available format. This leaves practice at the level of practice, as opposed to official policy and procedure. Should an institution be challenged in a court of law to defend its practice in a particular situation, it is written policy and procedure that will prove an important component of that school's defense. The flip side of this reality, of course, is compliance with one's own policy and procedure. Without official documentation of its business practices—in policy and procedure—an institution's integrity may rest on verbal allegation, opinion, and misinterpretation of intention.

Policy and procedure is addressed in greater detail in Chapter Six.

Interpretation and Explanation

A corollary of access to records is an implied responsibility for the record-keeper to provide some interpretation and explanation of the manner in which records are kept and the meaning of their content. The Code of Fair Information Practices keenly suspected that records might be maintained in such a manner as to make them unintelligible to anyone but employees of the recordkeeping entity. Many early recordkeeping computer systems used abbreviations and cryptic field names as a strategy for masking or hiding information from all but the initiated. To ensure that records do not remain suspect or cleverly concealed, the first two provisions of the Code of Fair Information Practices prohibit secrecy and mandate disclosure.

FERPA translates those provisions with a requirement for institutions to respond to "reasonable requests" for explanations and interpretations of its records (§99.10(c)). Such requests may come from individuals inspecting and reviewing the education records of an institution. Elucidation on the codes used in transcripts and other documentation would not be an unreasonable request. However, elaborating on circumstances or providing additional narrative or documentary evidence in support of official records may be an unreasonable request—especially where policy and procedure do not require the maintenance of such additional evidence.

> The educational agency or institution, or SEA or its component, shall respond to reasonable requests for explanations and interpretations of records.
>
> *§99.10(c)*

To eliminate the need for ad hoc explanations and to provide supporting disclosure to substantiate practice, institutions maintain a series of publications that compile such documentation. The institution's annual catalog is one such publication that has often been referred to as the business contract between the institution and the student, primarily because graduation requirements are often delineated in the catalog. But other publications and references may include student handbooks, program disclosures, pamphlets and booklets about activities, and individual policy disclosures.

Legends on the reverse of official documentation, such as transcripts and verifications, are a succinct method of providing information to the user or recipient of these documents for understanding the method of presentation and its content. Just be sure that instructions on legends are kept current and that the legends remain relevant to the presentation of data in the document they are intended to explain.

Search and Retrieval

Two fee structures are often associated with the production of records for inspection and review: one for search and retrieval and one for photocopies.

Charging a fee for the search and retrieval of student records is not permitted under FERPA (§99.11(b)) when the search and retrieval of records is in connection with a student's request to inspect and review education records. The guarantee regarding the inspection and review of education records has no qualifications, and the imposition of a fee to search for records may impede or even prohibit the student's ability to inspect and review his records.

> An educational agency or institution may not charge a fee to search for or to retrieve the education records of a student.
>
> *§99.11(b)*

The Code of Fair Information Practices sought to ensure that consumers would not be prevented from exercising their rights in regard to databases that contain their personally identifiable information. The practices detail explicit rights, and the influence on subsequent legislation was to ensure that no hindrances or impediments were introduced by government or other entities that would interfere with the administration of these rights.

It is with this understanding that search and retrieval fees are not permitted under FERPA when the request for records is made by the eligible student. This prohibition, however, does not affect the assessment of search and retrieval fees in other circumstances, such as in the production of records in response to a subpoena or other similar request.

Photocopies of Documentation

The regulatory writers were clever in their selection of language for this first guarantee because it is only about inspection and review. Institutions must provide students and individuals with authorized requests the ability to inspect and review education records—but that's it. There is no provision to require that recordkeepers provide photocopies or duplicates of those records.

Depending upon policy and procedure, an institution may, of course, provide photocopies of documents in its files—and may even charge a fee for that service. Photocopy fees should be consistent with other photocopy fees on campus and should not create a situation where a student may, by the imposition of fees, be denied the right to inspect and review her education records. If the student, for example, is out of the area—generally, 50 miles from the campus is considered a "reasonable" distance—and unable to come into an office to inspect her records, or if she is unable to pay the fee for photocopies, the institution should consider providing the photocopies without charge to ensure that the opportunity for inspection and review is provided.

> Unless the imposition of a fee effectively prevents a parent or eligible student from exercising the right to inspect and review the student's education records, an educational agency or institution may charge a fee for a copy of an education record which is made for the parent or eligible student.
>
> *§99.11(a)*

Many institutions, for various reasons, are sometimes reluctant to make photocopies of their records. And to be precise, institutions are not obliged by FERPA to make those photocopies at all. Institutions must only ensure that the eligible student is provided with an opportunity for inspection and review.

Institutions have been creative about providing inspection and review in situations that demand some sensitivity to other extenuating circumstances. If an institution prefers not to make photocopies and the student requesting inspection and review is in another state, long-distance inspection and review may be provided by mailing documents to another educational institution in the city where the student may now be living. The package of documents is sealed and sent to the registrar or other education official at the local institution. Once the student arrives at the local institution, the package of documents is opened in her presence and inspection and review takes place in the presence of the "deputy" education official. When the process is concluded, when the opportunity for inspection and review has been provided, the education official at the local institution repackages the documents and returns them to the originating institution. Photocopies were never provided. But more importantly, the first institution has complied with its obligation to provide the student with access for inspection and review of the education records.

If circumstances effectively prevent the parent or eligible student from exercising the right to inspect and review the student's education records, the educational agency or institution, or SEA or its component, shall—

1. Provide the parent or eligible student with a copy of the records requested; or

2. Make other arrangements for the parent or eligible student to inspect and review the records.

   §99.10(d)

While FERPA does not require institutions to provide photocopies of records, there are instances where photocopies may be required for legal or customer service considerations. In response to a court-ordered subpoena, photocopies of records may need to be provided to the attorneys of the opposing parties, sometimes with the registrar required to appear in court to formally provide the original documents.

For customer service considerations, institutions should consider individual circumstances before refusing to photocopy documentation from their student record files. In some cases, the original documentation may be returned to the student after the need for requiring that documentation has been served. This is especially beneficial to the student whose original documents were difficult to obtain in the first place. This is usually the case with international transcripts and documents containing the apostille (or official, usually governmental, certification) of another country.

While a document is in the custody of an institution, there is no prohibition against making a photocopy of that document and providing it to the student. Of course, you cannot imply an official issuance of a document for which you were not the original creator or recordkeeper. In such cases, a disclaimer should be stamped or attached to the document, indicating that the document is a photocopy of an original contained in your education records.

COPY

This is to Certify That the Document Herewith

Is a Facsimile or Photocopy

Of An Original Document

That is Contained in the Eduction Records Of

(Institution Name)

Another consideration in this regard may involve simply returning original documents to the student and maintaining only photocopies in your files. Most institutional policies require verification of certain qualifications but do not necessarily specify the retention of original documents as supporting evidence. And even if original documents are necessary, once the process for which the documents are required is satisfied, what purpose is there in retaining the original documents, especially when the documents may have been difficult for the student to obtain in the first place?

An alternative records management protocol may be to make a photocopy of the original document for the institution's files. Record on the photocopy that you have verified the original—for example, by documenting a date and initial. Then return the original documentation to the student. The

---

RECORDS MANAGEMENT CONCERNS: MAINTAINING ORIGINAL DOCUMENTS IN FILES

- Is it necessary to maintain original documentation in your education files?

- Is it enough to verify the existence of such documentation using photocopies or checklists?

- Will photocopies suffice in lieu of the original?

- Consider returning original documents to the student—especially documents that were difficult to procure.

- Consider what documents are retained and for how long. Note: documents retained in education records become education records themselves.

---

photocopy would be retained in the institution's file for as long as that part of the student record is maintained. Once the retention period is elapsed, the record would be destroyed along with other documents scheduled for destruction. But the original would be preserved in the custody of the student to whom the document belonged in the first place.

Whatever records management practices you adopt, be sure to add them to your written policy and procedure. You can then train and empower staff to make individual determinations regarding the maintenance of various documentation on behalf of both the institution and the student.

Holds and Denial of Service

When a student has outstanding financial obligations to an institution, a typical practice is to withhold or to deny services to the student until arrangements can be made to satisfactorily address those obligations. Verifications, transcripts, and continued enrollment are often the most visible and vital services to be denied students in these cases. Are such "holds" a violation of FERPA?

Remember that the guarantee under FERPA is to provide the opportunity for the inspection and review of education records. FERPA does not oblige institutions to provide any other service in this regard—only the opportunity for inspection and review. So while institutions may withhold services, they must, nevertheless, comply with a request for inspection and review.

Providing inspection and review to a student who is present in the registrar's office is not the difficulty, however. The problem arises in situations when the student is not able to come into the campus office to inspect and review his records. What if you need to provide photocopies in order to comply with the student's right to inspect and review?

According to the FPCO, there is nothing in FERPA to prohibit an institution from indicating on the photocopies provided to the student that outstanding financial obligations exist. The rationale here is that inspection and review is being provided directly to the student who already knows he has outstanding financial obligations to the institution. If the student had intended to share the documentation with anyone else, with a prospective employer, for instance, that's his business—and embarrassment. Presumably, however, the indication of outstanding obligations would be a deterrent from utilizing the records for anything other than the student's own inspection and review.

While not specifically a FERPA concern, there is another issue that arises in regard to holds that affects institutional practice. Institutions should take precautions when dealing with a student who has filed for bankruptcy. Bankruptcy laws prevent the continuation of debt collection efforts while

---

Andrews University v. Weiner Merchant

The 1992 6th Circuit Court of Appeals case of *Andrews University v. Weiner Merchant* (958 F. 2d 738) illustrates an important precaution that must be taken into account when holds are placed on student services for outstanding obligations.

An English citizen, Weiner Merchant attended Andrews University and applied for a financial aid loan through the Michigan National Bank. Just one year after her graduation, however, Merchant filed for Chapter 7 bankruptcy. The university paid off the bank and assumed Merchant's entire loan, adding to her obligations to the university and forcing the university to cease providing services, such as transcripts, to Merchant.

In its deliberations, the court concluded that the university's actions of withholding transcripts to Merchant was not lawful and a violation of 11 USC §362. That law regarding bankruptcy calls for a stay of debt collection efforts while a Chapter 7 bankruptcy is being adjudicated. The court judged the hold on transcripts placed by Andrews University was an attempt to collect a debt, putting it in violation of the debt collection stay. Andrews was forced to suspend its hold until the bankruptcy case had been settled, after which time it could reinstate its hold on services to Merchant.

The Court also found that Merchant's student loan could not be discharged under her Chapter 7 bankruptcy filing.

a case is under court consideration. Once bankruptcy has been filed, a "stay" on debt collection efforts is enacted while the bankruptcy court resolves the filing. Collectors must stand in line for reimbursement, if you will, depending upon the judgment of the court. And this stay affects not only collectors but the providers of services as well.

In the case of *Andrews University v. Weiner Merchant*, the enforcement of holds by the denial of transcripts was judged to be a debt collection effort. After all, the intent of a denial of service is to instigate some action toward repayment on the part of the individual with an obligation to the debtor. Institutions would be in violation of bankruptcy legislation by refusing to provide services such as transcripts to a student who has filed for bankruptcy. Under these conditions, the institution should suspend its holds on services while the bankruptcy case is in litigation. Once a judgment has been issued, the hold can always be reinstated on a student's account.

Exceptions to Inspection and Review: Letters of Recommendation

FERPA also specifies certain limitations—that is, when students do *not* have a right to inspect and review certain records that may be contained in their student files. Two types of records are specifically mentioned, one of which is given considerable treatment in the regulations so as to codify practice.

- Financial records of parents or guardians
- Letters of recommendation

In addition to the exceptions to education records (detailed in the discussion of the definition of education records in Chapter Two), the regulations withhold student access to records that may contain financial information about the student's parents or guardians. Financial regulations protect the privacy of financial information about individuals. While there is the familial relationship between the postsecondary student and her parent, the two entities are adults and, under the law, not entitled to information about each other's finances. Unless there is a requirement or distinct purpose to do so, the financial records of parents and guardians should not be maintained in the student's file and should never be provided to the student for inspection and review.

In the same section, the regulations also codify practice governing letters of recommendation.

A postsecondary institution does not have to permit a student to inspect and review education records that are:

1. Financial records, including any information those records contain, of his or her parents;

2. Confidential letters and confidential statements of recommendation placed in the education records of the student before January 1, 1975, as long as the statements are used only for the purposes for which they were specifically intended…

   §99.12(b)

Effective the first day of the year following the implementation of FERPA, letters of recommendations may be withheld from student inspection and review providing a few caveats are met. Those stipulations, defined in §99.12(b)(3), are the following.

- The student has, in writing, waived his right of access to the letters
- The letters of recommendation are in connection with admission to an institution, application for employment, or receipt of an honorary distinction

A postsecondary institution does not have to permit a student to inspect and review education records that are:
Confidential letters and confidential statements of recommendation placed in the student's education records after January 1, 1975, if:

i. The student has waived his or right to inspect and review those letters and statements; and

ii. Those letters and statements are related to the student's:

   A. Admission to an educational institution;

   B. Application for employment; or

   C. Receipt of an honor or honorary recognition.

   §99.12(b)(3)

Letters of recommendation have always generated substantial debate and controversy, particularly in regard to two points—student access and the ultimate usefulness of such letters.

There is widespread belief that if the composer of the letter could not be assured that a student would never see the letter, her comments in the correspondence would not be completely honest or be so diluted as to render the letter useless. This sentiment has led some faculty to insist that they will not write letters of recommendation *unless* the student waives his rights of access to the letter. On the flip side, some institutions advise students that they will not accept letters of recommendation *unless* the student has waived the right of access to those letters. Sadly, both of these positions and practices hark back to a more archaic time when academic communities considered themselves in a world set apart and not obligated to follow regulations enacted to protect the rights of all citizens in the greater society.

In the first place, the Code of Fair Information Practices insists that records cannot be kept secret and that individuals must be advised regarding what information is being created and communicated about them. The practices around confidential letters of recommendation, both academic and employment, are rooted in seeking frank evaluations of individuals about their performance and abilities. Unfortunately, political and other negative influences have not always kept their distance in regards to such evaluations, prompting the imposition of this meticulous procedure of waivers of rights of access that is currently in place.

The privacy—and civil—rights perspective on recommendations would certainly insist upon open and sincere communications that fairly and accurately assess an individual for a particular reason. The relationship between the evaluator and the subject of the evaluation should be such that an honest exchange of the content and reaction can take place *prior to* the composition of the letter. And the writer should provide to the person being evaluated a copy of that communication, even if the original must be sealed and forwarded under separate cover to another designated entity. The fact that a waiver has been enacted by a student should make no difference in regard to the extent of the letter's content or the candor with which it is expressed.

This is not to say that the practice of waiving rights of access to documents is without merit. From the perspective of the evaluator, some confidentiality should already be evident in the process. After all, in employment protocol, the interview process and the evaluation of candidates requires confidentiality on the part of the selection committee.

It can hardly be argued that either students or teachers shed their constitutional rights to freedom of speech or expression at the schoolhouse gates.

—JUSTICE ABE FORTAS

The legal and ethical point about how waivers are administrated is that individuals must never be forced to give up any of their rights. Students should never be coerced into giving up their privacy rights. Certainly, faculty members are not obliged to write letters of recommendations. The option to do so is entirely voluntary on the part of the faculty member. And for the student and the faculty member, the value of a letter of recommendation should arise from the relationship between the two and not from any political significance that may be derived from the letter's author. The invitation to write a letter of recommendation should come from the appreciation and value of the evaluator's comments in honestly assessing and counseling the subject's growth and potential.

For a faculty member to misuse the student's waiver of access as a condition of writing a letter of recommendation is not only immoral but illegal under the FERPA regulations. And the text of §99.12 goes on to establish qualifications for and limitations on the waiver of rights, defining the conditions under which a waiver of access is to be considered invalid or void.

A waiver under paragraph (b)(3)(i) of this section is valid only if:

i. The educational agency or institution does not require the waiver as a condition for admission to or receipt of a service or benefit from the agency or institution; and

ii. The waiver is made in writing and signed by the student, regardless of age.

§99.12(c)(1)

In §99.12(c)(1), the regulations qualify a valid waiver of access to a letter of recommendation on the lack of coercion between the parties involved—the student, the composer, and the institution—*and* on the existence of written evidence of waiving rights. The absence of either of these qualifications nullifies the waiver and allows the student to access the letter of recommendation for inspection and review like any other education record.

The second condition refers to the written documentation of a waiver of rights that must be kept with the original letter of recommendation. If the letter is to remain confidential, that waiver of access must be maintained with the letter itself. Without this attachment, a student has a right to inspect and review the letter of recommendation that is maintained in an education file.

There is no standard language for a waiver of rights of access. Text in regards to waivers is usually woven into standard forms provided to students by the requesting party. These forms tend to gloss over the confidentiality of the document to be produced and focus more on procedures

---

LETTER OF RECOMMENDATION WAIVER FORMAT RIGHT OF ACCESS DECLARATION

Check one of the following options.

☐ I waive my right of access to the contents of this recommendation letter. I understand that I may not request access to inspect, review, or receive copies of this letter, from either the composer or recipient of this letter.

☐ I do NOT waive my rights to access this recommendation letter or its contents. I understand that I may inspect and review this letter or copies of this letter wherever permitted by local policy and procedure or by other applicable regulations.

Student Signature _____

—INSTRUCTIONS TO THE COMPOSER AND TO RECORDKEEPERS OF THIS LETTER—

1. Per the Family Educational Rights and Privacy Act (FERPA), students have a right to inspect and review education records, except where the right of access to certain records has been waived. Education records are maintained by educational agencies and institutions. For all other entities, local regulations and other policies and procedures may apply.

2. To Composers of letters of recommendation: You may not insist on a student's waiver of access as a condition for writing a letter of recommendation.

3. To Recordkeepers of this letter: Maintain a copy of this Letter of Recommendation Request/ Waiver with each copy of the letter maintained in your files.

4. The absence of an attached Letter of Recommendation Request/Waiver allows a student to access copies of letters that are maintained in education records.

for composition and submission. A suggested text from Cliff Ramirez & Associates is provided in this section.

Because of the controversial nature of waiving rights of access to letters of recommendation, higher education policy and procedure would do well to be guided by best practices in records management. The area most related to letters of recommendation in higher education is that of letters of recommendation in human resources and employment.

First of all, letters of recommendations and the accompanying waiver should never be maintained with a student file. Remember, students have a right to inspect and review their education records at the institution. Keeping letters of recommendation separate from student files eliminates the possibility that, despite a waiver, a student may be given unintentional access to those letters.

Secondly, letters of recommendation should only be maintained for as long as their purpose requires. If the letters are used for admissions decisions, then the letters should be destroyed shortly after the admission decision has been made. The American Association of Collegiate Registrars and Admissions Officers (AACRAO) recommends that application files of individuals who are not accepted to the institution should only be maintained between zero and two years. Many institutions keep application files separate from the education records that are turned over to the registrar's office once the individual matriculates as a student. Further, only certain documents are transferred from the applicant file to the education record in the registrar's office. All other applicant documents are properly destroyed.

Faculty who maintain copies of the letters of recommendation that they have written must maintain a copy of any applicable waivers with those letters of recommendation. A faculty member's records are education records, with the exception of any sole possession records. In the absence of such waivers, these letters constitute education records, and students would have a right to inspect and review those records. If a student has waived rights of access and that written waiver is properly maintained with the letter to which it applies, the student would not have the right to inspect and review that letter.

It would be difficult for faculty to insist that their records of these letters of recommendation constitute sole possession records since the letter has already been communicated and shared with other education officials. Even for records maintained on private home computer systems, invoking sole possession may not be a sufficient legal defense against providing inspection and review. The faculty member is, after all, an education official for the institution and is maintaining records that directly relate to students. Without documentation of a waiver of access, sole possession is a difficult foundation on which to deny access.

In the case of *People Against Abuse in Schools v. Williamsport Area School District*, a Pennsylvania court ruled that a psychologist's records about grade school students, maintained on the psychologist's home computer, could not be excepted under the sole possession records rule. Despite the fact that no report was ever made to the school district based upon the information in those records, the court argued that the *intention* of those records was the sharing of critical information with the school and with the parents of the children involved. While the school did not insist on a formal report, the parents had every right to the content of the psychologist's investigation, and the fact that the records were maintained on a home computer in the home of the psychologist made no difference. In other words, the intent behind the existence of the records proved important in determining access to those notes. (The case of the *People Against Abuse in Schools v. Williamsport Area School District* is the focus of the sidebar on page 38 in the discussion of sole possession records.)

To avoid any problems, letters of recommendation, wherever they are kept, should be maintained with their applicable waivers. Without that waiver, a student has the right to request from an education official the opportunity to inspect and review his education records.

Because the issue of managing letters of recommendation is often fraught with confusion and emotional vehemence, guidelines from a records management perspective are provided in this section.

Records Retention

FERPA is not about records management, although certain practices are implied in the administration of its privacy regulations. There are a number of recordation requirements that are discussed in Chapter Six of this book; however, a related topic of some importance in this discussion of inspection and review is the simple availability of records for that inspection and review.

Records management strategies are incomplete if they do not address records retention and the destruction of records whose shelf-life has expired. Best practice obliges institutions to incorporate records retention guidelines in their policy and procedure, as well as to map out verifiable confidential records destruction protocols. Incumbent upon records managers, thereupon, is the monitoring of records retention and the destruction of records when policy compels their destruction.

MANAGING LETTERS OF RECOMMENDATION

Responsibilities of the composer of letters of recommendation

- Ask the student to provide you with a written declaration regarding rights of access to the letter being requested.

- Never force the student to waive rights of access as a condition of your writing the letter.

- Discuss the content you expect to include in your letter with the student.

- Once written, provide the student with a copy of the letter of recommendation—even if the student has waived rights of access.

- If you maintain a copy of the letter, you must maintain a copy of the student's declaration regarding rights of access.

Responsibilities of recordkeepers

- Maintain student declarations regarding rights of access with the letters to which they apply.

- Maintain letters and their applicable declarations only for as long as needed to serve their purpose.

- Do not file letters of recommendation and their student declarations with other education records.

- Students have a right to inspect and review letters of recommendation for which no declaration regarding rights of access have been submitted or retained.

- Properly destroy letters and their student declarations according to records retention policies and procedures.

Responsibilities of students

- When approaching a faculty member about a letter of recommendation, ask to discuss the potential contents of that letter before it is written. Remember that this is a mentoring experience and that comments are intended to guide your growth and development.

- Be sure that your wishes regarding access to letters of recommendation are written and submitted to the individual from whom you are requesting the letter of recommendation.

- Whether or not you waive your rights to a letter of recommendation, ask the composer if he is willing to share a copy of the letter with you.

- Read disclosures on applications and other documentation regarding entities collecting information about you to determine what rights of access you may have to information that is collected and maintained about you.

RECORDS MANAGEMENT CONCERNS: RETENTION

- Do you have a current records retention policy in place?

- Not every record in a file needs to be retained. Which are the specific records that need to be retained?

- What is the lifespan of a record—that is, for how long is it useful?

- What are your appropriate records destruction protocols?

Having policies and procedures in place—and policies and procedures to which there is faithful adherence—is solid legal protection for both public and private entities. When questioned in a court of law about records which you cannot produce because they are no longer in existence, you need only cite your written policy and procedures and refer to documented proof that records destruction protocols were appropriately followed.

It is up to the individual institution to define its own records retention policies, specifying what records are retained and for what period of time.

> The educational agency or institution, or SEA or its component, shall not destroy any education records if there is an outstanding request to inspect and review the records under this section.
>
> *§99.10(e)*

In regards to inspection and review, FERPA prohibits the destruction of any education records when the opportunity for a requested inspection and review has not yet been provided. Inspection and review must always be permitted in response to an authorized request. Destruction of a record when a request for inspection and review is still outstanding may be considered tantamount to the destruction of or tampering with evidence, and may have legal consequences beyond FERPA.

Right to Seek to Amend

The Code of Fair Information Practices guarantees individuals the right to correct or amend information that is being maintained about them. And the same right is carried over in FERPA.

FERPA guarantees eligible students the following rights:

- The right to inspect and review education records
- **The right to seek to amend education records**
- The right to have some control over the disclosure of information from education records
- The right to file a complaint for an alleged violation of their FERPA rights

Naturally, if institutions permit students to inspect and review their education records, the student may discover records or portion of records with which the student may disagree. The second right under FERPA is the right to seek to amend education records.

Criteria for Amendments

FERPA broadly qualifies the types of records for which a student may seek to amend. If the student believes that records are inaccurate or misleading, the student may seek to have those records corrected or changed. Students may also seek to amend records—or have records eliminated—on the grounds that a record or a portion of a record is an invasion of the student's privacy. Excluded from this list of criteria are grades.

> If a parent or eligible student believes the education records relating to the student contain information that is inaccurate, misleading, or in violation of a student's right of privacy, he or she may ask the educational agency or institution to amend the record.
>
> *§99.20(a)*

Every recordkeeper seeks to maintain accurate records; therefore, it goes without saying that inaccuracies should be corrected wherever they are detected. Admittedly, most of the information in education records is captured in databases where data entry is performed by individuals who are usually not the subject of the record. Unintentionally, errors will occur and, upon discovery, these errors should be rectified as soon as possible.

Because records are also being compiled from a variety of sources, the final representation may not be consistent with what was intended. Misleading or misrepresented information should be adjusted in the same way that inaccurate data is corrected.

Invasion of Privacy

Invasion of privacy is a cause of action in legal proceedings that was a concept that was largely developed by Samuel D. Warren and Louis D. Brandeis in 1890, when they published "The Right of Privacy" in the *Harvard Law Review*.

There are four primary areas in privacy that are identified in modern tort law.

- *Intrusion of solitude:* the physical or electronic invasion of a citizen's private quarters or space

- *Public disclosure of private facts:* the publication or dissemination of private information, however truthful, that a reasonable person would find objectionable

- *False light:* placing a person in a false light or dubious perspective through the publication or dissemination of facts that may, on their own, not be objectionable or defamatory

- *Appropriation:* the unauthorized use of a person's name, likeness, or other attributes to seek financial or other benefits

---

The more subjective portion of this provision has to do with what constitutes an invasion of the student's privacy or a violation of the student's privacy rights. FERPA does not suggest legal redress in this case but leaves deliberation entirely up to the institution. Consultation with campus counsel or an attorney may be suggested since "violation of the privacy rights of the student" is not confined to the jurisdiction of FERPA or education records. The grounds upon which the student feels that her privacy rights have been violated are vital for determining how the institution responds.

In the matter of grades, while the regulations do not mention them specifically, the FPCO has determined that grades are not covered under this FERPA guarantee. Grades are an assessment of academic performance by a faculty member and outside the jurisdiction of FERPA. While the inaccurate recording of a grade may be covered under the right to seek to amend, disputes about the assessment process or on what grounds a grade or evaluation was determined are beyond the scope of the regulations. While FERPA does not require it, institutions should establish their own policy and procedures to deal with complaints and disputes about grades and assessment.

Lastly in this consideration of criteria, while the regulations do not specify it, it can be implied that when FERPA guarantees to students the right to seek to amend education records, the responsibility is limited to those records created by the institution. The records maintained by the institution may include documentation received from other sources, such as transcripts and correspondence from other institutions or entities. Students who contest the contents of those records must direct their objection to the source or creators of those records.

While an institution may interpret records received from other sources in whatever manner it wishes, it may not alter those records. Institutions are only obliged to entertain requests for amendments that focus on records created by its own education officials and processes. In the case of a record received from another source, an unresolved dispute may be easily resolved by the elimination or exclusion of the contested record from the student's file.

Amendment Process

While defining the process for resolving amendment requests is up to each individual institution, the FERPA regulations do provide some broad guidelines for formal adjudication should the student be unsatisfied with the results of the institution's process.

Presumably, most situations are resolved when the creator of the record is made aware of the student's objection to the record. The creator would reevaluate the record and determine whether a change should be made to the record. The creator's decision is then communicated to the student, who must be satisfied with the results of the creator's review or have a means to contest that decision.

> The educational agency or institution shall decide whether to amend the record as requested within a reasonable time after the agency or institution receives the request.
>
> *§99.20(b)*

Generally, the student should be able to appeal to the supervisor of the creator of the record or to a formal body of representatives at the institution. It is at this point that FERPA interjects its requirements regarding the amendment of records.

A written statement should be submitted to the institution by the student, detailing all of his objections. FERPA directs the institution to make a determination "within a reasonable time" (§99.20(b)). Again, that time period is not defined by FERPA but should be expressly defined in the institution's policy and procedure.

If the decision of the institution is to amend or eliminate a record, the record should be dealt with accordingly. But if the decision is not agreeable to the student, the student needs to be advised of an appeal process and given the opportunity of a formal hearing.

An entire section in FERPA, §99.22, provides the minimum requirements for the hearing process. While some of the provisions are left to the discretion of local policy and procedure, such as the time frames for processing, there are other stipulations that are required of institutions in the process.

The hearing required by §99.21 must meet, at a minimum, the following requirements:

a. The educational agency or institution shall hold the hearing within a reasonable time after it has received the request for the hearing from the parent or eligible student.

b. The educational agency or institution shall give the parent or eligible student notice of the date, time, and place, reasonably in advance of the hearing.

c. The hearing may be conducted by any individual, including an official of the educational agency or institution, who does not have a direct interest in the outcome of the hearing.

d. The educational agency or institution shall give the parent or eligible student a full and fair opportunity to present evidence relevant to the issues raised under §99.21. The parent or eligible student may, at their own expense, be assisted or represented by one or more individuals of his or her own choice, including an attorney.

e. The educational agency or institution shall make its decision in writing within a reasonable period of time after the hearing.

f. The decision must be based solely on the evidence presented at the hearing, and must include a summary of the evidence and the reasons for the decision.

§99.22

Essentially, the student is entitled to a hearing or other proceeding to plead his case and argue his objection to the record in question. At his own expense, the student is allowed representation of his own choice, including legal representation. The official overseeing the proceeding must be a disinterested party and have no interest in the outcome or final decision. As with criminal court proceedings, only evidence presented in the process must be considered in arriving at a decision. And finally, the decision itself, whatever it may be, must be communicated to the student in writing, including the substantiating reasons for the decision.

If, as a result of a hearing, the educational agency or institution decides that the information in the education record is not inaccurate, misleading, or otherwise in violation of the privacy rights of the student, it shall inform the parent or eligible student of the right to place a statement in the record commenting on the contested information in the record or stating why he or she disagrees with the decision of the agency or institution, or both.

§99.21(b)(2)

If the student is still not satisfied with the results of the hearing, the student is provided with a final remedy.

The Fair Credit Reporting Act, consistent with the Privacy Act of 1974, provides consumers with an opportunity to amend information in their individual credit reports when that information is inaccurate, incomplete, or involves extenuating circumstances. Consumers write to the credit reporting agency, identifying the specific information in question. The credit bureau must investigate, usually writing to the creditor for justification of the content of its report. If the consumer's objection is substantiated, the record should be amended. But if the credit bureau finds no reason to change its record, the consumer still has an opportunity to provide a statement to the credit bureau that must be contained in and disclosed whenever the consumer's credit bureau report is disclosed. The same process is at work for the student here.

If an institution rules against a student's objection to a record or portion of a record, the student has a right to record his objection in a written statement. The statement must be submitted to the keeper of the record to which the student objects. As with the provisions for consumer credit reports, the student's statement must be filed with the contested record and disclosed whenever the contested record is disclosed. The student's statement must be maintained in the student's records for as long as the contested record is maintained.

Fair Credit Reporting Act

The first major reporting agency in the United States was the Retail Credit Company, established in 1899 to compile reports about consumers. Its business endeavors soon expanded to include selling reports to insurance companies and employers. But by the 1960s, credit reporting agencies began to be accused of using incomplete or outdated information, fabricating negative information, and furnishing lifestyle information to law enforcement and unauthorized entities. Lifestyle information included data about an individual's sexual orientation, marital status, drinking habits, and even personal hygiene.

The Fair Credit Reporting Act (FCRA) was passed in 1970 as a result of public exposure and congressional inquiry into the practices of the credit reporting agencies. Among its provisions was the right of consumers to access information in credit reports and to dispute incomplete or inaccurate information.

Numerous amendments have been made to the FCRA, including passage of the Fair and Accurate Credit Transactions Act in 2003, allowing consumers to request a free credit report once every 12 months.

Administration of the FCRA belongs to the Federal Trade Commission as well as to number of other government agencies.

These requirements regarding a student's statement in objection to a record are contained in §99.21(c) of the regulations and amount to only the second instance in which FERPA says something about records retention.

> If an educational agency or institution places a statement in the education records of a student under paragraph (b)(2) of this section, the agency or institution shall:
>
> 1. Maintain the statement with the contested part of the record for as long as the record is maintained; and
>
> 2. Disclose the statement whenever it discloses the portion of the record to which the statement relates.
>
> *§99.21(c)*

Anonymous Records

Anonymous records are records for which it is difficult or impossible to determine the identity of the creator of the record. Individuals, for reasons of their own, may seek to insert information into student records while eliminating any possibility of tracing the record back to themselves as the author.

Anonymous tips are unacceptable in the education environment. In fact, recordkeeping practices that have been spurred on by technology eliminate the potential for anonymous records by automatically recording the identity of the creator in an audit file whenever a record is created or amended. Audit trails track changes to vital information retained in the database and have been extremely useful in identifying the source of unauthorized disclosures of information.

Education officials should be discouraged from submitting anonymous records to education records. If a concern is critical enough to prompt any action, the observer should be encouraged to bring the concern to the attention of another education official, such as the individual's supervisor or a dean. Apart from legitimate educational interest, FERPA permits the communication of information where there may be a significant threat to the health and safety of a student or to other members of the educational community. A more comprehensive discussion of this topic is provided in Chapter Four.

Anonymous records serve no purpose. As part of a student's education record, they are subject to the student's inspection and review. Should the student object to the record and initiate a cause to amend the record, the institution would have no way to review the contested record with a creator. In such a predicament, the institution would be left with no other course of action than to eliminate the record from the student's file.

To avoid such embarrassing and time-consuming situations, the institution should prohibit the retention of any records for which the creator cannot be identified.

RECORDS MANAGEMENT CONCERNS: RELEVANCE OF RECORDS

- Retain only documents relevant to the purpose of the record or file being maintained.
- Records not relevant to the file being maintained should be referred to the appropriate office for disposition.
- Records of an articulable and significant threat to individuals or community safety must be referred to the appropriate office or official immediately upon discovery, detection, or receipt.
- The creator of a record should always be evident or easy to determine.

Right of Control over Disclosure

A predominating concern of the Code of Fair Information Practices focuses on how the personally identifiable information that is collected about individuals is used. Two of the five practices are concerned with usage and the prohibition of further disclosure without the prior consent of the individual identified by the record. And the last practice seeks to set standards for security and custodial responsibility.

Accordingly, the third of FERPA's guarantees to students is the right to have some control over the disclosure of information from their education records. Two important definitions are required here: disclosure and control.

FERPA guarantees eligible students the following rights.

- The right to inspect and review education records

- The right to seek to amend education records

- **The right to have some control over the disclosure of information from education records**

- The right to file a complaint for an alleged violation of their FERPA rights

---

Meaning of Disclosure

In its simplest sense, *disclosure* means to provide information, whether intentionally or unintentionally, from records that are kept in one's personal custody. It is important to note that the disclosure here refers to information that is derived from records in one's custody. Providing information from any other source may be personal knowledge but, more often than not, is only hearsay, secondhand information, or gossip. Depending upon the consequences and implications of transmitting such unfounded information, other legal repercussions may be entailed. FERPA applies specifically to the disclosure of information from education records.

Disclosure means to permit access to or the release, transfer, or other communication of personally identifiable information contained in education records by any means, including oral, written, or electronic means, to any party except the party identified as the party that provided or created the record.

§99.3

Disclosure is focused on the transmission of information from education records by any means, including oral, written, or electronic means. Electronic means may include images, data-bytes, audio and video transmissions, and other methods of electronic and digital communication.

The 2008 Amendments revised the Department of Education's understanding of disclosure, including an interpretation that addresses the need for institutions to verify the authenticity of documents that are purported to be issued by another educational institution.

Despite the growing use of security paper for printing official transcripts, the incidence of fraudulent or falsified documents has continued to be a concern. Security paper, the same kind of paper used for issuing checks, stocks, bonds, and other financially binding documents, contains its own tools for preventing and detecting fraud or attempts at falsification and tampering with the contents of a document. Merely photocopying the document reveals disclaimers that make the document unofficial and otherwise unacceptable. Further, the introduction or alteration of text and other content causes blemishes, discoloration, and instant evidence of criminal intentions.

The Battle against Fraudulent Credentials

For many years, the higher education community—and others—has been plagued by the rise of diploma mills. These purveyors of "novelties" that simulate the diplomas of reputable schools or purport to confer degrees for life experiences and undocumented work have created national distrust and suspicion. This was one of the reasons that institutions converted to issuing transcripts on security paper, thus protecting the authenticity of their own documents.

A 2003 article in the *Chronicle of Higher Education* estimated that half a million people lie on employment applications, which is why so many employers have turned to verifying degrees their prospective applicants claim to have earned. The same article lamented that the FBI ceased to investigate allegations of diploma mills because they were so hard to prosecute and were, in essence, victimless crimes.

In July 2007, Manhattan's Robert M. Morgenthau, of the Office of the New York County District Attorney, indicted ten individuals on an alleged scheme to sell degrees for cash. Months earlier, the office had been tipped off by Tuoro College. And among the indicted were Tuoro's former director of admissions, the former computer center director, and former students. All ten suspects were convicted in June 2009.

More and more, it is difficult to dismiss the work of diploma mills as victimless crimes. The cost increases in human resources processing as well as the unwarranted salaries paid to those undeserving individuals who successfully misrepresent their credentials are hardly insignificant. While the copyright infringement of logos and institutional names is evident, colleges and universities are, nevertheless, loathe to prosecute diploma mills because of the legal expense involved. Many prefer to leave the legal redress to those who are actually harmed by these crimes—leaving, in the end, no one to undertake the responsibility or leadership in such prosecutions.

Fraud and the Dilemma of Fraudulent Diplomas

While to many the issue of fraudulent diplomas is clearly a crime, the legal dilemma for institutions and law enforcement focuses on how to pursue and prosecute purveyors of such documents. Diploma mills often advertise their services as providing souvenirs, curios, or novelties. And who hasn't shopped for amusement park souvenirs that manipulate documents to give an individual an elevated sense of importance?

In most legal dictionaries, fraud is defined as intentional deception resulting in injury to another person. There are different kinds of fraud, including, among others, fraud in fact, positive fraud, swindling, cheating, rigging, and intrinsic fraud. In all versions, importance rests on identifying both intention and injury.

Clearly, the individual who presents a fraudulent diploma to another college or university or to an employer is intentionally misrepresenting her credentials. The reasons for such deception range from admission to highly competitive programs to acquiring high-paying or prestigious jobs.

The difficulty that paralyzes legal action is in identifying the injured party. Has an institutional name really been sullied? And is any institution really harmed by such isolated instances of misdirected cleverness? On the one hand, there are the copyright infringements and misappropriation of names and logos. But the expense of prosecution often deters institutions from pursuing action, especially when diploma mills go into and out of business so quickly.

The injury to society is perhaps the most compelling argument since the misrepresentation of credentials in certain fields can certainly imperil public and individual safety. Targeted action by law enforcement and local government provide the essential ammunition against diploma mills. With other types of fraud gaining the attention of regulators—even in FERPA—perhaps legislation will one day address the problem of fraudulent diplomas and the counterfeiters who produce them.

Security paper was a viable and heartily embraced solution when transcripts were mailed or hand-delivered. As web-based, student access systems have gained momentum and widespread acceptance, the desire for immediate, on-the-spot documentation has accelerated. Now, printouts from student access systems and the use of "unofficial" documents, while supplanting the wait time for the mailing of official transcripts, have added new potential for the spread of fraudulent and falsified information.

In discussing the need for revisions to the definition of disclosure in the *Federal Register* of March 24, 2008, the regulators intended to assist institutions in dealing with those situations where fraudulent documents are presented as valid or official transcripts from an institution.

Previously, because a prior written consent was required for the release of non-directory information, an institution could only verify for another institution whether a document it received was authentic or not. This left the second institution with no other option but to discredit the entire document without knowing what content of the document was manipulated or falsified.

Under the new understanding, supported by the expansion to the exception in §99.31(a)(2), referring to when a student seeks or intends to enroll, an institution has greater latitude in validating documents. The institution verifying the validity of a document it allegedly issued may now not only make a determination on authenticity, but it can also provide the inquiring institution with a valid, original document. The same applies for state and local educational agencies whose documents are misrepresented or altered.

> The disclosure is subject to the requirements of §99.34, to officials of another school, school system, or institution of postsecondary education where the student seeks or intends to enroll, or where the student is already enrolled so long as the disclosure is for purposes related to the student's enrollment or transfer.
>
> *§99.31(a)(2)*

The discussion in the March 24, 2008, issue of the *Federal Register* cites the exception in §99.31(a)(2), which allows an institution to disclose education records without prior written consent to an institution in which the student intends to enroll. If a fraudulent or falsified transcript is presented to an institution, the alleged originator of the document "may confirm or deny that the record is accurate and send the correct version" [FR 5576] to the inquiring institution.

The new interpretation and expansion on disclosure is a boon to institutions in attempting to circumvent the tide of fraudulent transcripts. In regards to disclosure, the *Federal Register* goes on to pointedly declare its intent.

The proposed amendment is needed to verify the accuracy of this type of information and to ensure that the privacy protections in FERPA are not used to shield or prevent detection of fraud. [FR 15576]

Some Control over Disclosure

What the FPCO describes as a student's right to have *some control* over the disclosure of information from education records is more cryptically worded in the regulations themselves. This right is contained in the list of items that an institution must include in its annual notification to students in attendance. And the wording in §99.7(a)(2)(iii) states only: "Consent to disclosures of personally identifiable information contained in the student's education records, except to the extent that the Act and §99.31 authorize disclosure without consent."

As already discussed in Chapter Two, FERPA divides information in education records into two categories—directory and non-directory information. A student, in exercising some control over disclosure of information from her education records, may request that the institution withhold disclosures in one of two ways.

An educational agency or institution may disclose directory information if it has given public notice to parents of students in attendance and eligible students in attendance at the agency or institution of:

1. The types of personally identifiable information that the agency or institution has designated as directory information;

2. A parent's or eligible student's right to refuse to let the agency or institution designate any or all of those types of information about the student as directory information; and

3. The period of time within which a parent or eligible student has to notify the agency or institution in writing that he or she does not want any or all of those types of information about the student designated as directory information.

§99.37(a)

According to §99.37, a student may request that directory information be withheld from public disclosure. Remember that once an institution identifies what data it considers directory information, it must disclose its definition of directory information to students in attendance through its annual notification. Thereafter, the institution may disclose such information without a student's prior written consent—*unless* the student has requested that such information not be disclosed. If a student suppresses the disclosure of directory information, the institution must deny all requests for directory information data about that student. Staff may respond to such inquiries with "I'm sorry, but that information is restricted and is not available to the public."

Recalling that §99.1(d) of the regulations stated that FERPA applies "to the recipient as a whole, including each of its components," it is important to mention that directory restrictions may impact business for academic departments and other components of the campus. When lists of students, photo montages, and group posters are compiled, education officials need to be wary of instances when students have requested that their directory information not be disclosed.

On most campuses, requests for suppressing the disclosure of information are submitted to the registrar's office and logged into a student records system that may or may not be accessible campuswide. Staff and faculty throughout campus need to be able to determine that the student has not restricted the disclosure of directory information before publicizing anything about a student. To unilaterally create disclosures about students without verifying the existence of directory restrictions is to create the potential for a FERPA violation.

From a different perspective, departments should notify students before creating publicity information about groups of students and allow individual students to opt out of being included in those lists or photographic directories. In the same way that publishers gather authorizations for student photographs and other inclusions in annuals and yearbooks, departments may wish to compile written authorizations from students electing to be included in a particular project from which there may be substantial public disclosure. In this way, departments and staff protect the campus against a potential violation of FERPA.

The second type of control students may exercise under this right is a request that no information whatsoever be disclosed about the student. This comprehensive request is often referred to as a "FERPA restriction." In essence, the student requests that his attendance and existence at the institution never be acknowledged or confirmed to the public. Institutions should respond to requests for information on these students by saying, "I'm sorry, I have no information about that person (or individual)." Staff responding to such inquiries must be careful not to use the word "student," since this may be interpreted as creating an implied relationship with the individual.

	Directory Restriction	**FERPA Restriction**
Requested/ Removed	In writing	In writing
Information Impacted	Specific directory information or all directory information	All information
Response to Inquiries	"I'm sorry. *That information* is not available to the public."	"I'm sorry. I have no information about that *person*."

FERPA restrictions are not common, and students need to be carefully counseled before the institution accepts a request for such a comprehensive restriction. Usually, compelling or extenuating circumstances require a FERPA restriction, as in the case of an individual participating in a witness relocation/protection program, a celebrity student, or an individual who is being stalked.

Institutions should counsel students to determine what kind of restriction is actually warranted for each individual situation. Once a restriction is placed, the institution cannot remove that restriction until the student submits a new request in writing, revoking the former restriction.

Students often forget to release restrictions before they graduate or leave the institution. This may place them in embarrassing and compromising dilemmas. For example, if a prospective employer calls the institution to verify the attainment of a degree, the institution would not be able to provide information until the student releases the restriction. The response to the potential employer would be, "I'm sorry, I have no information about that individual." And where would that leave the former student?

Once a FERPA restriction has been placed, even the institution must be wary of communications and requests received from that former student. If the former student writes to request some service from the institution, the institution may need to request that the individual provide copies of identification to substantiate the validity of the request. The request to remove a FERPA restriction from a student record requires positive identification and verification that the request, indeed, originated from the former student.

Because the FERPA guarantees are made to students in attendance, institutions are not required to accept requests for directory or FERPA restrictions from individuals who are no longer in attendance. This is not to say that the institution may not deem it prudent to accept such a request, depending upon the circumstances surrounding the former student's situation. FERPA, however, does not oblige the institution to accept the request and leaves determination of a response in such situations to the institution.

With regards to restrictions, then, it is important to remember several points.

- The institution is only required to accept requests for disclosure restrictions from students in attendance.
- Disclosure restrictions continue on student records until released by the student—even if the student has left the institution.
- Once a restriction has been placed, the restriction may only be revoked by the written authorization of the student.

> An educational agency or institution may disclose directory information about former students without complying with the notice and opt out conditions in paragraph (a) of this section. However, the agency or institution must continue to honor any valid request to opt out of the disclosure of directory information made while a student was in attendance unless the student rescinds the opt out request.
>
> *§99.37(b)*

In §99.37(b), included as part of the 2008 Amendments, FERPA specifies that institutions must continue to honor requests for disclosure restrictions that were placed by students while they were still in attendance at the institution. Even though the student may no longer be in attendance, the request remains in effect until it is revoked by the former student in writing.

The inclusion of this language was prompted by a 2006 complaint against the University of Cincinnati, where student information was passed on to an alumni office but without indication of directory and FERPA restrictions in place. When the university published its alumni website, including information about a student who had placed a restriction, the student complained and the university was found to be in violation of the regulations because the restriction request had not been honored by the institution nor revoked by the student.

Endurance of Restrictions: University of Cincinnati

In 2006, the Family Policy Compliance Office (FPCO) issued a letter to the University of Cincinnati (UC) that provides important guidance on the sustainability of restrictions placed by students while they are students.

A graduate student had placed a directory restriction on her records and did not revoke it upon graduation. When information was passed from the student records to the alumni office, restrictions were not transmitted. As a consequence, the student's information was published on InCircle, the school's alumni website.

Upon the complaint of the former student, the situation was investigated and the UC agreed to not only remove the information from the website but to set up protocols to guard against such errors in the future.

Continuity of Student Access

University Records Systems Access (URSA), the student access system at the University of California Los Angeles (UCLA), allows students and former students to complete a variety of transactions as well as have access to their academic records. Under the guidance of Registrar Anita Cotter, URSA has developed and undertaken the processing of such sensitive transactions as the recording and enactment of privacy options. The system authenticates identity and implements changes to directory restrictions overnight. Students must visit the Registrar's Office to request a full FERPA restriction. For students in attendance, changes are reflected in the electronic campus directory the next day. Further, URSA is available to former students for at least ten years after their departure from UCLA.

Whenever information is passed on to alumni relations and advancement offices, privacy restrictions should also follow the student record—or the record should not be transmitted at all. Of course, these offices need to be trained and cognizant regarding the meaning of directory and FERPA restrictions and be cautious about how student information with these kinds of restrictions is used.

Some institutions have utilized their student access systems to gather privacy information options from continuing students. When these systems are made available to former students, the authentication of requests to changes to privacy restrictions, and even the ordering of transcripts, can be greatly facilitated. The validity of the request and the identity of the former student making the request would be verified through the system's authentication protocols. In such cases, the student access system could manage privacy requests for students as long as updated information is passed along to administrators who may need to verify the existence of these kinds of restrictions.

Limits on Suppressing Directory Information

Another of the terms whose definition has been revised by the 2008 Amendments is that of attendance.

In the past, the working definition of attendance has focused on physical presence in a classroom. With advances in technology, however, classroom delivery methods have evolved. Attendance is no longer a physical requirement but can now be a virtual one. Attendance, as defined in the 2008 Amendments, includes participation in classroom or learning activities in a variety of ways, many of which no longer demand physical presence.

Attendance includes, but is not limited to—

a. Attendance in person or by paper correspondence, videocon-ference, satellite, Internet, or other electronic information and telecommunications technologies for students who are not phys-ically present in the classroom.

   §99.3

Because students need not be physically present for a classroom activity to take place, a disturbing situation has arisen that has drawn the attention of the faculty, schools, and the FERPA regulators. Students, whether intentionally or not, realize that they could avoid participating in classes if they suppress their directory information. With a directory restriction, name, contact information, and e-mail address cannot be distributed. For classes utilizing video conferencing technology, students with directory restrictions may not be photographed or appear on camera. These restrictions effectively eliminate student participation in classroom assignments and online discussions.

A parent or eligible student may not use the right under paragraph (a)(2) of this section to opt out of directory information disclosures to prevent an educational agency or institution from disclosing or requiring a student to disclose the student's name, electronic iden-tifier, or institutional e-mail address in a class in which the student is enrolled.

   §99.37(c)

To address this situation, §99.37(c) prohibits a student from placing a directory restriction to prevent the disclosure of contact information that may be necessary to distribute to a classroom community. As long as a student is enrolled in a class, the requirements for classroom participation supersede any restrictions that may have been placed by the student at the institution. In the March 24, 2008 issue, the *Federal Register* specifically declares the following.

…the right to opt out of directory information disclosures does not include a right to remain anonymous in class and, therefore, may not

be used to impede routine classroom communications and interactions by preventing a teacher from identifying a student by name in class, whether a class is held in a specific physical location or on-line through electronic communications. [FR 15590]

The discussion goes on to allow teachers to call students by name and even require students to place their names on sign-in sheets for the purpose of recording attendance. Students are required to disclose electronic identifiers or e-mail addresses so that teachers and other students enrolled in the class may communicate with one another in class work.

Note that this provision is strictly limited to information needed to identify and enable students to communicate in class, i.e., the student's name, unique electronic identifier, and institutional e-mail address. It provides no authority to disclose any directory information outside of the student's class. Further, no other kinds of directory information, including a student's home or campus address, telephone listing, or personal e-mail address not used for class communications, may be disclosed, even within the student's own class, if the parent or eligible student has exercised the right to opt out of directory information disclosures. [FR 15590]

Therefore, while a student cannot suppress the disclosure of directory information to abstain from participating in a class, if directory information has already been suppressed, only the specific information needed to participate in the course work may be shared with members of the classroom community. That information is limited to name, an electronic identifier, and an institutional e-mail address. Other information that may have been suppressed by the student could not be shared, and the student should not be required to disclose any other information with the classroom community.

Implied Consent

Recordkeepers, as the custodians of information, are in an enviable position to be able to confirm or deny the veracity of information that may be circulated in the community. As already seen, if confronted about the authenticity of one of its documents, an institution may not only deliver its judgment but provide an original replacement if a proffered document is shown to be fraudulent. This was the result of the 2008 Amendments' expansion on the definition of disclosure. And it was specific to the involvement of a document alleged to be issued by an institution in a situation where a student is seeking or intending to enroll in another institution.

When no document is involved, but only information has been circulated—verbally or in writing—what is a recordkeeper's responsibility? May the recordkeeper chime into the public forum to confirm or deny the veracity of information?

In the case of education records, the answer is a resounding negative. Without the prior written consent of the student, non-directory information may neither be confirmed nor denied, even if the disclosure was originally made by the student. In FERPA, there is no implied consent.

Implied consent is defined as follows.

consent when surrounding circumstances exist which would lead a reasonable person to believe that this consent had been given, although no direct, express, or explicit words of agreement had been uttered [Law.com Legal Dictionary]

Under FERPA, the prior written consent of the student is required for the disclosure of non-directory information from the student's education records. And, in fact, a prior written consent is the institution's clearance for the release of any information. It is a legal proof of authorization for the disclosure of information detailed in the consent language. As the FPCO has insisted on many occasions, when in doubt about whether you can release anything, ask for a prior written consent.

Without prior written consent, a recordkeeper may not confirm information or even give the impression of confirming non-directory information. This is because, under FERPA, a disclosure is a disclosure. FERPA does not take into account whether or not the information is already in circulation or

---

Implied Consent Laws

Implied consent is a controversial concept because detractors argue that implied consent defies the First Amendment of the Constitution. The First Amendment declares that "no person shall be compelled in any criminal case to be a witness against himself."

Implied consent is most often used by law enforcement in determining whether an individual has been driving under the influence (DUI) of alcohol or other drugs. If a driver is stopped, and the driver does not know his blood alcohol level, he must submit to a breathalyzer test or other test of blood, urine, or breath. Under the implied consent laws of many states, a driver cannot refuse to take such a test without incurring serious penalties or repercussions. According to state implied consent laws, a driver gives his consent to DUI testing from the moment of applying for and receiving a drivers license and through the act of getting behind the wheel of a motor vehicle.

Penalties for refusing to submit to DUI tests vary from state to state and can entail lengthy prison terms, especially where aggravated circumstances are involved, such as injury or death.

whether or not the information in circulation is true. To disclose information without prior written consent, or without the disclosure being permitted under the exceptions of §99.31, is to violate the regulations.

This understanding is underscored by the discussion surrounding the 2008 Amendments regarding the use of a social security number (SSN) in verifying student information. Institutions need to be cautious in issuing their verifications so that verifications of degrees, majors, or other enrollment information do not inadvertently confirm non-directory information such as the SSN.

Disclosures and the SSN

The December 9, 2008, issue of the *Federal Register* clarifies a number of issues regarding use of the SSN at institutions of higher education and advises caution when institutions affix their confirmation or certification of student information for third-party entities.

Institutions have long been in a quandary regarding use of the SSN as a student ID number. In fact, many have labored under the impression that schools could not even use an SSN as a student ID number (SID). The *Federal Register* confirms the following position on the part of the Department of Education.

> *In general, however, there is no statutory authority under FERPA to prohibit an educational agency or institution from using SSNs as a student ID number, on academic transcripts, or to search an electronic database so long as the agency or institution does not disclose the SSN in violation of FERPA requirements. [FR 74808]*

The spirit of this assertion is more concerned with the protection of the SSN. In the same paragraph, moreover, the *Federal Register* goes on to insist on a position that may at first seem contradictory.

> *FERPA does prohibit using the student's SSN, without consent, to search for records in order to confirm directory information. [FR 74808]*

What are the regulators trying to accomplish? And what are the specific requirements on institutions?

The concern about the use of the SSN goes back to the Privacy Act of 1974 and has been fueled by 21st century concerns regarding identity theft. Some states have, in fact, passed legislation prohibiting institutions from using the SSN as an identification number for individuals. The passage of the Identity Theft Red Flags and Address Discrepancies Rules, or Red Flags Rules (see Chapter Six) effective August 2009, are an indication of the level of continuing federal concern for identity theft.

For many years, the Department of Education erroneously interpreted the use of the SID as tantamount to an SSN. This was not surprising, since the SSN was often used as the SID at many institutions. But the two are not on an equal par, and this realization has prompted the clarifications included in the 2008 Amendments.

The Department of Education's position on the SSN has not changed. Institutions cannot designate the SSN as directory information and, because it is non-directory information, cannot disclose an SSN without the prior consent of the student. With regard to the SID, the department does not recommend designation of the SID as directory information. But the student user ID (see Chapter Two), which may be an SID, is permitted to be directory information if the data element by itself does not provide access to non-directory information or other personally identifiable information.

The difference in treatment has to do with the kind of information that can be accessed through these data elements. The concern is that if these data elements provide a gateway to personally identifiable information about a student, they cannot be designated as directory information. The only way in which these items would provide sufficient protection for non-directory information is if they use a two-factor authentication protocol that consists of a logon ID and a password or personal identification number (PIN). And even then, directory information designation should be considered carefully and made only if there is a demonstrated operational need to do so.

Use of the SSN should be restricted to internal usage and to those situations where use of the SSN is permitted by legislation, such as in the processing of financial aid. For all other usage, the prior written consent of the student is required in order to use or disclose an SSN.

The caution with regards to unintentional disclosure focuses on the processing of verification requests received from third parties. To facilitate a verification request, a third party may provide a form that supplies information about a student and asks for a certification signature from an education official at the institution. These forms may be used to request confirmation of attendance, majors, degrees, and graduation dates. Space is generally provided for the institution's verification, requesting a signature, the printed name of the certifying official, contact information, the date, and may even require the imprint of a seal.

At face value, it could be interpreted that the signature is attached to the information supplied to the form by the education official. But from a different perspective—and a legally contestable one—the signature could be interpreted as confirming *all* of the information presented in the document about the student. If an SSN is listed, that verification could be interpreted to include the SSN itself. And without a signed authorization from the student, such a disclosure is a potential violation of FERPA.

Discussion in the *Federal Register* indicates that the legislators are aware of these kinds of situations.

> *A school is not required to deny a request for directory information about a student, such as a confirmation whether a student is enrolled or has received a degree if the requestor supplies the student's SSN (or other non-directory information) along with the request. However, in releasing or confirming directory information about a student, the school may not use the student's SSN (or other non-directory information) supplied by the requestor to identify or locate the student's records unless a parent or eligible student has provided written consent. This is because the confirmation of information in education records is considered a disclosure under FERPA. [FR 74809]*

The Department of Education's recommendations for dealing with these kinds of verification requests are not specific but instructive.

> *There is no authority in FERPA to require a school to notify requestors that it is not confirming the student's SSN (or other non-directory information) when it discloses or confirms directory information. However, when a party submits a student's SSN along with a request for directory information, in order to avoid confusion, unless a parent or eligible student has provided written consent for the disclosure of the student's SSN, the school may indicate that it has not used the SSN (or other non-directory information) to locate the student's records and that its response may not and does not confirm the accuracy of the SSN (or other non-directory information) supplied with the request. [FR 74810]*

There are several ways of addressing these situations.

One strategy is for the institution to develop its own official response to requests for verifications. The third party's form would not be used. Instead, the institution would utilize its own form, inserting the appropriate information requested by the third party. Providing your own verification document eliminates the potential for misinterpretation of the data you are confirming.

During the 1990s, UCLA developed a document it called a "Verification Transcript," thus creating its own official verification document. Conceived by Registrar Anita Cotter, the concept was rooted in the fact that information on the document was derived from the student's official record at the university—that is, from the transcript. Whereas the "Academic Transcript" provides non-directory information and requires the prior consent of the student for release, the "Verification Transcript" lists only directory information and, barring any directory restrictions, could be provided to third parties willing to pay the transcript fee. (Since the "Verification Transcript" was printed on security paper, the regular transcript fee was charged.)

But what if you do have to utilize the form provided by the third party? If you must use the third-party form, and the form contains an SSN or other personally identifiable information that the institution cannot disclose, you must indicate clearly what information is being verified by the institution. You may need to tag each data element you confirm or provide a separate notation, initial, or stamp. The official verifying the specific information would need to check mark the data element supplied and initial as evidence of having provided the information.

✓ Verified by _____

An alternative strategy would be to provide a stamp near or over the signature line of the third party's form. The stamp would disclose, specify, or limit the data being confirmed by the institution.

VERIFICATION CERTIFICATION

This is to certify that [the institution] verifies and confirms only the information provided by the education official completing this form. [The institution] makes no judgment or disposition on other data included in this form, which may or may not have been used in the processing of this verification or confirmation.

Signature _____

Date _____

Institutions are not unfamiliar with third parties who insist that their own forms must be used or completed to provide information. Some of these entities may cite their own policies and procedures and contend that forms will be incomplete or unacceptable without your compliance in utilizing their forms. Institutions cannot be responsible for the policies and procedures of other entities. You are responsible only for your own protocols. So, if your official verification is the only form you produce in response to such requests, there is nothing to prevent you from insisting that you are complying with your own policies and procedures.

Policies and procedures exist not only to keep your processes compliant but to protect you and your practices from legal assault. A more extensive discussion about policies and procedures is provided in Chapter Six.

Right to File a Complaint

The fourth guarantee to students is the right to file a complaint for an alleged violation of the student's FERPA rights.

FERPA guarantees eligible students the following rights:

- The right to inspect and review education records
- The right to seek to amend education records
- The right to have some control over the disclosure of information from education records
- **The right to file a complaint for an alleged violation of their FERPA rights**

Complaints are submitted in writing to the Family Policy Compliance Office (FPCO), which is the office of the U.S. Department of Education, charged with interpreting, investigating, and adjudicating issues involving FERPA.

FPCO Authority to Investigate

The FPCO is introduced in §99.60(a), from which the regulations go on to describe the responsibilities designated by the Secretary of the U.S. Department of Education to the FPCO. In the regulations, those responsibilities are basically two.

- Investigate complaints and violations
- Provide technical assistance and guidance

The enforcement responsibility is essentially inferred and altogether missing from the regulatory language. Enforcement, to be sure, belongs to the Secretary of the U.S. Department of Education.

The Secretary designates the Office to:

1. Investigate, process, and review complaints and violations under the Act and this part; and

2. Provide technical assistance to ensure compliance with the Act and this part.

§99.60(b)

In defining the FPCO's investigatory responsibility, the regulations detail "investigate, process, and review complaints and violations" (§99.60(b)(1)). The structure of the language infers that the FPCO reacts to complaints and violations. In §99.63 and §99.64, the regulations talk about the submission of complaints and alleged violations.

In the first citation, §99.63, the regulations identify the FPCO as the official recipients of complaints "regarding an alleged violation under the Act." In this section, complaints are submitted by parents and eligible students—the parties to whom FERPA rights are guaranteed under the act. With the 2008 Amendments, however, this restriction on the source of complaints is eliminated and expanded with the revisions to §99.64.

§99.64 undergoes a tremendous revision with the 2008 Amendments, including a key revision to its interrogatory title. The question, "What is the complaint procedure?" has been changed to substitute the word "investigation" for "complaint." The question becomes, "What is the investigation procedure?"

The paragraph goes on to ameliorate the first two of its four provisions.

> A complaint must contain specific allegations of fact giving reasonable cause to believe that a violation of the Act or this part has occurred. A complaint does not have to allege that a violation is based on a policy or practice of the educational agency or institution.
>
> *§99.64(a)*

The requirement of "specific allegations" remains in §99.64(a), since these facts form the basis for a complaint. The FPCO needs to know what specific actions prompted the accusation that a violation of FERPA has occurred. What is significant in the amendment to §99.64(a) is the second sentence, which essentially eliminates any need for complainants to provide substantiating information that might prove or support an allegation of a violation. That endeavor is left to the FPCO and its investigation process. The complainant need only state specifically the allegation or the reason that she feels a violation of FERPA rights has occurred.

While complainants may understand their basic rights under FERPA, they are not expected to compose briefs detailing violations and ascribing source policies or procedures as the bases for those violations. That is the work of the FPCO. If you will, complainants need only explain the articulable and significant sense that a violation has occurred. Committing the facts to a written document addressed to the FPCO provides the FPCO with a basis on which to launch an investigation or offer an interpretation of the events described.

It is §99.64(b) that offers the most important change to the enforcement provisions of FERPA and to the authorities of the FPCO.

> The Office investigates a timely complaint filed by a parent or eligible student, or conducts its own investigation when no complaint has been filed or a complaint has been withdrawn, to determine whether an educational agency or institution has failed to comply with a provision of the Act or this part. If the Office determines that an educational agency or institution has failed to comply with a provision of the Act or this part, it may also determine whether failure to comply is based on a policy or procedure of the agency or institution.
>
> *§99.64(b)*

First, the source of complaints is expanded. Parents and eligible students have always had the right to file a complaint for alleged violation of their FERPA rights. It is, after all, their fourth guarantee under FERPA. But in the new language of §99.64(b), investigations by the FPCO can be triggered by sources other than the complaints of parents or eligible students. The FPCO may choose to investigate a situation even if a complaint which had been filed is later retracted. The fact that a complaint was submitted in the first place signifies that actions or policies may have been misunderstood. And if it happened once, it can happen again. Depending upon the situation, the FPCO may investigate, if only to offer guidance and clarification of responsibilities under FERPA.

That the FPCO may choose to launch an investigation on its own initiative is a momentous change. When first proposed in March 2008, education officials wondered if the U.S. Department of Education was considering undertaking surprise audits of institutions to ensure compliance with the FERPA regulations. After all, the revised language expands the authority of the FPCO and permits the FPCO to intervene in campus operations where the potential for FERPA violations may exist. The original reactionary approach to investigations has suddenly become proactive.

In the March 24, 2008 issue, the *Federal Register* declared the following.

While not a widespread problem, the Department needs to establish in its regulations that the Office may investigate allegations of non-compliance provided by a school official or some other party who is not a parent or eligible student because sometimes parents and students are not aware of an ongoing FERPA problem that needs to be addressed. [FR 15591]

In citing its reasons for this particular amendment, the Department of Education referred to its documentation in the *Gonzaga University v. Doe* case (see the sidebar on page 25). So many administrators were involved in the unofficial investigation of the student in question that, if any one of them had raised a concern about whether FERPA or other ethical practices supported the investigation and the actions taking place, the situation might have been circumvented early on.

The second sentence of §99.64(b) alludes to what has been called the adjudicative role of the FPCO. In other words, the FPCO is interested in determining the root cause of violations and alleged violations in an effort to eliminate any future misunderstandings or wrongful commissions. To be sure, the goal of an FPCO investigation is not to convict an institution of a FERPA crime and strip it of its federal funding. Rather, the FPCO seeks to determine the cause of violations or potential violations and provide assistance in bringing policy, procedure, practice, or training into line so that no future incidents occur.

Submission of Complaints

§99.63 asks the question "Where are complaints filed?" and goes on to provide instructions.

A parent or eligible student may file a written complaint with the Office regarding an alleged violation under the Act or this part.

§99.63

Complaints are submitted to the Family Policy Compliance Office in writing. They may be sent through the U.S. mail to the address provided in §99.63 or they may be faxed. But they must be in writing.

§99.64(a) stated that the complaints "must contain specific allegations of fact giving reasonable cause to believe that a violation" has occurred. The regulations do not, in fact, provide guidelines for what would constitute the contents of a complaint other than the request for "specific allegations." But complainants can take some direction from the instructions the

---

SUBMITTING COMPLAINTS TO THE FPCO

Complaints should be submitted in writing as follows.

U.S. mail

> Family Policy Compliance Office
> U.S. Department of Education
> 400 Maryland Avenue SW
> Washington DC 20202–5920

Fax: (202) 260–9001

FPCO has often given to institutions whenever interpretation or guidance has been sought.

Typically, there are three requirements whenever inquiries are submitted by an institution.

- Contact information for the inquiring official
- Name and complete address of the institution involved
- Specific question or complete details of the situation requiring guidance

First of all, the FPCO needs contact information from the inquiring party so that the guidance or interpretation can be properly addressed. Secondly, the name of the institution and its complete address is required. This is because state and local regulations, not just FERPA, may have implications in regard to the situation posited. The FPCO will not be able to provide a complete response without some consideration for local authority. And lastly, the situation itself must be described as completely as possible.

From these instructions to education officials at institutions, basic elements or components of a complaint alleging FERPA violations can be compiled. They include the same essential informational items: contact information; identification of the institution involved, including its complete address; and a full statement of the facts involved. Without this minimum information, the FPCO cannot respond to a complaint. The FPCO may even have further questions, which is why providing valid contact information is so vital.

Contents of a Complaint for an Alleged FERPA Violation	
Preliminaries	• Identify the individual(s) whose rights were allegedly violated. Identify the institution involved—name, city and state location.
The Facts	• What happened? Describe events in detail, including dates, locations, conversations, incidents. • Who is involved? Identify all parties—education officials, parents, eligible students, and others. • Why do you feel there has been a FERPA violation? Although it is not required, provide supporting documentation, if available.
Contact Info	• Provide your contact information, including full name, complete address, and a telephone number. If possible, provide contact information for the institution and for education officials involved.

Processing of Complaints

The second two parts of §99.64 are about the processing of complaints by the FPCO and a definition of the term *timely complaint* used in §99.64(b).

§99.64(c) defines a timely complaint as one that is submitted within 180 days of the alleged violation or within 180 days of the date that one would reasonably become aware of the alleged violation. It is important to note that the six-month time frame is as of the date of the alleged violation. Attempts may have been made to file complaints at the institution for resolution of the issues involved. If the resolutions are unsatisfactory, so that an individual feels compelled to complain to the FPCO, the 180 days begins with the alleged violation itself and not the most recent date of the unsatisfactory resolution by the institution or anyone else.

> A timely complaint is defined as an allegation of a violation of the Act that is submitted to the Office within 180 days of the date of the alleged violation or of the date that the complainant knew or reasonably should have known of the alleged violation.
>
> *§99.64(c)*

Is the 180 days a firm period? Can the FPCO accept complaints regarding alleged violations that have occurred beyond the six-month time frame? A simple response is provided in the last section of §99.64 and it is an affirmative one.

> The Office may extend the time limit in this section for good cause shown.
>
> *§99.64(d)*

The investigatory and enforcement perspective of complaints regarding alleged violations of FERPA is covered in Chapter One.

Chapter 4

FERPA Exceptions for Parents and Safety

THE GUARANTEES THAT FERPA makes to students are essentially a straightforward adaptation of the Code of Fair Information Practices to the education environment and follow in much the same format as other privacy legislation. The challenge for those who must comply with the regulations, however, surfaces in the decision-making process of a real-world context, where the rigid guidelines of legal language blur and succumb to a myriad of interpretation and application.

Beyond the basic rights of any legislation is consideration of the exceptions or unusual circumstances that require evaluation of individual situations and formal or informal decision making. Depending upon the parties, events, and needs entailed, arriving at a determination of how FERPA should be enforced may confound a strict or literal interpretation of those basic rights.

It is important to maintain perspective. Exceptions are exceptions because they can and often do impinge upon the rights established as the foundation of the legislation. There must always be valid and compelling reasons for invoking any exception because to do so is to abridge or encroach upon the rights of citizens.

In its discussion of the 2008 Amendments, in the March 24, 2008 issue of the *Federal Register*, and also in the announcement of the final regulations in the December 9, 2008 issue of the *Federal Register*, the Department of Education frequently reminds readers that the purpose of the regulations is to protect the privacy of education records. Parents and eligible students are the only individuals guaranteed access and rights in regards to education records. In the postsecondary environment, that means only students.

The fact that third-party access—even by education officials—to education records is folded into a discussion of exceptions to the primary guarantees is significant and instructive for local policy, procedure, and decision making.

Legal Age and In Loco Parentis

Higher education administrators and parents often find it difficult to think of college-age students as legal adults. The transition from high school to college or university is often broken only by a summer vacation, a very natural intermission in the education calendar to which students and parents have become accustomed. But there is an even more important transition—a rite of passage, if you will—that occurs between secondary and postsecondary education—one that is acknowledged not only by FERPA but by the U.S. legal system as a whole. It is the formal recognition of an individual's becoming a legal adult.

Legal age is defined as follows.

Legal age is the age at which a person is responsible for his/her own actions (including the capacity to enter into a contract which is enforceable by the other party), for damages for negligence or intentional wrongs without a parent being liable, and for punishment as an adult for a crime. [Law.com Legal Dictionary]

Legal Age in the United States

Age	Activity	Comments
18	Legal age	National norm
18	Voting	Ratified 1971, 26th Amendment to the Constitution
21	Drinking/buying alcohol	National norm
—	Marriage, with or without parental consent Abortion, right to choose Driving Prosecution for crimes Liability for damages	Varies from state to state

If an individual were not attending college or university, he would be a working or nonworking member of the general society, responsible for himself and to society as a whole. Nationally, the legal age is considered to be 18 years of age. And what is most critical about this distinction is the assignment of responsibility for consequences. After a person reaches 18 years of age, mommy and daddy can no longer be held liable or responsible for whatever the individual does. The individual becomes solely responsible for his or her actions.

Obscuring our realization of this fact in higher education are two oft-manipulated concepts: in loco parentis and the definition of the parent or parents of a dependent child.

Legal dictionaries define in loco parentis as "a person or institution that assumes parental rights and duties for a minor" [legal-dictionary.org], or, more expansively, as follows.

In loco parentis is the legal doctrine under which an individual assumes parental rights, duties, and obligations without going through the formalities of legal adoption. [West's Encyclopedia of American Law, *Free Dictionary by Farlex, http://legal-dictionary.thefreedictionary.com/]*

Adopted from English Common Law by the colonial Puritans, in loco parentis was, in large part, responsible for the perceived separation of the academic environment from the real world. Schools were viewed as assuming an educational and moral responsibility for the rearing of children—a concept that takes on a significant interpretation in Aldous Huxley's 1932 futuristic novel *Brave New World.*

For well into the 19th century, courts and local authorities were reluctant to interfere in what was happening in the school—even when appeals were voiced by students and parents to external authority. The academic environment was considered almost sacred. For a court to become involved in a school setting was considered taboo, in much the same way that interfering between a parent and child was considered unconscionable.

America and the world in the post–World War II environment changed that.

After World War II, attitudes toward institutions changed radically. The secularization of schools fueled a departure from in loco parentis and eventually fostered the emergence of student rights in the 1960s and 1970s. In 1961, the case of *Dixon v. Alabama State Board of Education*, which revolved around the unjustified expulsion of six African American college students, extended due process to students at tax-supported schools. No

---

Due Process

Due process is the notion that legal and court procedures must be fair. In America, this idea is ingrained in the Fourteenth Amendment, which guarantees citizens that they cannot be deprived of liberty or property without due process of law.

The original notion of due process, however, originates in the Magna Carta (1215 AD). And the phrase "due process of law" is first found in a statutatory rendition of the Magna Carta that was circulated in England in 1354.

Dixon v. Alabama State Board of Education

The story of *Dixon v. Alabama State Board of Education* (24 F. 2nd 150) began with a sit-in demonstration at a public restaurant by 29 African American students of Alabama State College. A number of other demonstrations followed, prompting the president of the college to provide the names of the demonstrating students to the Alabama State Board of Education. The result was the expulsion of John St. Dixon and five other students for "unspecified reasons."

The 1961 federal case has been called the most significant legal action establishing the right of due process for students in public higher education. The court overturned the rulings of the lower courts on the basis that the students could not be expelled without due process.

The case has also been called the death of in loco parentis. The college based its action of expulsion on the doctrine of in loco parentis, expelling the students without ever holding a hearing. The court, however, held that the college could not act in this manner to discipline or expel students—especially at a state institution.

---

longer could students be expelled for misconduct without notice and without the opportunity to defend themselves in a formal hearing.

Later in the 1960s, students found their political voice and began to become more and more vocal about and involved in national issues. The escalation of the Vietnam War divided the nation and incited protests and demonstrations in various sectors of our society. The educational arena was not immune. Students in colleges and universities often staged angry and violent protests that could hardly be ignored. Media and journalistic attention focused on a citizenry that was suddenly immersed in a national dialogue for which silence was not an option.

The political turmoil was not confined to the postsecondary environment, however. High schools experienced their own coming of age as teenagers took up the banners of protest against the war. If postsecondary institutions expressed their own exclusivity to dealing with discipline within their halls, secondary schools were swift and punitive in their strategies to control students who were still minors. But their parental-like discipline was not always seen as constitutional nor in alignment with the ideals that shaped the United States two centuries prior.

Student protests at the secondary school level were viewed as misbehavior, and such action was often judged disobedient, disruptive, and unsocial. These were minors, after all. No one expected minors to have political scruples. Then, the expulsion of three Des Moines high school students protesting the Vietnam War drew the attention of the U.S. Supreme Court. The students and their parents had not even considered contesting the expulsion of the students until approached by the Iowa Civil Liberties Union. In the 1969 case of *Tinker et al. v. Des Moines Independent Community School District*, the Court

Tinker et al. v. Des Moines Independent Community School District

The 1969 case of *Tinker et al. v. Des Moines Independent Community School District* (393 US 503) is often cited as a precedent in the constitutional rights of students—in particular, free speech and First Amendment rights.

The case revolved around three students who, in December of 1965, wore black armbands to school to protest the U.S. involvement in Vietnam. John F. Tinker, 15, his friend Christopher Eckhart, 16, and John's 13-year old sister wore the armbands to their high school and junior high school. Despite their quiet and passive protest, the students were immediately suspended until after the holidays—coincidentally, when the students' protest was scheduled to end.

The students' parents did not take action until approached by the Iowa Civil Liberties Union. The case was heard in November 1968, with a ruling that was passed the following February. The decision was a 7–2 vote in favor of the students.

In the court dialogue, Justice Abe Fortas, who wrote for the majority of the justices, prefaced his remarks by declaring, "It can hardly be argued that either students or teachers shed their constitutional rights to freedom of speech or expression at the schoolhouse gates."

The case gave rise to the phrase "the Tinker test," referring to an evaluation of disciplinary proceedings to determine whether a student's First Amendment rights have been violated.

ruled in favor of the students and affirmed that students do not "shed their constitutional rights . . . at the schoolhouse gates."

That in loco parentis refers to parental rights over minors fundamentally divorces the concept from application to higher education. After all, postsecondary students are, for the most part, no longer minors. And so as not to place undo burden on postsecondary education officials attempting to determine whether FERPA applies to a particular student, the language of the regulations uses an either/or definition when it defines eligible student.

Eligible student means a student who has reached the age of 18 years of age or is attending an institution of postsecondary education.

§99.3

According to §99.3, the eligible student—the individual to whom the FERPA rights are guaranteed—is the student who is 18 years of age *or* who attends a postsecondary institution. Consequently, every student of a college or university, or other postsecondary educational institution, is an eligible student and, therefore, guaranteed rights under FERPA.

To underscore this point, FERPA further declares that the rights assigned to parents in K–12, because the student was a minor, transfer from the parent to the student when the individual becomes an eligible student (§99.5). In effect, at the point when an individual matriculates at a college or university, that individual assumes all of his or her own privacy rights and the responsibilities guaranteed under these regulations. The regulations continue to say "parent or eligible student" throughout the legislation since the regulations apply to K–12 as well. But for postsecondary education institutions, it is the eligible student who has sole possession of privacy rights under the act.

> When a student becomes an eligible student, the rights accorded to, and consent required of, parents under this part transfer from the parents to the student.
>
> *§99.5(a)*

In documenting this right of passage, the FERPA regulations are rightfully positioned among other federal and state legislation binding upon and benefiting U.S. citizens. For the eligible student, an adult citizen in the eyes of our legal system, the FERPA regulations assign rights and responsibilities in the same way that other legislation codifies the rights of citizens. In essence, to deprive an eligible student of his FERPA rights is tantamount to divesting the individual of legally and constitutionally assured rights

---

Resurgence of In Loco Parentis

While free speech protests and the secularization of schools did much to diminish the application of in loco parentis in the nation's schools, the end of the 20th century witnessed a resurgence, principally due to efforts to ensure the safety of students in schools. Local and state courts, and the U.S. Supreme Court, were called in to make decisions regarding punishment, the use of drugs and other controlled substances, and weapons on campus. Among the generated legislation were the following:

The Drug-Free Schools and Campuses Act, which grew out of President Reagan's war on drugs, prohibited the possession, distribution, and use of drugs and alcohol on K–12 and postsecondary campuses. The 1989 law applies to both students and employees of the institutions.

Vernonia School District v. Acton provided the arena for the 1995 U.S. Supreme Court's decision that the drug testing of athletes did not violate the constitutional rights of students. Drug testing would later be extended to any student who wished to participate in a school's extracurricular activities. The view was espoused that students in school were under the direct supervision of the state, which had responsibility for the welfare of all students.

Amidst a deluge of other legislation targeting hate speech, intolerance, and dress codes, Congress passed the Gun-Free Schools Act of 1994. The act required schools to expel students found in possession of guns or other firearms. The act spurred a number of lawsuits, most of which were denied, with the courts maintaining the responsibility of the schools to ensure a safe environment.

and privileges. This is why the issue of Section 1983 rights—the right to sue—is often raised in situations of alleged FERPA violations.

Despite the clarity of §99.5(a) and its pronouncement of the reassignment of FERPA rights to the eligible student, the playing field in higher education operations remains clouded by other considerations and relationships—one of which arises from yet another piece of federal legislation.

Complicating the discussion and adding further nuances to the consideration of privacy rights is the identification of dependent children for tax-reporting purposes and the exceptions permitted under FERPA for the parents of those dependent students.

Parents and the Parents of Dependent Students

When FERPA defines the term *parent*, it does so in light of other legislation, federal and otherwise, where minors, legal age, and individual responsibility have significant bearing.

Parent refers to natural parents, guardians, or other individuals who take upon themselves the responsibilities of parents or guardians—that is, those individuals assuming responsibilities for minors. In its presentations, the FPCO elaborates on this definition to include those individuals responsible for minors in nuclear and extended families, divorced and single-parent families, domestic partnerships, same-sex marriages, custodianships, and other roles of guardianship. All of these forms of parenting are intended to be covered by the definition of parent in FERPA.

> Parent means a parent of a student and includes natural parent, a guardian, or an individual acting as a parent in the absence of a parent or guardian.
>
> §99.3

Under the law, parents are responsible—physically, emotionally, socially, and financially—for their minor children. The failure of a parent in any of these areas can invoke or cause the intervention of external authorities, up to and including the assumption of guardianship over minors by the state or other local authorities.

When the child reaches the age of 18, however, that parental responsibility, at least for legal purposes, ceases. The child becomes an independent entity. Essentially, the child becomes an adult, and established institutional and social conventions must respect that transfer of responsibility and accountability in various ways.

FERPA's acknowledgment comes in the form of a simple reassignment of rights and responsibilities, tied to the child's entry into the postsecondary environment. After defining an eligible student, in §99.3, the regulations go on to transfer rights from the parents to the eligible student. For all intents and purposes, parental rights disappear when an individual becomes a student in a postsecondary institution.

> When a student becomes an eligible student, the rights accorded to, and consent required of, parents under this part transfer from the parents to the student.
>
> §99.5(a)

But the parents themselves don't disappear, as many college administrators know. Parents remain involved emotionally and financially with their children. And over the years, changing attitudes on the roles of parents have given rise to involvement in the postsecondary environment at varying levels. At one time, parents sent their sons away to university, where they became men equipped and ready to assume responsibilities in society or to enter military service. Sexist as the statement may seem, that was, nevertheless, the prevailing attitude and social expectation.

Late in the 20th century, the phenomena of the "helicopter" parent— or "dive bomber" parent, as one military school administrator put it— characterized the parent as more intricately involved in the progress of the student through college or university. Hovering and guiding the child's progress, the helicopter parent becomes involved as needed, sometimes stepping in for the student so as not to detract the student from her studies. Frequently, the intervening parent demands a customer service response as if the institutional relationship to the parent had existed all along.

The changing role of parents has encouraged many institutions to create parent relations offices or to implement other outreach—or intermediary— strategies at the campus. In some instances, the parent-teacher associations of the K–12 setting have morphed into new parent alliances in the postsecondary environment. Some of these alliances are affiliated directly with the institution, but others are independent. External organizations and associations, such as College Parents of America, attempt to build peer support among parents and often take on lobbying efforts regarding concerns such as institutional accountability and government positions on financial aid and campus safety.

College Parents of America

College Parents of America (www.collegeparents.org) has dedicated itself to providing government advocacy, timely information, and vital resources to a national community of parents, colleges and universities, K–12 school systems, corporations, and other associations and organizations. Its goal is to ensure that higher education remains an accessible and successful part of American culture.

In addition to legislative lobbying efforts, the organization streamlines access to information for parents and families regarding scholarship opportunities, resources, and money-saving strategies. The organization has even convened a panel of experts willing to share their expertise and respond to questions one-on-one from members.

College Parents of America is headed by President James A. Boyle, formerly the vice president of brand marketing and corporate communications for Sallie Mae. Before becoming president in 2003, Boyle worked as a press secretary on Capitol Hill and for the National Cable Television Association, WorldGate, Discovery Communications, and NBC.

The multiple challenges of a more complex and competitive adult world have, no doubt, fueled a curious desire to extend adolescence. A generation of parents who have experienced firsthand the successes and disappointments of dealing with the intricacies of postsecondary education curricula, job market expectations, and qualification by credentials underlies the recent swing of the in loco parentis pendulum. Anxious to guide their children on the swiftest road to professional and financial success, many parents are pointedly and intimately involved in their children's lives right on through college and university. (An alternative reaction is provided in the Afterthoughts.)

For postsecondary institutions, striking the legal, moral, and ethical balance is not always as clearly defined as it is in regulation or institutional policy. FERPA, aware of institutional traditions that have embraced parental relationships to varying degrees, seems to offer a measure of acknowledgment in §99.5(a)(2).

Nothing in this section prevents an educational agency or institution from disclosing education records, or personally identifiable information from education records, to a parent without the prior written consent of the eligible student if the disclosure meets the conditions in §99.31(a)(8), §99.31(a)(10), §99.31(a)(15), or any other provision of §99.31(a).

§99.5(a)(2)

Specifically addressing the postsecondary environment, the regulations state that nothing in this section—and remember the FERPA regulations are Section 99 of the Code of Federal Regulations (CFR)—prohibits institutions from sharing personally identifiable information with parents provided certain conditions are met. And the conditions of this caveat are contained in the portion of the regulations that deal with exceptions. Such disclosure actions should always be considered exceptions and have solid, legal foundation for their undertaking.

By law, the student in higher education is an adult, fully entitled to the same inalienable rights as other adult U.S. citizens. To interfere with, diminish, or otherwise deny those rights is a serious legal and civil rights violation—a matter that can be argued as extending to and implicating the very foundations of the Constitution itself.

In the eyes of the law, it does not matter that parents are supporting their children through college or university. Such financial affiliations may encumber the student to the parent, but that is the extent of the relationship. The institution must maintain its relationship directly with the adult student. The institutional catalog, after all, is essentially written as a contract between the institution and its programs with the student in attendance. For a third party to become involved—even if that other party is a parent—is an intrusion into that relationship. This interjection of a third party in the institution-student relationship must be dealt with by exception alone.

The reason most often used as justification for providing information access to parents is that of the claim of the parents of dependent children. Parents insist that, because they are still supporting their college-age children, financially and otherwise, they are entitled to access the personally identifiable information about their children that is held by the education institution. Parents seek assurance that their children are successfully progressing through their expensive college educations and that their encouragement and psychological support are effective.

Indeed, these reasons do not even take into account those cultural and traditional influences of parental involvement that often drive the participation of parents whose origins are not American or even from the Western Hemisphere. In many parts of the world, the involvement of the parent is integral in the educational process, regardless of age or other external and legal rights.

So, FERPA details a number of exceptions—situations in which disclosure of non-directory information is permitted without prior consent to parents on a one-time basis.

FERPA EXCEPTIONS REGARDING PARENTS

99.31(a)(8)	Parents of a dependent student
99.31(a)(10)	Health and safety emergency
99.31(a)(15)	Violations governing use or possession of alcohol or other controlled substance

---

The first of the parent exceptions has to do with providing information, without the prior written consent of the student, to the parents of dependent children. FERPA lists this as an exception which may be utilized by postsecondary institutions. But no institution is required to grant such access to parents. It is an individual decision on the part of the institution—a process that is permitted, but not required.

> The disclosure is to parents, as defined in Sec. 99.3, of a dependent student, as defined in §152 of the Internal Revenue Code of 1986.
>
> *§99.31(a)(8)*

The *privilege* of being a parent of a dependent student is confined to the benefits and liabilities of the Internal Revenue Code (§152 of Title 26 of the U.S. Code). It is, in essence, a tax benefit, allowing deductions for the financial support of children under conditions specifically outlined in §152 of the code. This tax benefit status, however, has no other rights or privileges beyond the Internal Revenue Code. Other regulations may utilize this status as a benchmark for identifying or classifying other rights, privileges, or responsibilities, but tax dependency status has no other intrinsic benefits or implications.

In this context, FERPA recognizes and affirms the rights of the eligible student. But FERPA also says that the institution *may* make an exception and provide personally identifiable information to the parents of dependent children *if* the institution determines that it needs to make such disclosures.

Initially, the understanding of this exception was that, like other exceptions, it referred to considerations on a case by case basis. Parents were required to make a formal request for specific information about their dependent students every time that the information was desired. In return, institutions had to verify that the student was a dependent on the parent's IRS Form 1040 or federal income tax return filing. This verification needed to be completed each time that information was requested because tax status could change at any time. Finally, as with the notification to students when their records are subpoenaed, the student needed to be notified and given an opportunity to quash or prevent the disclosure.

Because the use of this exception has been frequent for some institutions, the FPCO advised that institutions could make it a practice of disclosing information to the parents of dependent students if this practice is disclosed in the institution's annual notification. Recordkeepers are still required to verify that the student is a dependent of the parent at the time of disclosure, but utilization of this exception as a practice allows institutions to continue some of their traditions of parental notification and involvement of the past.

While the language of the regulations has not changed, even despite the 2008 Amendments, the interpretation and guidance of the FPCO has relaxed somewhat in the area of sharing information with the parents of dependent students. The FPCO now permits institutions to accept blanket waivers or authorizations that allow the institution to share personally identifiable information with the parents of dependent students. The student may identify herself as a dependent in such a waiver and authorize the institution to share information with her parents. The authorization would continue to be valid until revoked or cancelled by the student or until the student graduates or departs the institution. This is the same process that has been used by student accounting and financial aid offices, but previously confined to the disclosure of financial or accounting information.

However the exception is adopted into regular practice at the institution, the FPCO, nevertheless, continues to insist that if such a practice is regularly utilized at the institution, the practice needs to be disclosed in the institution's annual notification. A statement would be added to the annual notification that informs students in attendance that information from education records is disclosed to the parents of dependent students and specifies the conditions under which such disclosure would occur.

The utilization of web-based student access systems (SAS) has added a new dimension to providing access to non-directory information for parents. Although students have been advised that logon IDs and passwords are confidential and should not be shared with anyone, institutions know that students have shared access credentials with parents and other significant relations. Sometimes these discoveries have been accidental, such

AUTHORIZATION FOR PARENTAL ACCESS

I, (student name), declare that I am the tax dependent of (names), who is/are my (relationship), and hereby authorize (institution) to grant said individual(s) access to my student information, including directory and non-directory information. This authorization is effective until (date) or until revoked in writing, whichever occurs first.

_____

Student Signature and Date

as when a parent calls the registrar's office with a question about degree progress information that is displayed on student portal pages. Despite the precautions about compromising logons and passwords, the ultimate responsibility for their confidentiality remains with the adult student.

> The parent or eligible student shall provide a signed and dated written consent before an educational agency or institution discloses personally identifiable information from the student's education records, except as provided in §99.31.
>
> *§99.30(a)*

For the institution, disclosures of personally identifiable information to anyone other than the student require a prior written consent, unless the regulations permit an exception. On this basis, the University of Southern California (USC) has utilized its student access system (SAS) to facilitate the process between students and their parents. In 2005, Associate Registrar Robert Morley introduced a guest access function to USC's SAS, which is called OASIS. USC students now authorize and grant access to parents and other guests so that these third parties can directly utilize OASIS to access personally identifiable information about the student.

The beauty of the USC system is that the technology reinforces the need for student authorization to access the student's non-directory information. The prior consent of the student, required for disclosure in §99.30(a), is underscored. As a further administrative benefit, by giving the authority directly to the student, the number of requests for documents and information received in the registrar's office is significantly reduced.

OASIS at the University of Southern California

The student access system at the University of California (USC) has evolved over the years, constantly working to meet the needs of its students. Under the leadership of Associate Registrar Robert Morley, OASIS has taken on a variety of services for current students, including enrollment and the compilation of book lists, evaluating degree progress and commencement documentation, ordering verifications and transcripts (including pdf transcripts), processing financial aid and transfer credit, and updating personal information.

A distinctive feature of the USC system is the availability of a guest access function within OASIS. Introduced in 2005, the new functionality conferred on students the ability to authorize and permit guests to access selected information from their education records. Guests may include parents, guardians, or even individuals contributing financially toward their matriculation at USC. Students make the determination themselves, assigning logons and passwords. Further, the student can revoke access at any time or set time parameters for the guest access.

When initially implemented, questions were raised about the guest access function since FERPA requires prior written consent for the disclosure of non-directory information to third parties. However, with the passage of the ESign Act and the authentication process inherent in the system (logons and passwords), the guest access function in OASIS is not only FERPA compliant but an elegant and individually empowering way to develop student appreciation of their privacy rights and responsibilities.

Notification of Drug and Alcohol Violations

Two other parent-related exceptions are listed in §99.31 of the FERPA regulations: the provisions for health and safety and for violations of drug and alcohol laws. Because health and safety have implications beyond the involvement of parents, those provisions will be considered separately in the next section. The issue of notifying parents when their students commit certain violations, however, continues our discussion of parental disclosures.

The Higher Education Amendments of 1998, made to the Higher Education Reauthorization Act of 1965 and signed into law by President Bill Clinton, included numerous provisions that provided changes, enhancements, and additions to higher education funding programs. One of the spotlights of the amendments focused on the use of alcohol, drugs, and other controlled substances at colleges and universities.

The College Initiative to Reduce Binge Drinking and Illegal Alcohol Consumption, §119 of the Higher Education Amendments, was intended to demonstrate government support for local school initiatives that assumed responsibilities for and introduced programs to help curb alcohol and drug abuse among students. The legislation advocated the adoption of zero tolerance policies, strenuous disciplinary sanctions, and the use of internal and outsourced counseling referrals for students involved with the illegal consumption of alcohol and drugs.

Higher Education Reauthorization Act of 1965

The Higher Education Reauthorization Act of 1965 was part of President Lyndon Johnson's Great Society domestic agenda. When signed into public law (PL 89–329), it established programs to strengthen higher education in the United States. These programs included financial assistance for students (Title IV), scholarships and low interest loans, and the National Teachers Corps.

Programs have been renewed in subsequent reauthorizations (Higher Education Amendments)—in 1968, 1972, 1976, 1980, 1986, 1992, 1998, and 2008. With each reauthorization, new strategies and amendments to existing provisions have attempted to keep the programs current and relevant to the challenges faced by the higher education community.

While significant in that no previous legislation had addressed alcohol and drug abuse at colleges and universities, the initiative failed to provide any penalties or sanctions on institutions for failure to take action. Joel Epstein, senior associate and attorney for the Higher Education Center for Alcohol and Other Drug Prevention, explained the Higher Education Amendments in the June 1999 edition of the *Prevention Updates Newsletter*. In the newsletter, he lamented, "While Section 119 is an important statement of congressional support for a college initiative, the section has no force of law."

§120 of the Higher Education Amendments codified the Drug-Free Schools and Communities Act (DFSCA) and established biennial reviews, grants, and rewards for innovative drug prevention programs. But it was §484 of the amendments that had the most striking impact.

Drug-Free Schools and Communities Act

Conditions for the receipt of federal funding by institutions of higher education (IHE) were established in 1990 by the Drug and Alcohol Abuse Prevention Regulations, §86 of the Education Department General Administrative Regulations (EDGAR). The mandate requires IHEs to certify the adoption and implementation of programs to prevent the unlawful possession, use, or distribution of illicit drugs and alcohol by students and employees.

The requirements on institutions are:

- An annual notification of standards of conduct, including sanctions for violations, and descriptions of health risk and available treatment options

- A "sound method" for distribution of this annual notification

- A biennial review of the effectiveness of the institution's alcohol and drug prevention programs

- Maintenance of the biennial review until requested, if requested, by the U.S. Department of Education

Support for institutional efforts in alcohol and drug prevention is available from the Higher Education Center for Alcohol and Other Drug Abuse and Violence Prevention (www.higheredcenter.org).

§484, called the Suspension of Eligibility for Drug-Related Offenses, targeted eligibility for financial aid. The Aid Elimination Provision added an important question to the Free Application for Federal Student Aid (FAFSA). Applicants were asked if they had ever been convicted of a drug crime while they were a recipient of federal financial aid. A response was required. Individuals who responded in the affirmative, or who failed to answer the question, were immediately disqualified as a beneficiary of grants, loans, and participation in work-study programs. A period of ineligibility was prescribed based upon the severity of the student's record of offenses. This period of ineligibility could range from as short as one year to permanent disqualification.

Periods of Ineligibility for Financial Aid Resulting from Drug-Related Offenses

For *possession* of a controlled substance		For the *sale* of a controlled substance	
Offense	**Period of Ineligibility**	**Offense**	**Period of Ineligibility**
First conviction	1 year	First conviction	2 years
Second conviction	2 years	Second conviction	Indefinite
Third conviction	Indefinite		

But eligibility for financial aid was not the only area targeted by national efforts to combat drugs and controlled substances on the campus.

At the same time, an amendment was proposed by Senator John Warner of Virginia that made its way into the Higher Education Amendments as §952, the Alcohol or Drug Possession Disclosure. The Warner Amendment, as it would be called, impacted FERPA and added another exception to the disclosures that could be made to the parents of postsecondary students. This

John William Warner

The Republican senator from Virginia since 1979, John William Warner, Jr. was born on February 18, 1927, and attended Washington and Lee University and the University of Virginia Law School. He enlisted in the United States Marine Corps during the Korean Conflict and later served as Secretary of the Navy between 1972 and 1974. Before entering politics, he had a private law practice and was an assistant U.S. district attorney between 1956 and 1960.

Senator Warner has been involved with a number of political committees concerned with the environment and public works, intelligence and homeland security, and pensions and benefits. An advocate of pro-choice, embryonic stem cell research, and gun control laws, Senator Warner was a supporter of the Brady Bill and in 2004, voted to expand the definition of hate crimes to include sexual orientation.

Controlled Substances

The federal Controlled Substances Act (CSA) was enacted as part of the Comprehensive Drug Abuse Prevention and Control Act of 1970. The CSA is particularly concerned with the manufacture, importation, distribution and sale, and possession of certain drugs listed in the act. The CSA defines five categories of controlled substances. Generally, the categories are as follows:

- High potential for abuse, not accepted as medical treatment, safety risk if not under medical supervision—examples: cannabis, heroin, mescaline

- High potential for abuse, accepted as medical treatment, may incur severe, psychological dependencies—examples: cocaine used as a topical ointment, opium, morphine, amphetamines, and short-acting barbiturates

- High potential for abuse, may be accepted medical treatments, may incur moderate levels of various kinds of dependencies—examples: anabolic steroids and intermediate-acting barbiturates

- Low potential for abuse, accepted medical treatments, may lead to temporary dependence—examples: long-lasting barbiturates, such as Phenobarbital, and certain anti-diarrheal drugs

- Low potential for abuse, accepted medical treatments, some potential for dependence—examples: cough suppressants

Alcohol, caffeine, and tobacco were excluded from the list of controlled substances.

The CSA has had a number of amendments since it was passed. Enforcement of the CSA belongs to the Drug Enforcement Administration (DEA).

---

exception focused on student violations of policies and procedures in regard to the possession, sale, and usage of alcohol or controlled substances.

The Warner Amendment changed and expanded FERPA §99.31(a)(15)(i) so as to permit institutions to make certain disclosures to parents in regard to violations by their students of institutional policies regarding the possession, use, or sale of alcohol and other controlled substances.

The disclosure requirements under the Warner Amendment, introduced into FERPA at §99.31(a)(15)(i), include two caveats.

- A violation must have been determined.
- The student must be under the age of 21 at the time of disclosure.

First, the provision specifies that a violation needs to be involved. The student must have been found guilty of violating federal, state, or local laws or of violating institutional policies. The expansion to include violations of institutional policy was a hallmark of the 1998 amendment. Violation, of course, means that the institution must have some formal policy regarding drugs and alcohol and that some form of disciplinary action or hearing would have taken place to formally determine the violation.

> The disclosure is to a parent of a student at an institution of postsec-
> ondary education regarding the student's violation of any Federal,
> State, or local law, or of any rule or policy of the institution, govern-
> ing the use or possession of alcohol or a controlled substance if—
>
> A. The institution determines that the student has committed a dis-
>   ciplinary violation with respect to that use or possession; and
>
> B. The student is under the age of 21 at the time of the disclosure to
>   the parent.
>
>   *§99.31(a)(15) (i)*

Secondly, disclosure of a violation of a policy regarding alcohol or other controlled substance could only be made to a parent as long as the student is under the age of 21 at the time of the disclosure.

Reaction to the new provision was mixed and, in some instances, contro-versial. In the perspective of the student press and civil liberties advocates, in loco parentis was experiencing a serious revival because postsecondary students were again being viewed and treated as minors, robbed of their adult rights and privacy.

Warner's amendment was incorporated into FERPA under the excep-tions provisions of §99.31, which means that institutions would be permit-ted, but not be required, to make such disclosures to parents. If an institution wishes to make such a disclosure to parents, an exception is permitted so long as the provisions of the amendment are met—namely, that a violation had been determined *and* that the student involved be under the age of 21 at the time of the disclosure to parents.

The specifications of the amendment are important. Since many stu-dents turn 21 while attending college or university, adult rights—citizen rights—need to be protected. And, as indicated earlier, 21 is the national norm for the minimum age to purchase, possess, and consume alcohol.

To guard against unwarranted or unjustified disclosures, the regula-tions specify that a violation must have been formally determined. Implicit in the provision is a requirement that institutions cease from relying solely on federal, state, or local regulations to provide authority in these kinds of situations, particularly since larger campuses often employ their own law enforcement units. Colleges and universities need to codify their own policies in regard to the possession and use of alcohol and other controlled substances by students on their campuses.

In effect, the mandate requires institutions to impose regulations on post-secondary students similar to the kinds of laws and regulations that govern

> Disciplinary action or proceeding means the investigation, adjudi-
> cation, or imposition of sanctions by an educational agency or insti-
> tution with respect to an infraction or violation of internal rules of
> conduct applicable to students of the agency or institution.
>
> *§99.3*

social responsibility for other adults in the nonacademic environment. Just
because an individual is attending college or university does not mean that
the student is immune from social responsibility and legal compliance.

Further, with respect to the disclosure to parents, there must be a
formal disciplinary process involved that would have investigated and
deliberated the alleged charge against a student or students. Disciplinary
action was already defined in §99.3, the section of FERPA devoted to the
definition of terms.

Threats to Health and Safety

Indeed, the importance of institutional policy and procedure, not only
in regard to alcohol and controlled substances, but to a host of other organizational and disciplinary issues should be clearly evident. Recall that
should the FPCO or the Department of Education investigate issues at
any campus, one of the tools of adjudication involves the production and
review of campus policy and procedure.

In the decade prior to the sudden aerial attacks on the United States
on September 11, 2001, numerous initiatives and legislation were initiated in regard to various forms of violence that had their impact on the
education sector. Some imposed reporting requirements on schools while
others affected provisions to campus policies and procedures, including
amendments to FERPA.

> The disclosure is in connection with a health or safety emergency,
> under the conditions described in Sec. 99.36.
>
> *§99.31(a)(10)*

Disclosures based upon health and safety had long been a part of
FERPA, contained in §99.31, the section on exceptions, and elaborated upon
in its own section, §99.36. But the problem for many education officials has
been the word *emergency*, which is often defined as an event with a specific
time frame that requires urgent and immediate action.

Nothing in this act shall prevent an educational agency or institution from—

1. Including in the education records of a student appropriate information concerning disciplinary action taken against the student for conduct that posed a significant risk to the safety or well-being of that student, other students, or other members of the school community;

2. Disclosing appropriate information maintained under paragraph (b)(1) of this section to teachers and school officials within the agency or institution who the agency or institution has determined have legitimate educational interests in the behavior of the student; or

3. Disclosing appropriate information maintained under paragraph (b)(1) of this section to teachers and school officials in other schools who have been determined to have legitimate educational interests in the behavior of the student.

§99.36(b)

In §99.36, the regulations go on to detail the kinds of disclosures to which it refers under this health and safety emergency provision. And, in fact, schools are provided with substantial latitude for disclosing information within the educational *system*—not merely within the educational agency or institution—about student conduct determined to pose a significant risk to the community.

The instructions of §99.36(b), however, are placed between two other clauses. In §99.36(a), disclosure is specified "to appropriate parties in connection with an emergency if knowledge of the information is necessary to protect the health and safety" of individuals. Common understanding of "appropriate parties" in this clause has often referred to police and other law enforcement officials responding to the emergency. At the other end of the paragraph, §99.36(c) cautioned, "Paragraphs (a) and (b) of this section will be strictly construed."

The 2008 Amendments introduced significant changes to paragraphs (a) and (c) of §99.36, prompted primarily by the official assessments of the 2007 Virginia Tech tragedy. The March 2008 *Federal Register* quoted the June 13, 2007, "Report to the President on Issues Raised by the Virginia Tech

---

Virginia Tech Tragedy

Two separate shooting attacks took place on April 16, 2007, on the campus of Virginia Polytechnic Institute and State University (Virginia Tech) in Blacksburg, Virginia. The perpetrator was 23-year-old Seung-Hui Cho, an undergraduate English student at Virginia Tech. During his two barrages, Cho killed 5 faculty members and 27 students. Other individuals were injured: 17 due to gunshot injuries, and 6, who leapt from a second story window during the attacks. At the end of the assault, Cho committed suicide.

Cho's problems began when he was in middle school, where he was treated for a severe anxiety disorder. His treatment continued until he was a junior in high school. At college, Cho was accused of stalking two female students and had also been declared mentally ill. Nevertheless, Cho had been able to purchase the two handguns used in the Virginia Tech attack.

The incident prompted numerous concerns and criticisms regarding the university's handling of the situation. Could the school have anticipated and prevented the tragedy that occurred? An investigative panel was formed that included Tom Ridge, former Director of Homeland Security. In the latter half of 2007, HR 2640 was passed, mandating improvements to the national criminal background check system. And on March 24, 2008, amendments were proposed to FERPA clarifying privacy issues and recasting the health and safety emergency exception to the threat level.

As a memorial to the victims, 32 pieces of hokie stone were placed on the Virginia Tech drill field. Each stone commemorates one of the victims. The massacre is the deadliest shooting incident to be orchestrated by a single gunman in U.S. history.

Tragedy," citing misunderstanding and fear on the part of campus officials regarding interpretation of their responsibilities under FERPA, HIPAA, and the relationship of these regulations to state law.

The first of these 2008 Amendments, to §99.36(a), was not lengthy as far as verbiage is concerned—in fact, a mere phrase. Yet, the inclusion of "parents of an eligible student" in §99.36(a) expands the disclosure permissions in a crucial way because the involvement of family members may often be key to understanding and even deterring problematic behavior or incidents of concern.

> An educational agency or institution may disclose personally identifiable information from an education record to appropriate parties, including parents of an eligible student, in connection with an emergency if knowledge of the information is necessary to protect the health or safety of the student or other individuals.
>
> *§99.36(a)*

The sentence that was §99.36(c) was replaced entirely in the 2008 Amendments. And it is in this section that the intent and tone of the disclosure provision changes from an emergency to a level of threat. The exception of disclosing information from education records is recast to those situations where an "articulable or significant threat to the health and safety" of individuals is involved. And disclosure is expanded to permit disclosure "to any person whose knowledge of the information is necessary to protect the health and safety" of individuals.

In making a determination under paragraph (a) of this section, an educational agency or institution may take into account the totality of circumstances pertaining to a threat to the safety or health of a student or other individuals. If the educational agency or institution determines that there is an articulable or significant threat to the health or safety of a student or other individuals, it may disclose information from education records to any person whose knowledge of the information is necessary to protect the health and safety of the student or other individuals. If, based on the information available at the time of determination, there is a rational basis for the determination, the Department will not substitute its judgment for that of the educational agency or institution in evaluating the circumstances and making its determination.

§99.36(c)

With the revision to §99.36(c), institutions are empowered to deal responsibly with threats to the health and safety of their community members by making disclosures that allow officials to consult with individuals and agencies whom they feel will help protect the community. Institutions need not wait until there is an emergency that requires urgent reaction. The accent is now on disclosures where those disclosures are necessary to prevent harm to members of the education community. As long as an "articulable and significant threat" is determined, the institution may take whatever action it deems necessary.

To underscore this empowerment and the imperative for dealing with threats to health and safety, the regulations go on, in §99.36(c), to place complete confidence and trust for the determination of threats at the local level—that is, with the institution that takes action based upon its determination. The regulations insist that "the Department [of Education] will not substitute its judgment for that of the educational agency or institution" in the evaluation of circumstances that prompt any action in response to an "articulable and significant threat." In other words, the reasons that prompt institutional action in response to a threat against health and safety will not be reevaluated or judged by the FPCO.

The wording and assurance of §99.36(c) emphasizes the responsibility of the institution in dealing with a local threat to health and safety, but at the same time, underscores the confidence of the government in the institution's ability to determine *when* action and response are necessary. Certainly, the unexpectedness of the violence and tragedy at Columbine High School and Virginia Tech demonstrate the inability of government to prognosticate and legislate for every potential situation that may impede the daily operation of an educational community. The use of "an articulable and significant threat" is purposely imprecise because situations may vary in their intensity and potential as a threat to health and safety. What may be easily dismissed in one environment may engender serious cause for alarm in another. Therefore, the responsibility for determination when action should be taken rests appropriately at the local level, with the institution.

In some ways, the phraseology is appropriate as guidance for the institution and for education officials at institutions. When behavior, incidents, or other knowledge disturbs an education official or other individuals so that a concern is exchanged—when something becomes *articulable*—then that is the time when evaluation and appropriate action should be contemplated and taken.

Columbine High School Massacre

The massacre at Columbine High School, near Denver, took place on Tuesday, April 20, 1999. A total of 12 students and a teacher were shot and killed, and another two dozen individuals were injured. The perpetrators were two of Columbine's own students—Eric Harris, 18, and Dylan Klebold, 17—both of whom committed suicide at the conclusion of their rampage.

The incident focused attention on gun control laws and mental health but also raised concern for the gothic subculture, the effect on young people of violence in films and video games, extensive usage of the Internet, and teenage access to antidepressants and other prescription medications.

At the very least, education officials should communicate their concerns to supervisors, department heads, deans, and other institutional officials. In thoughtful and responsible dialogue, a determination can be made to take action or to escalate concerns to a higher authority.

Safe Campus

Concerns for health and safety focus not only upon the catastrophic but also upon attempts to ensure safe campuses for day-to-day operations. Sadly, though, the impetus for safety and crime prevention legislation affecting campus policy and procedure, including FERPA, has often arisen as a reaction to tragic incidents throughout the country.

Perhaps the most well-known legislation affecting campus safety is the Clery Act. But a number of other crimes and crime legislation have impacted campus safety, including another provision in the 2008 Amendments to FERPA.

Originally passed as the Crime Awareness and Campus Security Act of 1990, the Clery Act was named for Jeanne Clery, a first-year student who was raped and murdered in her own residence hall bedroom at Lehigh University four years earlier. During the investigation, it was revealed that the Lehigh campus had experienced a history of violent crimes, none of which was known to Jeanne, Clery's parents, or to other

---

Jeanne Clery

Jeanne Anne Clery was a first-year student at Lehigh University who was assaulted, raped, and murdered while she slept in her dorm room on April 5, 1986. The assailant was another student with whom Jeanne was not acquainted. Entering the building through a door which had been propped open, the perpetrator expected to burglarize property when the rape and murder occurred.

The subsequent investigation revealed that Lehigh actually had a history of violent crimes—38 in the three years prior to Jeanne's death. The discovery angered Howard and Connie Clery, Jeanne's parents, who launched a campaign to compel institutions to disclose statistics about campus crimes. Originally a Pennsylvania initiative, the cause was taken up by Congress in 1990 and passed as the Crime Awareness and Campus Security Act of 1990. It became known as the Jeanne Clery Disclosure of Campus Security Policy and Crimes Statistics Act within the Higher Education Amendments of 1998.

The Clery Act requires institutions that receive federal funding to publish annual crime statistics by October 1 of each year and to disclose security policies to current and prospective students, as well as to employees.

CRIME REPORTING SPECIFICATIONS OF THE CLERY ACT

Crime Categories

Criminal homicide

- Murder and non-negligent manslaughter
- Negligent manslaughter

Sex offenses

- Forcible sex offenses, including rape
- Nonforcible sex offenses

Robbery

Aggravated assault

Burglary

Motor vehicle theft

Arson

Incident Types

Liquor law violations

Drug law violations

Illegal weapons possession

Geographical Areas

Campus

Campus residence facilities for students

Noncampus buildings

Public property (streets, sidewalks)

members of the campus community. Angered at this discovery, Howard and Connie Clery, the parents of the murdered girl, launched a campaign to force colleges and universities to publish their crime statistics on an annual basis.

When it was passed by Congress in 1990, the Clery Act posed three basic requirements to institutions that receive federal funding.

- An annual disclosure of crime statistics
- Disclosure of security policies to students—current and prospective—and to staff
- Issuance of timely warnings when the potential for unsafe conditions on campus present themselves

Specifications for crime statistics reporting were detailed in the Clery Act, identifying seven crime categories, three types of incidents, and several geographical areas or zones that should be covered by the statistics. Reporting was required to cover a three-year period and annual disclosures would be required by October 1 of each year.

It was not until the Higher Education Amendments of 1998, however, that institutions were required to submit their crime statistics to the Department of Education for disclosure to the public. The amendments that

Security on Campus, Inc.

In 1987, Howard and Connie Clery founded Security on Campus, Inc. The nonprofit organization was formed to provide assistance to victims of crimes on campus. When the Clery Act was passed, the organization took on additional responsibilities for assisting individuals with the submission of official complaints about campus safety under the act. Assistance is free. Contact information is:

Website: www.securityoncampus.org

E-mail: cleryact@securityoncampus.org

Phone: (888) 251–7959

were enacted by President Bill Clinton added the requirement that institutions with their own police departments create and maintain daily crime logs that would be available to parents and to the public. And incidentally, it was not until the adoption of these amendments in 1998 that the act took on the name of Jeanne Clery.

With the assignment of recordkeeping authority to the Department of Education, the Clery Act also provided for the processing of complaints under its provisions. All complaints are to be directed to the Department of Education (www.ed.gov). Security on Campus, Inc., a nonprofit organization founded by the parents of Jeanne Clery, provides free assistance to individuals in the preparation and submission of complaints under the Clery Act.

In 1992, an amendment was proposed to the Clery Act by Congressman James Ramstad of Minnesota. The amendment was passed to ensure that institutions would provide specific and basic rights to both the victims and the alleged perpetrators of sexual assaults on campus. These rights included the following:

- The right to a disciplinary hearing for the accuser and the accused
- Disclosures of hearing results to the accuser and the accused
- Options for law enforcement reporting for the accuser
- All students should be advised about on- and off-campus counseling, mental health, and other services for victims of sexual offenses
- Students should also be advised of options for making changes to academic and living situations

The amendments to FERPA in regard to crimes of violence and nonforcible sex offenses came with the Higher Education Amendments of 1998. And the amendments resolved a dilemma that had been created by the 1992 Ramstad Amendment.

Guided by the FPCO, institutions had been directed that disclosures of the final results of a disciplinary hearing involving a crime of violence or sex crime could only be disclosed to the victim. The concern quickly arose, however, about the results being disclosed beyond the victim and the accuser. What was to prevent the alleged victim, for instance, from disclosing the results to other students or even to the public? Certainly, such a disclosure could not be prevented, especially since the same amendments provided for advising the victim regarding other law enforcement remedies.

The disclosure, subject to the requirements in §99.39, is in connection with a disciplinary proceeding at an institution of postsecondary education. The institution must not disclose the final results of the disciplinary proceeding unless it determines that—

A. The student is an alleged perpetrator of a crime of violence or nonforcible sex offense; and

B. With respect to the allegation made against him or her, the student has committed a violation of the institution's rules or policies.

§99.31(a)(14)(i)

The amendment to §99.31(a)(14)(i) essentially permits the institution to disclose to the public the results of a disciplinary hearing provided the disciplinary hearing is in relation to a crime of violence or nonforcible sex offense *and* a determination of a violation has been made. In regard to such disclosures, the regulations refer to the identity of the alleged perpetrator where a violation is determined to have occurred.

But again, the placement of this amendment is within §99.31, the section on exceptions. The upshot is that institutions are permitted to make such disclosures but are not required to do so.

As an additional stipulation, the regulations protect the identity of the victim and other students who may be involved in the incident, perhaps as witnesses. In §99.31(a)(14)(ii), FERPA prohibits the disclosure of the names of other students involved without their prior written consent. Specifically, the prohibition is written in regard to the institution and says nothing about the ability of the institution to contain or prohibit disclosures that may be made by the alleged victim or the other students involved.

Nonforcible Sex Offenses

The term *nonforcible sex offenses* refers to sexual acts and conduct with individuals who, under the law, are judged incapable of giving their consent to sexual activity. Minors and those who are underage, as well as individuals who are physically and cognitively incompetent, are considered unable to give appropriate consent for sexual activity. In a court of law, allegations of consent from such individuals are considered invalid and inadmissible.

Variations from state to state in the laws regarding nonforcible sex offenses differ on the determination of the age of consent and levels of intoxication producing temporary mental incompetence. States are also not consistent in the prosecution of certain acts, such as fornication, adultery, and consensual sodomy, some of which have been eliminated from local rosters of criminal offenses.

> The institution may not disclose the name of any other student, including a victim or witness, without the prior written consent of the other student.
>
> *§99.31(a)(14)(ii)*

Campus Sex Crimes Prevention Act

Among the 2008 Amendments to FERPA is the introduction of a clause under §99.31 to address the disclosure of information about registered sex offenders.

§99.31(a)(16) permits, but does not require, the disclosure of information about registered sex offenders, provided the disclosure is in compliance with federal legislation about the disclosure of sex offender information. In its guidance, the FPCO goes on to emphasize that institutions are neither required nor encouraged to collect and maintain information about registered sex offenders. Since the information is already available to communities through registries established under Megan's Law, there is no need for institutions to duplicate the effort. They need only make information available to the education community regarding where to access information about registered sex offenders.

> The disclosure concerns sex offenders and others required to register under section 170101 of the Violent Crime Control and Law Enforcement Act of 1994, 42 USC 14071, and the information was provided to the educational agency or institution under 42 USC 14071 and applicable federal guidelines.
>
> *§99.31(a)(16)*

The history behind the introduction of §99.31(a)(16) is a long and tragic one, culminating primarily in the Campus Sex Crimes Prevention Act (CSCPA), which was established October 28, 2000. The CSCPA was §1601 of the Victims of Trafficking and Violence Protection Act of 2000, PL 106–386. Sponsored by Senator John Kyl of Arizona, the CSCPA required the tracking of registered sex offenders who are enrolled as students at postsecondary institutions or who are working or volunteering to work on campus.

The nation was awakened to the need to track sex offenders after the 1989 disappearance of 11-year old Jacob Wetterling. In 1994, Congress passed the Jacob Wetterling Crimes Against Children and Sexually Violent Offender Registration Act. The Jacob Wetterling Act, as it came to be known, was part of the Federal Violent Crime Control and Law Enforcement Act of 1994.

The Jacob Wetterling Act requires and established a national registry to track sex offenders and perpetrators of crimes against children. Two years later, Megan's Law amended the Jacob Wetterling Act, requiring states to establish a community notification system of information contained in the registries.

Established in 1996, Megan's Law required law enforcement authorities to make available to the public information about registered sex offenders. This information included the following.

- Name of the sex offender
- Picture, photograph, or likeness of the individual

Jacob Wetterling

The Jacob Wetterling Crimes Against Children and Sexually Violent Offender Registration Act of 1994 takes its name from a young boy who was the subject of a 1989 incident in St. Joseph, Minnesota.

On October 22, 1989, two brothers—Jacob, 11, and Trevor, 10—and an 11-year-old friend, Aaron, had gone to a convenience store. While riding their bicycles home, the boys were accosted by a masked man who forced the boys to abandon their bicycles and flashlights in a ditch. He made the boys lie face down on the ground and, at gun point, demanded to know the age of each boy. Trevor was released immediately and after inspecting Aaron's face, the masked man released Aaron, too, telling them to run into the woods and not look back. Jacob was led away and never heard from again.

During the investigation, it was discovered that halfway houses in the St. Joseph area were regularly housing sex offenders recently released from prison. Just 10 months prior to Jacob's disappearance, a young boy had been kidnapped, forced into a car, sexually assaulted, and then released into the woods with the instruction not to look back.

After his disappearance, Jacob's mother, Patty Wetterling, became an advocate for missing children and, with her husband Jerry, formed the Jacob Wetterling Foundation. As a member of a task force appointed by the governor, Patty worked for stronger sex offender registration laws in Minnesota. In 1994, Congress passed the Crimes Against Children and Sexually Violent Offender Registration Act in Jacob's name. The act required states to implement registries for sex offenders and perpetrators of crimes against children.

Megan Nicole Kanka

A 7-year-old girl, Megan Nicole Kanka, was the namesake for Megan's Law. She lived in Hamilton Township, New Jersey. On July, 29, 1994, a 36-year-old neighbor named Jesse Timmendequas invited Megan to his home to see a new puppy. No one knew that Timmendequas was a pedophile with a record of two convictions. He raped and strangled Megan with a belt, stuffing her body into a toy box and dumping it in a neighborhood park.

In 1996, Megan's Law amended the Jacob Wetterling Act, requiring states to establish community notification systems regarding the location of sex offenders and perpetrators of crimes against children.

Timmendequas was sentenced and incarcerated at the New Jersey State Prison in Princeton.

- Address of residence
- Incarceration date
- Nature of the crime committed

Further, individuals convicted of sex crimes are required to report updated information to law enforcement officials regarding changes to address or employment. While the focus of the law was on sexual offenses committed against children, some states expanded the registry reporting requirements to include all types of sexual offenses.

Megan's Law was amended further in 2006 by the Adam Walsh Child Protection and Safety Act. This act established new registry requirements and proposed a system of three tiers for classifying sex offenders according to the risk they posed to their communities. The changes in legislation were prompted by the 1981 disappearance of six-year old Adam Walsh from a Florida shopping mall. After the gruesome discovery of the boy's severed head, Adam's father, John Walsh, became an activist for child protection laws, founding a national center for missing and exploited children and establishing a television series, *America's Most Wanted*, to aid in the tracking and capture of criminals.

Two other pieces of legislation are relevant to this discussion: the Sexual Offender Tracking and Identification Act of 1996 and the Campus Sex Crimes Prevention Act.

The Sexual Offender Tracking and Identification Act of 1996 was named for Pam Lychner, a Houston real estate agent who was attacked in 1990 by a workman with prior convictions as a rapist and as a child molester. This act amended the Jacob Wetterling Act by establishing *lifetime* registration requirements for recidivists and for offenders who perpetrate certain aggravated acts or crimes.

Adam Walsh

On July 27, 1981, 6-year-old Adam Walsh went shopping with his mother Reve at Sears in Hollywood, Florida. While Mom went to look for lamps, young Adam stayed in the toy department, fascinated by video games, which were the rage of the early 1980s. At length, a 17-year-old female security guard asked four boys to leave the toy department because of the disruption they were causing. Adam was believed to be one of the boys.

Adam disappeared and an intense search for his whereabouts began. Sixteen days after the abduction, Adam's severed head was discovered in a drainage canal about 100 miles from his home. Police suspected serial killer Ottis Elwood Toole of perpetrating the crime, but the investigation into the boy's death was so badly mishandled, the case could not be closed. From his prison cell, Toole confessed twice to Adam's murder but also recanted those confessions. On December 16, 2008, Toole's niece confirmed to Adam's father that in 1996, on his prison deathbed, Toole had finally confessed to Adam's murder.

John Walsh, Adam's father, became an activist and advocate for child protection laws. He founded the National Center for Missing and Exploited Children (NCMEC) and lobbied for legislation along with Patty Wetterling, the mother of Jacob Wetterling, an 11-year-old boy who disappeared in 1989. The Adam Walsh Child Protection and Safety Act was passed in 2006.

John Walsh is known as the creator and host of the syndicated Fox Television series *America's Most Wanted*.

Additionally, a 1998 amendment to the Jacob Wetterling Act was prompted by §115 of the General Provisions of Title I of the Commerce, Justice, and State, the Judiciary, and Related Agencies Appropriations Act (CJSA). This act heightened requirements for registration to include not only sexually violent offenders but federal and military offenders, nonresident workers, and students, all of whom must be tracked in the National Sex Offender Registry (NSOR).

The Campus Sex Crimes Prevention Act (CSCPA) of 2000 was yet another amendment to the Jacob Wetterling Act, requiring sex offenders to report enrollment or employment at any institution of higher education. The

National Sex Offender Registry

The National Alert Registry at www.registeredoffenderslist.org is a program of the U.S. Department of Justice and a component of the Bureau of Justice Statistics (BJS) National Criminal History Improvement Program. The registry was established to track the location of individuals who have been convicted of sex crimes against children. In 2003, the U.S. Supreme Court authorized the posting of this information on the Internet.

The National Alert Registry provides additional information on child safety as well as for guiding users on utilizing the information in the registry.

Pam Lychner

One day in 1990, real estate agent Pam Lychner had arranged to show a vacant home to a prospective buyer. Arriving at the Houston area property, she was met by William David Kelley, a workman who had returned to the house claiming to have forgotten to clean under a sink. A convicted rapist and child molester, Kelley brutally assaulted Pam and would have killed her if her husband had not arrived at the house to save her life.

Recovering from the incident, Pam went on to organize Justice for All (www.jfa.net), an advocacy group for victim rights. The organization lobbied for tougher sentences for perpetrators of violent crimes. Pam also worked with Senators Lindsey Gramm and Joe Biden on a bill that would establish a national database to track sex offenders.

In July 1996, Pam and her two daughters, Katie, 8, and Shannon, 10, were killed in the TWA Flight 800 explosion off Long Island. When Congress passed the Sexual Offender Tracking and Identification Act later that year, it was named in memory of Pam Lychner.

Kelley was convicted after plea bargaining to be tried for aggravated kidnapping with the intent to commit sexual assault. He was sentenced to 20 years in prison.

CSCPA goes on to require the enactment of procedures to share such information with statewide data systems and with law enforcement units that have jurisdiction over the communities in which the institutions are located. Effective October 2002, the CSCPA requirements are enforced through state eligibility for federal funding and codified through state law.

CSCPA, in turn, amended the Clery Act. Institutions of higher education, already required to disclose campus crime statistics on an annual basis, must now disclose to their communities where law enforcement information about sex offenders can be obtained. This information may be included in the annual security report and began with campus 2003 reports.

National Center for Campus Public Safety

On February 3, 2009, the U.S. House of Representatives passed HR 748, a bill that seeks to establish a National Center for Campus Public Safety. The center would act as a clearinghouse for campuses across the nation to coordinate the sharing of information, collaborate on policy development, and promote best practices in the field of campus safety. The center would also conduct its own research.

The concept of the center was developed and lobbied for by the International Association of Campus Law Enforcement Administrators. First proposed in 2004, the idea had an initial victory in 2007, when a bill advocating for the creation of the center was passed in Congress. The bill was never forwarded to the Senate, however, prompting the reemergence in the 2009 bill.

The International Association of Campus Law Enforcement Administrators cites the Virginia Tech situation, mounting pressures as a result of economic depression, and the continuing concerns of homeland security as reasons for the funding and support of the center.

USA PATRIOT Act

A discussion of campus safety would be incomplete without some attention to the USA PATRIOT Act.

The events of September 11, 2001, were a tremendous shock to the nation and to every facet of American society. While the economy and the federal government were the primary physical targets of the Islamic terrorists that day, the devastation wrought reached to every area of American life and to each and every citizen and immigrant in the nation.

There was no business as usual that day. In addition to the grounding of all air travel, everything seemed to stop as cities, commerce, and iconic U.S. landmarks braced for potential attack if the assaults on New York and Washington, D.C. continued into other areas of the country.

In education communities, a similar paralysis struck. Classes were cancelled and, where possible, students were sent home. In higher education, attention turned toward attempting to understand the events, the causes and motivations behind the attacks, and the implications for a nation needing to move forward beyond recovery.

9/11

The tragic events of September 11, 2001, changed America forever. That morning, four separate commercial airline flights, departing from Boston, Newark, and Washington, D.C., were hijacked by 19 al-Qaeda terrorists and redirected toward New York and Washington, D.C.

At 8:46 am EST, the North Tower of the World Trade Center was struck by American Airlines Flight 11. Less than 20 minutes later, at 9:03 am, United Flight 175 plowed into the South Tower. Before the attacks were over, the twin towers of the World Trade Center would collapse and disappear forever from the Manhattan skyline.

Two other flights were diverted by their Islamic terrorist hijackers with courses set for Washington, D.C. At 9:37 am, American Flight 77 crashed into the Pentagon in Arlington County, just outside the District of Columbia.

The last airliner, United Flight 93, was presumed to be bound for the Capitol or the White House. Both locations were evacuated as news of the New York and Pentagon attacks were reported on broadcasts throughout the nation. The passengers of United 93, learning of the earlier attacks through cell phone and other emergency communications, attempted to regain control of their flight. But their efforts were unsuccessful. The flight crashed into a rural Pennsylvania field outside Shanksville.

The devastation at all of the crash sites made it difficult for authorities to determine the number of victims who had lost their lives in the 9/11 attacks. In addition to the airline passengers and employees of the World Trade Center and Pentagon, many of the victims were firefighters, police, and New York Port Authority officers. Initial statistics logged the count at 2,974, but the final list exceeded 3,000 in the wake of clean-up efforts and casualties from the toxic fumes of the collapsed structures.

On October 26, 2001, just 45 days after the terrorist attacks of 9/11, President George W. Bush signed the United and Strengthening America by Providing Appropriate Tools Required to Intercept and Obstruct Terrorists (USA PATRIOT) Act of 2001 (USAPA). Much of the legislation had already been written before 9/11 and had, in fact, been the subject of great controversy and debate. Many of the proposals that made it into the USAPA were extracted from the Anti-Terrorism Act (ATA) of 2001, which focused on the monitoring of communications and personal information by law enforcement.

The tense consciousness of the nation and the need for Congress to react quickly to the events of 9/11 propelled the approval of the USAPA. The USAPA made sweeping amendments to at least 15 other statutes. And despite the inclusion of a sunset, or expiration, clause, the USAPA was not perfect. In its analysis and assessment of the USAPA, the Electronic Privacy Information Center (www.epic.org) concluded the following.

> *The Act did not, however, provide for the system of checks and balances that traditionally safeguard civil liberties in the face of such legislation.*

The regulatory language of the legislation was too imprecise in some of its critical areas regarding authority and just cause. Privacy advocates objected that the USAPA created opportunities and the potential for abuse of the investigative rights by law enforcement. Without oversight, the civil rights of American citizens and, in particular, immigrants of certain ethnic and national origins, were suddenly at peril.

One of the provisions added to the final legislative language of the USAPA was a sunset clause, a determination of when the legislation would essentially expire unless it were renewed or extended by Congress. USAPA was supposed to sunset at the end of 2005. Renewed controversy questioned the need to continue the expansive authorities given law enforcement now four years after the devastation of 9/11. President Bush argued that the War on Terror had been aided by the USAPA's strengthening of the Department of Justice and pointed to the lack of any further attacks on U.S. soil. Further, the discovery and foiling of other suspected terrorist activity proved that the USAPA was not only working but necessary to the nation's continued War on Terror.

On March 9, 2006, the President signed the USA PATRIOT Improvement and Reauthorization Act of 2005, effectively passing much of the original legislation into law.

Electronic communication, finance and banking, immigration, and education have all been affected by the provisions of USAPA. As far as

---

Patriot Act Reauthorization

The reauthorization of the USA PATRIOT Act, signed into law by President George W. Bush on March 9, 2006, included a number of new provisions.

- Per a recommendation of the Weapons of Mass Destruction (WMD) Commission, a new Assistant Attorney General for National Security was created.

- "Hawalas," or informal money transfer networks, were added to the targets for penalties on terrorism financing.

- Transportation via land, air, and water are protected through tougher penalties for terrorist attacks.

The Combat Methamphetamine Epidemic Act of 2005 is included, requiring tracking on the part of pharmacies and other retailers for over-the-counter sales of drugs that might be used to manufacture methamphetamines.

---

education and the education environment are concerned, there were several important impacts to privacy and an amendment to FERPA.

- *Ex parte* orders and subpoenas
- Secret searches and seizures by law enforcement
- Surveillance
- Immigration and foreign visitors

Secret Searches and Records Production

Immediately after 9/11, institutions across the nation were confronted by federal investigators scrutinizing the lives and interests of students and researchers who might be involved in potential terrorist activity. Some investigators presented *ex parte* orders, while others used the health and safety exception in FERPA §99.31(a)(10) as justification for their inquiry.

> The disclosure is in connection with a health and safety emergency, under the conditions described in §99.36.
>
> *§99.31(a)(10)*

In the wake of the 9/11 attacks, there certainly was cause for institutions to urgently comply with such requests on the basis of the national emergency. And it was not just education that faced and dealt with these kinds of investigations either. Banks, financial institutions, medical and biological research laboratories, warfare and weaponry research facilities, libraries, commercial retailers, online vendors, and private-living facilities were all approached in those tenuous days following 9/11. To ensure federal authority to continue such activity in the name of safeguarding America beyond the immediate emergency, however, specific legislation was needed. And so the USAPA was passed.

The most evident impact on FERPA is the inclusion of a clause regarding *ex parte* orders in the exceptions paragraph regarding subpoenas. But the implications of this amendment, the health and safety emergency exception, and the USAPA go beyond court orders and the production of records.

> An *ex parte* order obtained by the United States Attorney General (or designee not lower than an Assistant Attorney General) concerning investigations or prosecutions of an offense listed in 18 USC 2331.
>
> *§99.31(a)(9)(ii)(C)*

USAPA codified the ability of the government and law enforcement to conduct "secret searches," to seize tangible evidence, and to conduct surveillance essentially without the requirement of demonstrating probable cause to anyone. While the language of the legislation referred to "delayed notification" to the subject of searches, the period of such delay was defined as only "reasonable," with extensions or renewals of the delay permitted by the act. As long as "reasonable necessity" exists, the courts could authorize seizure of tangible property and records in these investigations.

Investigations were also not simply restricted to the education records in the registrar's office. Just about any kind of information from any area of the campus could be demanded. Library records, Internet searches, research data and inquiries, housing records, and even medical and psychological records could be targeted. And just as records could exist in any form and format, the USAPA defined no limitations on the records of its interest. Under its seizure provisions, investigators could take into custody computers and other work that may provide critical evidence or contribute to their investigation.

In essence, USAPA approved the FBI's use of Carnivore. Carnivore, which was first revealed in July 2000, is a tool that allows the FBI to access the communications activity of all subscribers of an Internet provider that

Carnivore

The controversial Carnivore is a Microsoft Windows-configured workstation that resides on an Internet provider's network. Through its packet-sniffing software, it is able to monitor and track electronic communications, which are recorded on a removable disk.

The Federal Bureau of Investigation (FBI) first announced its implementation of Carnivore in July 2000. Approved by Attorney General Janet Reno under the Clinton Administration, the FBI's announcement was met with immediate concern. The day after the announcement, the Electronic Privacy Information Center (EPIC) filed a request for disclosures under the Freedom of Information Act (FOIA). Among the demands was public disclosure of the FBI's records regarding the software, Carnivore's source code, and other technical details.

In other disclosures, the FBI admitted that it did not use Carnivore or the rebranded version of the software known as DCS-1000. It did admit to using commercially available Internet surveillance products between 2002 and 2003. Then in January 2005, the FBI announced that it was abandoning pursuing the use of Carnivore in its surveillance activities.

the agency may be monitoring. Controversial about this ability is that the access is not localized to suspect subjects or persons of interest. With Carnivore, the communications—e-mail, searches, web surfing activity, and any other types of electronic communication—of *every* subscriber, even law-abiding citizens, are available to federal investigators.

Expanded Surveillance Permissions

While the use of Carnivore covers electronic communication and information, other amendments to the Wiretap Statute, the Foreign Intelligence Surveillance Act, and the Pen Register and Trap and Trace Statute expanded the provisions on traditional surveillance operations.

Law enforcement was given increased authorities to install pen registers and trap and trace devices where vital to an investigation. These surveillance tools function by capturing information from communication devices, such as a telephone. But the USAPA expanded coverage to include new technology then emerging to enable communication between parties via any transmission media.

Pen register refers to the capture of the *outgoing* destination information in communications. Trap and trace refers to the capture of *incoming* communication information. A caller ID system is an example of a trap and trace device. With the USAPA, the nature of the devices used in surveillance operations was expanded beyond the telephone and other traditional monitoring devices to include the ability to capture information such as computer routing, Internet addresses, and electronic signaling.

UPDATED DEFINITIONS FROM THE USA PATRIOT ACT

Pen register: a device or process which records or decodes dialing, routing, addressing, or signaling information transmitted by an instrument or facility from which a wire or electronic communication is transmitted

Trap and trace: a device or process which captures the incoming electronic or other impulses which identify the originating number or other dialing, routing, addressing, and signaling information likely to identify the source of a wire or electronic communication

Many of these covert activities have long been associated with espionage and the Foreign Intelligence Surveillance Act (FISA) and have traditionally focused on foreign intelligence and counterintelligence. With the changes espoused by the USAPA, the potential subjects of federal surveillance activities may now include Americans and surveillance operations within the boundaries of the United States itself. And, of course, targets of interest would immediately include research facilities at higher education institutions focusing on knowledge and activities that might enable terrorism.

Before the USAPA, surveillance orders and search warrants were restricted to the jurisdiction of the court in whose locality the surveillance device was to be installed. This made securing warrants somewhat cumbersome and time consuming for investigators. As a result of USAPA, however, such orders may now be approved and issued by any court nationwide.

In making a determination under paragraph (a) of this section, an educational agency or institution may take into account the totality of the circumstances pertaining to a threat to the health or safety of a student or other individuals. If the educational agency or institution determines that there is an articulable and significant threat to the health or safety of a student or other individuals, it may disclose information from education records to any person whose knowledge of the information is necessary to protect the health or safety of the student or other individuals. If based on the information available at the time of the determination, there is a rational basis for the determination, the Department will not substitute its judgment for that of the educational agency or institution in evaluating the circumstances and making its determination.

§99.36(c)

PATRIOT ACT BLAMELESS CLAUSE

An educational agency or institution that, in good faith, produces education records in accordance with an order issued under this subsection shall not be liable to any person for that production.

—*USAPA §507(j)(4)*

For the educational institution, the potential exists for surveillance and search activities regarding students and other members of the academic community. When approached by the FBI or other federal investigators, authority will likely be justified by an *ex parte* order or other order issued under the FERPA exception for health and safety. A good faith effort to comply and cooperate with the investigators is required. And at the same time, the exemptions and blameless clause of §99.36(c) apply.

To FERPA's concurrence can be added the protection clause from the USAPA itself, which frees from liability any institution that cooperates with a USAPA federal investigation in good faith.

SEVIS

With the expansion of surveillance and covert tracking operations under the USAPA, the government refocused its scrutiny and management of foreign nationals visiting and migrating into the United States. Immigration and port of entry monitoring operations were folded into a new office, the Department of Homeland Security, which was created with the primary goal of protecting the nation from potential attacks like the ones that occurred on 9/11. The former operations of the Immigration and Naturalization Service (INS), which ceased to exist on March 1, 2003, were reenvisioned and realigned under the new U.S. Immigration and Customs Enforcement (ICE).

The impact on life in the United States after 9/11 was severe and significant. Various sectors of our society were affected in different ways, particularly travel and the security of mass transportation systems. Finance and commerce were affected, along with foreign trade. Privacy, in many respects, took a back seat to national security.

ICE introduced new measures and protocols to more closely monitor the entry and activities of visitors to the United States. In higher education, the revised procedures affected how foreign students are treated administratively, with the institution responsible for reporting requirements that, for some, seemed to deputize institutions as extensions of the ICE.

In 2003, the Student and Exchange Visitor Information System (SEVIS) was implemented to track the activities of nonimmigrant students (F and M visa) and exchange visitors (J visa) who enter the United States. Established as an Internet-based reporting system, SEVIS is moderated by the Student and Exchange Visitor Program (SEVP). In order to qualify as hosts or sponsors of nonimmigrant students, educational agencies and institutions must qualify and be approved by the U.S. Department of State (DoS).

ICE regulations were published in an issue of the *Federal Register* dated December 11, 2002, and sought to provide guidance on the utilization and goals of SEVIS. Educational institutions were taken aback by the extensive information required by SEVIS. The information on nonimmigrant students sought by SEVIS included directory and non-directory information, including data not previously recorded or required of native and international students. While USAPA amended FERPA to permit institutions to cooperate with federal investigators probing potential terrorist activity, SEVIS' data gathering efforts tested and even threatened the basic rights to privacy of human beings—citizens or not.

REPORTING REQUIREMENTS PER ICE REGULATIONS

Per 8 CFR §214.3(g), as amended in 67 Federal Register 76256 (December 11, 2002), designated school officials must make the following information or documents about nonimmigrant students available to any ICE officer upon request:

- Name
- Date and place of birth
- Country of citizenship
- Current address where the student and the student's dependents reside (Mailing address acceptable if mail cannot be received at a current address)
- Current academic status
- Date of commencement of studies
- Degree program and field of study
- Certification for practical training (if applicable), including beginning and end dates
- Termination date and reason, if known
- Documents referred to in §214.3(k)
- Number of credits completed each semester or term
- Photocopy of student's I-20 ID copy

On behalf of colleges and universities throughout the nation, Jerry Sullivan, president of the American Association of Collegiate Registrars and Admissions Officers (AACRAO), submitted to the Family Policy Compliance Office (FPCO) a request for guidance and clarification regarding the responsibilities of educational institutions in regard to SEVIS. On August 27, 2004, Director LeRoy S. Rooker responded in a Dear Colleague Letter that is available in the electronic library of the FPCO's website.

Sullivan's concerns were two-fold: first, the FERPA implications of the actual disclosures to ICE and the DHS, and secondly, the use of outsourced contractors to facilitate the collection of information for submission to ICE and the DHS. In his response, however, Rooker addressed a number of additional issues.

SEVIS FACTS AND STATISTICS

The General Summary Quarterly Review for the period ending September 30, 2008, reported the following facts and statistics.

- Over 1.1 million active students in the system

- 36% of all approved schools are in California (1,195), New York (685), Florida (569), Texas (535), and Pennsylvania (418)

- Top approved schools (by population): Cornell University, Houston Community College System, Santa Monica College, San Francisco State University, and Northern Virginia Community College

- Top F-1 schools: City University of New York, University of Southern California, Columbia University in the City of New York, Purdue University, and University of Illinois

- Top M-1 schools: Pan Am International Flight Academy, Sabena Airline Training Center, STMC Training Institute, Bethel School of Supernatural Ministry, and Sierra Academy of Aeronautics – International Training Center

- 51% of active students are in six states: California, New York, Texas, Massachusetts, Illinois, and Florida

- Largest number of active students come from South Korea, followed by India, China, and Japan

- Largest percentage of students in approved schools: female

- Leading major of active students: business, followed by engineering, basic skills, and computer and information sciences

- 67% of active students are enrolled in a bachelor's, masters, or doctoral program, followed by language training and associate programs

First of all, Rooker pointed out that FERPA does not apply to foreign students as far as SEVIS is concerned.

With regard to the broader question concerning access by ICE to education records of foreign students and exchange visitor program participants, §641(c)(2) of the Illegal Immigration Reform and Immigrant Responsibility Act of 1996 (IIRIRA), as amended, (8 USC §1372) provides that FERPA shall not apply to aliens described in subsection (a) of §641 to the extent that the Attorney General determines necessary to carry out the SEVIS program. In the December 11 regulations, the Attorney General made such a determination. 67 Fed Reg 76256, 76270 (December 11, 2002). In effect ICE regulations, 8 CFR §214.1(h), state with respect to F and M nonimmigrant students and J nonimmigrant exchange visitors, the FERPA provisions that might impede the proper implementation of 8 USC §1372 or 8 CFR §214.3(g) are waived to the extent that 8 USC §1372 or 8 CFR §214.3(g) requires the educational agency or institution to report the information. [Dear Colleague Letter, 27 August 2004]

In his letter to AACRAO, Rooker explains that any FERPA requirements that might impede a school's cooperation with ICE and the SEVIS program are "waived" so that institutions can report the information required by the program and the attorney general. The administration of SEVIS was transferred to the assistant secretary of the Bureau of Border Security under the Homeland Security Act of 2002 (PL 107–296, Title IV, §442).

Approved SEVIS Program Sponsors

The U.S. Department of State (DoS) processes, evaluates, and approves schools wishing to become approved Student and Exchange Visitor Program (SEVP) sponsors. There are three primary qualifications which schools must meet.

- Previous experience in the field of international exchanges
- Financial requirements
- Technological ability to utilize SEVIS

The first two requirements are conditions for consideration that have been defined by the Department of Homeland Security. The final requisite is unconditional since the SEVP works entirely in an electronic environment. Participating schools must be able to access the Internet and submit data through the SEVIS program.

Instructions and links to information about SEVP and SEVIS are available from the DoS Bureau of Educational and Cultural Affairs website http://exchanges.state.gov/jexchanges/sevis.html.

Rooker went on to say that it does not matter if the data collection responsibilities have been outsourced to an external contractor. FERPA has never prohibited the use of outside contractors or service providers as long as these providers comply with FERPA in the same way that the institution would comply with FERPA.

In summarization, Rooker states the position of the U.S. Department of Education and the FPCO.

> *We believe that Congress did not intend for the privacy protections under FERPA to impede ICE in carrying out the SEVIS program. Therefore, our advice to AACRAO is that institutions generally may not use FERPA in order to refuse to comply with requests from ICE relative to participation in SEVIS. [Dear Colleague Letter, 27 August 2004]*

It should be noted that ICE documents generally require the nonimmigrant student or exchange visitor to endorse and agree to a statement that permits ICE to obtain *any* information from institutions and other entities without the prior consent of the visa applicant.

Chapter 5

Other Exceptions and FERPA Concerns

SIMPLIFICATIONS ARE DANGEROUS because they often overgeneralize the intent of the subject at hand. In many ways, however, the structure of the FERPA regulations is a simple one.

Clear and simple, all privacy rights over education records belong to either parents or eligible students. Where third parties are concerned, the regulations recognize certain operational functions and processes that are part of the business of education. But there is no singular or overall recognition of rights assigned to any party other than those to parents and eligible students. Instead, FERPA contains a list of exceptions where disclosures *may* be permitted. Disclosures to these entities or in these situations are *not* required. It is up to the institution to determine whether disclosure is appropriate, given the circumstances at hand and the conditions detailed in the regulations.

Because parents and potential threats to health and safety are often the first concerns that come to mind in any discussion of exceptions to privacy rights in education, they were addressed first in Chapter Four of this book. In this chapter, consideration is given to all of the other operational questions and situational issues that arise in complying with FERPA on a daily basis.

Under what conditions is prior consent not required to disclose information?

An educational agency or institution may disclose personally identifiable information from an education record of a student without the consent required of Sec. 99.30 if the disclosure meets one or more of the following exceptions.

1. The disclosure is to other school officials, including teachers, within the agency or institution whom the agency or institution has determined to have legitimate educational interest.

   §99.31(a)(1)(i)(A)

To underscore the seriousness of the sweeping assignment of privacy rights in FERPA, consider the extensiveness and particularity of the exceptions in §99.31. The first exception focuses on education officials, clearly enforcing the notion that access to education records is neither a right nor a privilege but dependent upon legitimate educational interest and the administration of one's responsibilities as an education official (see Chapter Two). If education officials do not have a limitless right to access education records, how much more serious a determination is necessary when deciding whether to disclose or refuse to disclose education records to third parties!

When in doubt, think prior written consent.

—LEROY ROOKER,
former Director of the Family Policy Compliance Office

In his FERPA training programs, former FPCO director LeRoy Rooker has often said, "When in doubt, think prior written consent." That is, when an education official is uncertain whether disclosure is authorized or permitted, the official can always ask for a prior written consent. A prior written consent is authorization to release whatever records are specified in the consent.

Certainly, prior written consent is the standard by which disclosure is permitted to third parties. Operationally, however, there are a myriad of regular tasks and undertakings in education that make prior written consent questionable, if not altogether impossible. For these often unique situations, FERPA attempts, in §99.31, to detail a host of conditions that *may* be exceptions to the prior written consent rule. Again, it is up to the institution to make a final determination regarding disclosure.

In this chapter, attention is given to a number of these permitted exceptions, especially those affected by the 2008 Amendments.

Disclosures to Other Educational Agencies and Institutions

An important implication arises out of the 2008 Amendments to §99.31(a)(2).

Institutions were previously permitted to provide non-directory information to an institution "where the student seeks or intends to enroll" (§99.31(a)(2)). The only qualification in this regard was evidence that, indeed, the student had submitted an application to another institution, whether for admission or transfer.

Education officials have traditionally interpreted the language of the exception very narrowly and precisely. That is, the exception was interpreted to refer solely to the period during which the student was seeking admission to another institution. Once the student was admitted and enrolled, once that student had matriculated at the other institution, relationships were suddenly redefined and the exception was deemed inapplicable.

This kind of interpretation is quite understandable, given the strictness of other clauses in the regulations. In light of the April 2007 tragedy at Virginia Tech, however, such a restriction, if only implied, contributes to the creation of potentially dangerous situations for unsuspecting institutions.

> The disclosure is, subject to the requirements of §99.34, to the officials of another school, school system, or institution of postsecondary education where the student seeks or intends to enroll, or where the student is already enrolled so long as the disclosure is for purposes related to the student's enrollment or transfer.
>
> *§99.31(a)(2)*

The 2008 Amendments, therefore, added the clause "or where the student is already enrolled" to clarify that information can still be shared with another institution *even after* the student has matriculated. In the March 24, 2008, edition of the *Federal Register*, the regulators explained their interpretation and rewriting of this exception.

> *This proposed exception to the consent requirement is intended to ease administrative burdens on educational agencies and institutions by allowing them to send transcripts and other information from education records to schools where a student seeks or intends to enroll without meeting the formal consent requirements in §99.30. We have concluded that authority to disclose or transfer information to a student's new school under this exception does not cease automatically the moment a student has actually enrolled. [FR 15581]*

Even after a student has begun classes at another institution, the student's former school may communicate additional information to the second institution as long as that information is related to the student's enrollment or transfer to that second institution. In the *Federal Register* discussion, "transcripts and other information" is intended to include disciplinary records and other critical data about which the accepting institution should be aware. With reference to the Virginia Tech situation, the *Federal Register* went on to elaborate.

> *Under §99.31(a)(2) and §99.34(a), FERPA permits school officials to disclose any and all education records, including health and disciplinary records, to another institution where the student seeks or intends to enroll. [FR 15581]*

§99.34 is the section in FERPA that discusses the disclosure of information to other educational agencies or institutions.

An educational agency or institution that discloses an education record under §99.31(a)(2) shall:

Make a reasonable attempt to notify the parent or eligible student at the last known address of the parent or eligible student, unless:

i. The disclosure is initiated by the parent or eligible student; or

ii. The annual notification of the agency or institution under Sec. 99.7 includes a notice that the agency or institution forwards education records to other agencies or institutions that have requested the records and in which the student seeks or intends to enroll.

§99.34(a)(1)

Essentially, if an institution discloses non-directory information to another institution, an attempt must be made to notify the student involved, unless the disclosure was initiated by the student. Students initiate such disclosures through transcript requests or by signing waivers attached to admission and transfer applications that permit the admitting institution to seek information from the school in which the student was formerly or is currently enrolled. An exception to this requirement is provided in (ii), which states that if the first institution discloses to students in its annual notification that it provides information to schools in which students seek or intend to enroll, no additional notification is expected or required.

§99.34 goes on to stipulate that the disclosing institution must give to the student, upon the student's request, a copy of the record or records that were disclosed (§99.34(a)(2)) and provide the opportunity for a hearing (§99.34(a)(3)) should the disclosure be challenged.

> An educational agency or institution may disclose an education record of a student in attendance to another educational agency or institution if:
>
> 1. The student is enrolled or receives services from the other agency or institution; and
>
> 2. The disclosure meets the requirements of paragraph (a) of this section.
>
>   *§99.34(b)*

The section goes on to provide permission for disclosures to another institution where a student may be concurrently enrolled or receiving services.

Because students may be enrolled in classes at more than one institution, FERPA permits the disclosure of information from education records between the institutions. The only requirement here is that the potential for disclosure of information between institutions in which a student is concurrently enrolled must be acknowledged in the annual notification of the institution providing the information.

Subpoenas and *Ex Parte* Orders

Requirements of Subpoena Processing

A subpoena is a court order for the production and delivery of records to a court and may, in some cases, require a personal appearance for testimony under oath. Failure to comply with a subpoena is tantamount to contempt of court and carries penalties that differ from state to state.

Under §99.31(a)(9), compliance with a subpoena or a court order is an exception under FERPA. This is because the rules and regulations regarding compliance requirements with subpoenas may differ between states and from one court district to another.

> The disclosure is to comply with a judicial order or lawfully issued subpoena.
>
> *§99.31(a)(9)(i)*

Subpoenas are binding upon the party addressed, whether or not the subpoena is delivered in person or sent through the U.S. Postal Service. Institutions must have formal procedures for dealing with different types of subpoenas. Because the registrar is considered the official custodian of academic records, requests involving student records or the interpretation of information in education records are often directed to the Registrar's Office. And the registrar is also the expert witness designated to testify in court about academic records—or the lack thereof.

Policies, procedures, and local regulations that deal with subpoenas are guided by privacy regulations and the rights assured to citizens under the Constitution. The constitutional right is one of "due process" (see the sidebar on page 123) for any proceeding against a citizen. FERPA makes reference to these rights in its guidance on compliance with a judicial order or subpoena involving education records.

The educational agency or institution may disclose information under paragraph (a)(9)(i) of this section only if the agency or institution makes a reasonable effort to notify the parent or eligible student of the order or subpoena in advance of compliance, so that the parent or eligible student may seek protective action, unless the disclosure is in compliance with—

A. A Federal grand jury subpoena and the court has ordered the existence or contents of the subpoena or the information furnished in response to the subpoena not be disclosed; or

B. Any other subpoena issued for a law enforcement purpose and the court or other issuing agency has ordered that the existence or the contents of the subpoena or the information furnished in response to the subpoena not be disclosed.

§99.31(a)(9)(ii)

Whenever a duly authorized subpoena is received, it should first be inspected to ensure that the party served is, in fact, the addressee of the subpoena. The subpoena may order the production of records, originals or facsimiles, giving a date for surrender to a court. Except for the most extreme cases, dates are usually set to provide sufficient time for the recordkeeper to compile the requested documents and to deliver them to the court.

GENERAL GUIDELINES FOR PROCESSING SUBPOENAS

1. Verify that the subpoena is lawfully executed and properly addressed to you. Acknowledge the subpoena, usually through a signature of receipt, and advise the party issuing the subpoena when documents may be released. This date must be in compliance with state regulations for the production of records in response to a subpoena.

2. Unless the subpoena directs otherwise, notify your student that records have been subpoenaed. You must make a good faith effort to notify the student, using the last address you have on record—even if that address may be years old. Be sure to retain returned mail in your subpoena file. Advise the student when records will be released in compliance with the subpoena.

3. If the student notifies you that he/she will attempt to quash the subpoena, you must not deliver records unless the student fails to provide you with evidence that the subpoena has been quashed.

4. Release records in compliance with the subpoena on the appointed date. Generally, records are packaged and addressed to the court that issued the subpoena for records. In some cases, records must be delivered in person and surrendered under oath as exhibits in a court proceeding.

Before the institution surrenders documents, however, the individual or individuals whose records have been subpoenaed should be notified of the order to produce records. This is done to provide the party an opportunity to contest the subpoena and formally quash, or dismiss, the subpoena through a separate court order. Upon receipt of the subpoena, institutions should make an attempt to notify the student or former student regarding the subpoena order and advise the individual of the date when records are to be surrendered to the court. A "reasonable" or good faith effort means that a notification through the U.S. Mail to the last known address on file is sufficient.

A quash is a court order that nullifies a previous subpoena order. Individuals who feel that a subpoena of records is inappropriate or irrelevant to a particular case or court matter may petition the court to quash a previously issued order. When a quash request is granted, the court issues a formal, written order and recordkeepers should attempt to obtain copies of such orders when the institution is released from complying with a subpoena. The order may be issued to the requesting party, and institutions should request a copy from the student or former student for the institution's records.

Motion to Quash

The ability of individuals to quash court-ordered subpoenas is guaranteed in the U.S. Code of Federal Regulations.

> Any person against whom a subpoena is directed may file a motion to quash or limit the subpoena setting forth the reasons why the subpoena should not be complied with or why it should be limited in scope. The motion shall be filed with the administrative judge within 20 days after service of the subpoena. [4 CFR §28.47]

Contingent with this right is the responsibility of the complainant to specify reasons to a judge substantiating the petition to quash. The regulatory language also specifies a time frame of 20 days within which such an action must be filed.

It should be noted that the regulation refers to a "motion to quash or limit the subpoena." Individuals may seek to either have the subpoena dismissed entirely—a quash—or have the scope of evidence demanded reduced to what may be more appropriate to the nature of the case at hand.

When the student or former student receives the institutional notification of a subpoena having been served, the student may notify the institution that he or she will attempt to quash the subpoena. At this point, the institution is generally not required to surrender documents as ordered in a subpoena. But this is only a temporary stay in the process. Unless a subpoena is formally withdrawn, only another court order can quash the subpoena.

While a student's intent to quash a subpoena may be communicated by phone, a written note to this effect is helpful should the student encounter delays in the process. The written note is used as documentation should the institution be approached again about complying with the subpoena. The student should be required to provide a copy of the court's order to quash the subpoena for the institution's records as soon as possible. If no such order is provided, and the institution is pressed by a court for compliance, records must be surrendered.

In some cases, particularly where suspected terrorist activity or potential threats to health or safety are concerned, law enforcement officials may conduct investigations that depend upon sensitivity and the confidentiality of the existence of an investigation. Subpoenas and court orders may stipulate that the institution not disclose the existence of the subpoena or the investigation to the party whose records are being requested. Institutions must comply with such orders but are only required to do so should the court order or subpoena express this requirement within the document. When a verbal request is made at the time a court order or subpoena is delivered, institutions would be within their rights to insist that the order or subpoena contain this directive in writing. If the order or subpoena does not include such language, a revised order or a new subpoena should be required.

Questions about compliance with unusual or particularly sensitive subpoena matters should always be referred to campus counsel.

Ex Parte Orders

In the aftermath of 9/11, institutions nationwide were approached by federal investigators with inquiries about the activities of potential and suspected terrorists. These investigations, in the tension following the attacks in New York and Washington, were clearly covert and demanded the utmost confidentiality and secrecy. Institutions quickly became familiar with the term *ex parte* order.

The Latin term *ex parte* simply means "from (by or for) one party." Therefore, an *ex parte* is defined as follows.

> *a proceeding, order, motion, application, request, submission, etc., made by or granted for the benefit of one party only; done for, in behalf of, or on application of one party only [Law Libraries, New York State Unified Court System]*

Generally, *ex parte* orders refer to investigations where the subject of the investigation is not notified or made aware of the investigation. *Ex parte* orders are used in the United States, Canada, the United Kingdom, and Australia. They are usually reserved for urgent matters or situations where notification requirements may subject a particular person or persons to substantial and irreparable harm if existence of the investigation is disclosed.

In the United States, *ex parte* orders, despite the USA PATRIOT Act, are limited by the right of due process guaranteed through the Fifth and Fourteenth Amendments of the Constitution. The passage of the USA PATRIOT Act (USAPA) greatly expanded government rights in its investigatory activities of citizens and other parties. In addition to student records, educational institutions saw investigations extend to library records, research accounts, biometric access records, and clinical, laboratory, and experimental involvements. Surveillance through a variety of media, including phone, Internet, video, and electronic communications were all utilized.

The USAPA amended FERPA to codify compliance with *ex parte* orders. With the 2008 Amendments, the implications of the USAPA for FERPA are formally assimilated into the language of the regulations. To the exceptions of §99.31(a)(9), the section regarding court orders and subpoena, language about *ex parte* orders has been introduced, along with the appropriate qual-ifications or conditions for compliance. For FERPA, *ex parte* orders must be signed by an assistant attorney general or above.

> An *ex parte* court order obtained by the United States Attorney Gen-eral (or designee not lower than an Assistant Attorney General) concerning investigations or prosecutions of an offense listed in 18 USC 2332b(g)(5)(B) or an act of domestic or international terrorism as defined in 18 USC 2331.
>
> *§99.31(a)(9)(ii)(C)*

The USAPA included a provision of its own—§507—that provided im-munity for an institution that cooperated with an investigation initiated under the USAPA. The act went on to define protections for institutions and other entities that cooperate in good faith with federal investigations concerned with the protection and security of the nation.

The spirit of the hold blameless clause of the USAPA is reflected in §99.36(c) of the FERPA regulations. Disclosures in compliance with *ex parte* orders and federal investigators often carry implications for health or safety to some degree. In its discussion of disclosures based upon determination of "an articulable and significant threat," the regulations, at §99.36(c), insist that the Department of Education will not "substitute its judgment" for that of the local institution making its determination. (See Chapter Four for discussion of the health or safety implications in FERPA.)

The USAPA was passed into law as PL 107–56 on October 26, 2001. While the act sunset at the end of 2005, a number of the original provisions were renewed by Congress and continue in effect. (More discussion about the USAPA is presented in Chapter Four.)

PATRIOT ACT BLAMELESS CLAUSE

An educational agency or institution that, in good faith, produces education records in accordance with an order issued under this subsection shall not be liable to any person for that production.

—USA PATRIOT Act §507(j)(4)

Redisclosures and Service Providers

The secondary usage provision of the Code of Fair Information Practices effectively prohibits the use of data for a purpose other than that for which the data was collected in the first place. Further, the redisclosure of information is permitted only with the prior written consent of the individual to whom the records refer.

The FERPA regulations establish guidelines and permissions when redisclosure without prior written consent might be possible. And it is the recordkeeper, or custodian of the record, who makes the final determination about the appropriateness of redisclosure.

Redisclosure is always a concern in the context of information that has already been disclosed to a third party. Third parties may include entities within the institution, but most often the reference is to entities outside the institution. Under the Code of Fair Information Practices and the stipulations of the regulatory language for prior written consent (§99.30), a third party may only use information for the purpose disclosed in the consent and cannot release information further—that is, to any other party or parties. Should such redisclosure, called *further disclosure*, be discovered, the institution may not provide information from education records to the offending party for a period of five years.

> If the Office determines that a third party outside the educational agency or institution improperly rediscloses personally identifiable information from education records in violation of this section, the educational agency or institution may not allow that third party access to personally identifiable information from education records for at least five years.
>
> *§99.33(e)*

The FPCO has often recommended that when institutions release information to a third party, based upon a prior written consent or other written agreement, some notice about the privacy of the information should accompany the data. Such a disclosure may be composed as follows.

The information provided herewith contains personally identifiable information from education records and is protected by the federal Family Educational Rights and Privacy Act (FERPA) and other applicable privacy regulations. This information cannot be used for purposes other than that for which the information has been requested and disclosed. Further disclosure is prohibited, except as prescribed or permitted under FERPA. When no longer required, this information must be properly destroyed. Failure to comply with these conditions will result in the termination of your right to request personally identifiable information from the education records of this institution for a period of not less than five (5) years.

Over the years, a distinction has been required in regard to third parties and is now incorporated in the language of §99.33(e). That refinement has to do with the applicability of the five-year moratorium on the disclosure of education records. That penalty only applies to third parties outside the institution. If the penalty were to apply to entities within the institution, this requirement might well impede the ability of an institution to conduct its own administrative and educational business.

While the moratorium does not apply to entities within the institution, the responsibility for guarding against unauthorized disclosure of information still pertains. Earlier in its regulatory language, FERPA had specified its applicability to the recipient of federal funding "as a whole, including each of its components (such as a department within the university)" (§99.1(d)). The penalty for further disclosure for incidents within the institution would not entail the five-year moratorium but may very well call into question an institution's compliance with FERPA and, consequently, its eligibility to participate in and receive federal funding.

When education records are disclosed to third parties outside the institution, there may be situations where redisclosure may be appropriate or even mandated by other laws and regulations. The growing use of service providers, external to the institution, may involve the delegation of these service providers to act on behalf of the institution for such disclosures. The clearest example of this kind of entity is the National Student Clearinghouse, which provides a variety of services for and on behalf of institutions—such as processing student loan verifications, verifying attendance and degrees, and other data collection and reporting.

TO THE RECIPIENT OF THESE STUDENT RECORDS

This information is protected by the federal Family Educational Rights and Privacy Act (FERPA) and cannot be further disclosed. When no longer required, these documents must be properly destroyed. Failure to comply with these conditions may result in the termination of your right to request records from this institution for a period of five years.

Paragraph (a) of this section does not prevent an educational agency or institution from disclosing personally identifiable information with the understanding that the party receiving the information may make further disclosures of the information on behalf of the educational agency or institution if:

i. The disclosure meets the requirements of §99.31; and

ii. The agency or institution has complied with the requirements of §99.32(b).

§99.33(b)(1)

The 2008 Amendments revised §99.33(b)(1) to update practice and the relationships of institutions to third-party service providers. The qualifications in this section refer to the list of exceptions to prior written consent, detailed in §99.31 of the regulations, and other requirements in §99.32. The requirements of §99.32(b) specify *legitimate interest* in the disclosure of information with an injunction that the institution maintain documentation regarding the release of information to the third party.

If an educational agency or institution discloses personally identifiable information from an education record with the understanding authorized under §99.33(b), the record of the disclosure required under this section must include:

1. The names of the additional parties to which the receiving party may disclose the information on behalf of the educational agency or institution; and

2. The legitimate interests under §99.31 which each of the additional parties has in requesting or obtaining the information.

§99.32(b)

The next clause, §99.33(b)(2), goes on to specify that the party releasing information in response to a court order or subpoena must follow the requirements detailed in §99.31(a)(9)(ii)—namely, making a reasonable effort to notify the student that records have been subpoenaed. The third party, similar to the institution, must follow the subpoena process detailed in FERPA, including making a reasonable attempt to notify the student or former student of the party's receipt of the subpoena.

A party that receives a court order or lawfully issued subpoena and rediscloses personally identifiable information from education records on behalf of an educational agency or institution in response to that order or subpoena under §99.31(a)(9) must provide the notification required under §99.31(a)(9)(ii).

§99.33(b)(2)

Business and industry utilize written agreements or contracts to bind parties in formal service relationships. Certainly, with all of the requirements under FERPA and additional specifications that may be delineated between an institution and a service provider, documentation of service-level agreements is not only important but imperative between the institution and its third-party service provider.

The FPCO has long recommended that such agreements with outsourced, third-party service providers, involving the disclosure and use of personally identifiable information from education records, specifically declare the protections and applicability of FERPA. This recommendation has been made both for ongoing disclosures as well as for ad hoc or temporary disclosures, such as those made for the purpose of educational studies or research (see the next section in this chapter).

Finally, the timbre of the 2008 Amendments with regards to contracted, third-party service providers is essentially one of operational, business empowerment. Realizing that these entities are often functioning in roles that might otherwise be reserved for an institutional employee, FERPA,

A contractor, consultant, volunteer, or other party to whom an agency or institution has outsourced institutional services or functions may be considered a school official under this paragraph provided that the outside party—

1. Performs an institutional service or function for which the agency or institution would otherwise use employees;

2. Is under the direct control of the agency or institution; and

3. Is subject to the requirements of §99.33(a) governing the use and redisclosure of personally identifiable information from education records.

§99.31(a)(1)(i)(B)

in §99.31(a)(1)(i)(B), now permits such service providers to be considered education or school officials.

The designation of education official is important because it allows service providers access to education records based solely upon legitimate educational interest—or legitimate business interest, based upon the tasks for which the provider has been hired to perform. With such access comes the responsibility of acting as an education official, meaning that these service providers must fully comply with all of the provisions of FERPA.

But these service providers are not familiar with FERPA. Further, these service providers do not receive federal funding and would not otherwise be bound by FERPA. How is control to be maintained?

The March 24, 2008, issue of the *Federal Register* discusses this point with some concern, although its final conclusion is to place ultimate responsibility with the institution that contracts with the provider in the first place.

Educational agencies and institutions are responsible for their outside service providers' failure to comply with applicable FERPA requirements. [FR 15579]

The implication is that institutions must educate their service providers, as they do with education officials on the campus, about FERPA and its requirements with regards to the privacy and protection of education records. This is why contracts and agreements include reference to FERPA. Service providers should consult with the institution whenever operational questions arise that involve privacy, disclosure, access, and redisclosure of information from education records. If they do not consult with the institution, then they should educate themselves about the applicable FERPA regulations.

Ultimately, the responsibility for FERPA compliance rests with the institution that employs the outside service provider. When employees inappropriately disclose protected information, the consequence is disciplinary action, up to and including termination. The consequence for the breach of a business agreement is termination of that agreement. Including caveats to this effect in service provider agreements with the institution satisfy the requirement that the service provider be "under the direct control of the agency or the institution" (§99.31(a)(1)(i)(B)(2). Under such a contract, the institution exercises control by making it a contingency of the contract's continuance that the outside service provider comply with FERPA.

Must the institution provide on-site training to its service providers regarding FERPA? While there is no stated requirement to do so, it is nevertheless implied, as in the case of educating officials on the campus. But training can also be evidenced by merely referencing appropriate resources and by making it a contingency of the business relationship that the third party educate itself on FERPA. The agreement might go on to require the service provider to train all staff members who will have legitimate business responsibilities involving information from the education records that have been disclosed by the institution.

Studies and Research

The 2008 Amendments have made a number of changes to the exception in §99.31 dealing with studies that are conducted for or on behalf of educational agencies and institutions. Studies conducted for institutions may examine any number of issues, initiatives, or strategies relevant to education, a local community, or the greater American society. Often these broader surveys are conducted by organizations outside the institution and may or may not have a relationship to federal or state governments. Institutions may also conduct their own studies as part of self-assessment, program evaluation, or long-term strategic planning. In all of these cases, the need for access to non-directory information from education records raises FERPA concerns when the study or research is conducted by third parties.

FERPA makes an exception to the requirement of prior written consent for studies that are conducted for or on behalf of the institution. Codified at §99.31(a)(6), the section includes extensive provisions and new, operating requirements that arise from the 2008 Amendments.

> For the purposes of paragraph (a)(6) of this section, the term organization includes, but is not limited to, Federal, State, and local agencies, and independent organizations.
>
> *§99.31(a)(6)(v)*

Throughout §99.31(a)(6), the term *organization* is used to refer to the entity conducting a study or studies using information from education records. These third parties may be federal or state governmental agencies or even local agencies. But they may also be organizations external to government and education. No matter the characteristics of these entities, the provisions of §99.31(a)(6) apply.

In the first subparagraph, at §99.31(a)(6)(i), the regulations identify some purposes for which studies might be conducted. The validation of tests, the administration of financial aid, and the improvement of pedagogy are specifically mentioned. Curiously, this list is not open-ended.

> The disclosure is to organizations conducting studies for, or on behalf of, educational agencies or institutions to:
>
> A. Develop, validate, or administer predictive tests;
>
> B. Administer student aid programs; or
>
> C. Improve instruction.
>
> *§99.31(a)(6)(i)*

In the next section, the provisos for disclosing information are listed. There are three.

First of all, the organization must protect the privacy of the individuals whose records are disclosed for the study. Only employees of the organization to whom the education records are disclosed may access the information—and even then, only employees with "legitimate interest in the information" may access the data. Reminded of the qualification of legitimate educational interest for access on the part of education officials, "legitimate interest" here connotes a limitation of access to employees of the organization who are actually involved in the study itself. Access is not given broadly. In other words, only representatives of the organization with a demonstrated need to know or need to access the information may be given that permission.

The second proviso is a requirement that the data be destroyed once the study has concluded or when the data is no longer needed. The regulations

CONCERNS REGARDING DISCLOSURES FOR STUDIES AND RESEARCH

- Privacy of the education records and their subjects
- Destruction of records when they are no longer needed for the study or research
- Formal agreement between the institution and the organization receiving information from education records

expand on this provision in the next requirement, which is a written agreement or contract between the institution and the organization conducting the study. The regulations specifically call for a written agreement, which legally means a document in writing signed by the parties involved, setting out provisions for the relationship between the two parties.

An educational agency or institution may disclose information under paragraph (a)(6)(i) only if—

A. The study is conducted in a manner that does not permit personal identification of parents and students by individuals other than the representatives of the organization that have legitimate interests in the information;

B. The information is destroyed when no longer needed for the purposes for which the study was conducted; and

C. The educational agency or institution enters into a written agreement with the organization…

§99.31(a)(6)(ii)

And what are the provisions that should be included in that written agreement? These are detailed in the requirements of §99.31(a)(6)(ii)(C). Remember that a prior written consent specifies the information to be disclosed, the purpose of the disclosure, and identifies the party or parties to whom disclosure is to be made. The requirements of §99.31(a)(6)(ii)(C) follow these same specifications, subtly incorporating concerns from the Code of Fair Information Practices.

The first requirement of the written agreement is that it must specify the information to be disclosed and the purpose of the disclosure. It is important to be as specific as possible when setting the purpose to paper, for it is this purpose that defines the limitations for use of the information to be disclosed. Usage of that information for any other purpose outside the original intent, as stated in the agreement, is a violation of the contract and carries a penalty that is defined later in the paragraph.

The second component of the agreement obliges the receiving organization to use the information that the institution discloses only for the purpose stated in the agreement. In many ways, this is the most critical element of the agreement. Without wording that definitely commits the organization

The educational agency or institution enters into a written agreement with the organization that—

1. Specifies the purpose, scope, and duration of the study or studies and the information to be disclosed;

2. Requires the organization to use personally identifiable information from education records only to meet the purpose or purposes of the study as stated in the written agreement;

3. Requires the organization to conduct the study in a manner that does not permit personal identification of parents and students, as defined in this part, by anyone other than representatives of the organization with legitimate interests; and

4. Requires the organization to destroy or return to the educational agency or institution all personally identifiable information when the information is no longer needed for the purposes for which the study was conducted and specifies the time period in which the information must be returned or destroyed.

    §99.31(a)(6)(ii)(C)

to the provisions of the agreement, the document might be taken as mere guidelines. In other words, herein lies the legal crux of the agreement.

The third provision requires the organization to protect the privacy of the information that is disclosed and specifically to protect the identification of the parents or students whose records are involved. The organization must ensure that only representatives of the organization may access the information—and, more precisely, only representatives with legitimate interests in the data for purposes of the study.

Lastly, the regulations require destruction of the information by the organization when the data is no longer needed for the purpose(s) of its study or studies. The regulations are very careful here and specific in the options for this requirement.

- The organization must destroy the information when it is no longer needed, or return the data to the educational agency or institution.
- The agreement must detail a specific time period for the destruction or return of the data. This time frame may be based upon the expected duration of the study or studies.

COMPONENTS OF THE WRITTEN AGREEMENT REGARDING STUDIES

• Identify the information from education records requested

• Specify the purpose(s) of the study or studies

• Restrict use of personally identifiable information to the purposes of the study

• Limit access to information to organizational representatives with legitimate interest

• Prescribe an expiration date for destruction or return of the data

• Require the receiving organization to comply with the agreement

• Declare the applicability of FERPA and its privacy protections

• Disclose penalty for breach of contract

This last stipulation forces the institution to set an expiration date for the disclosure of information for the purpose of the study. Many institutions will not wish to set up tickler files to track when data should be returned by organizations, so the specification of a destruction date will undoubtedly be the most desirable option. For the receiving organization, the destruction date should force communication with the institution should extensions to the contract become necessary. Both the institution and the organization are reminded that sensitive information is still out there and must be dealt with in a proper and appropriate manner.

As it did with contracted service providers, the FERPA regulations make institutions responsible for the actions of the organization to which information from education records has been disclosed. Discussion in the December 9, 2008, issue of the *Federal Register* stated:

> *In this regard, it should be noted that educational agencies and institutions are responsible for any failures by an organization conducting a study to comply with applicable FERPA requirements. [FR 74827]*

This statement underscores the importance of the written agreement. Whereas there is no right of action under FERPA, institutions may have other legal avenues to pursue a breach of contract should the organization fail to comply with FERPA and with the provisions of the agreement. In fact, FERPA provides its own penalty for the failure of organizations to comply in §99.31(a)(6)(iv)—the inability of the organization to access education records from the institution for a period of five years.

> If this Office determines that a third party outside the educational agency or institution to whom information is disclosed under this paragraph (a)(6) violates paragraph (a)(6)(ii)(B) of this section, the educational agency or institution may not allow that third party access to personally identifiable information from education records for at least five years.
>
> *§99.31(a)(6)(iv)*

As a spending statute, FERPA has enforcement authority through its controls on federal funding to educational agencies and institutions. But FERPA has no authority over organizations that do not receive federal funding. FERPA must exert its authority indirectly. Therefore, the penalty in §99.31(a)(6)(iv) is structured as a directive to the institution but with no less of a dire impact on the organization involved.

FERPA declares that should the FPCO determine that an organization has violated its agreement, the institution is prohibited from disclosing information from education records to that organization for a period of not less than five years. The penalty should be included in the written agreement as a disclosure of the consequences for failure of the organization to comply with the agreement. For organizations whose life blood involves studies and analysis of student data from the education records of institutions, a five-year moratorium on its ability to receive information from an educational institution would be a crippling and devastating blow to its business endeavors.

From a different perspective, for an institution to continue doing business with an organization which has violated FERPA is for the institution to be in violation itself. And being in violation, the institution would be subject to the penalties described in FERPA—the potential loss of federal funding for its institutional programs.

The 2008 Amendments introduce a new sentence into §99.31(a)(6), dispelling any relationship between the institution and the organization conducting the study or with the study itself. At §99.31(a)(6)(iii), the regulations state that no institution is required to initiate a study. Further, an institution is not required to agree with or to endorse the conclusions of a study, even if it discloses information from education records for the benefit of the study.

> An educational agency or institution is not required to initiate a study or agree with or endorse the conclusions or results of the study.
>
> *§99.31(a)(6)(iii)*

The establishment of the written agreement maintains a distance between the institution and the organization, a separateness represented by the business relationship. No collusion is implied through the provision or access of the same education records.

Still and all, the use of FERPA-compliant contracts should not be adopted as a practice for the nondiscriminate disclosure of education records to third parties. The FERPA regulators do not wish to imply that student records vaults are now open to anyone who agrees to a FERPA contract. The institution must still make a determination and a decision to disclose education records. After all, these provisions are exceptions in §99.31 and not meant to be operational practice. The *Federal Register* of December 9, 2008, makes this clear.

> *…the existence of a written agreement is not a rationale in and of itself for the disclosure of education records. As a privacy statute, FERPA requires that parents and eligible students provide written consent before educational agencies and institution disclose personally identifiable information from students' education records. [74826]*

For the institution, as it does with the presentation of a prior written consent, a decision must be made whether there is sufficient reason to disclose personally identifiable information from education records for any reason. Under FERPA, an institution's allegiance remains to the privacy of the education records for which it has been entrusted. Any decision to participate in studies, regardless of the source, must not be taken lightly.

For questions about the appropriateness of disclosures for the benefit of any study or research, institutions may always consult with the FPCO, their state Department of Education, or with their individual campus counsel.

Recordation Requirements for Disclosures

While FERPA does not provide directions to institutions on what kinds of records to keep or how long to maintain them, there are instances in the regulations where specific requirements are made or implied regarding records.

RECORDS RETENTION IN FERPA

- Records cannot be destroyed when a request for inspection and review is outstanding.

- Statements from students regarding records considered inaccurate, misleading, or otherwise an invasion of privacy must be maintained and disclosed with the objectionable record.

- Access to and disclosures from education records must be recorded and made available to parents or eligible students upon request.

- Disclosures made under the health or safety exception must be recorded.

- Names of federal, state, and local educational authorities that can make further disclosures from education records must be recorded.

The first instance, connected to the right to inspect and review education records, is recorded in §99.10(e). When a request has been received to inspect and review education records, the requested records cannot be destroyed until the opportunity for inspection and review of those records has been provided to the requesting party. In other regulations having to do with subpoenas and court orders for the production of evidence, the recordkeeper may not destroy records or documents requested. Such actions on the part of the recordkeeper may entail legal and even criminal penalties, such as for destroying or tampering with evidence.

> The educational agency or institution or SEA or its component shall not destroy any education records if there is an outstanding request to inspect and review the records under this section.
>
> *§99.10(e)*

The second example referring to records retention arises in respect to the right to seek to amend education records that the student considers inaccurate, misleading, or otherwise an invasion of privacy (see Chapter Three). §99.32 of the regulations details requirements for a hearing, allowing the parent or eligible student to challenge a decision on the amendment of records. If, at the end of the hearing, the complainant is still not satisfied, the student may record his or her objections in a statement that must be submitted to the recordkeeper. The recordkeeper, per §99.21(c), is required to maintain the statement for as long as the record to which the student objected is maintained. Furthermore, the recordkeeper must disclose the student's statement each and every time that the objectionable record is disclosed.

> If an educational agency or institution places a statement in the education records of a student under paragraph (b)(2) of this section, the agency or institution shall:
>
> 1. Maintain the statement with the contested part of the record for as long as the record is maintained; and
> 2. Disclose the statement whenever it discloses the portion of the record to which the statement relates.
>
> *§99.21(c)*

A third instance occurs in regard to the right to have some control over the disclosure of information from education records. In fact, §99.32 is devoted to the recordkeeping requirements under FERPA, a section that was expanded with the 2008 Amendments to include the maintenance of disclosures made to educational authorities—federal, state, and local—as well as disclosures made under the health or safety exception (§99.36).

> An educational agency or institution must maintain a record of each request for access to and each disclosure of personally identifiable information from the education records of each student, as well as the names of State and local educational authorities and Federal officials and agencies listed in §99.31(a)(3) that may make further disclosures of personally identifiable information from the student's education records without consent under §99.33(b).
>
> *§99.32(a)*

FERPA has always required institutions to maintain a record of disclosures of information from education records. The regulations have been specific about the kind of documentation that needed to be maintained, requiring at minimum, an identification of the party or parties to whom information was provided and the reasons for providing that information. These requirements are itemized in §99.32(a)(3).

For each request or disclosure, the record must include:

i. The parties who have requested or received personally identifiable information from the education records; and

ii. The legitimate interests the parties had in requesting the information.

§99.32(a)(3)

The information that must be recorded is similar to the components required of a prior written consent—namely, specification of the records to be disclosed, a statement of the purpose for disclosure, and identification of the party or parties to whom disclosure is made. For the purposes of recordation here, it is only necessary to identify the parties to whom disclosure was made and the basis—the legitimate educational interest—for that disclosure.

There are significant changes to the remainder of §99.32 and to §99.33 that arise from the 2008 Amendments.

Paragraph (a) of this section does not prevent an educational agency or institution from disclosing personally identifiable information with the understanding that the party receiving the information may make further disclosures of the information on behalf of the educational agency or institution…

§99.33(b)(1)

Because third parties are now authorized, per §99.33(b)(1), to disclose information from education records, the student, who is the subject of those records, has a right to know to whom further disclosures were made. FERPA stipulates that the third party making the disclosure must maintain a record of those disclosures. Upon request of the institution on whose behalf the disclosures were made, the third party must provide a record of the disclosures it has made in regard to a particular student.

An educational agency or institution must obtain a copy of the record of further disclosures maintained under paragraph (b)(2) of this section and make it available in response to a parent's or eligible student's request to review the record required under paragraph (a)(1) of this section.

§99.32(a)(4)

The mechanics of these requirements are not as complicated as they may appear on a first read. The institution discloses education records to a third party or service provider, which can make further disclosures on its behalf. That third party must keep a record of the further disclosures it makes. These records can be communicated back to the parent institution on a regular basis, or they may be maintained by the third party until requested. In its annual notification, the institution must disclose to students the names of the third parties to whom it discloses education records and the fact that these third parties can make further disclosures on behalf of the institution.

When a student requests inspection and review of her records, she may request to review a record of those further disclosures made by the third party or parties. If those records have been supplied by the third party on a regular basis, the institution may share those disclosures. If no regular transmission of information has been received from the third party, however, the institution must request the record or records from the third party and provide it to the student for inspection and review.

The other recordation requirement added as a result of the 2008 Amendments has to do with disclosures made under the health or safety exception. §99.32(a)(5) is added to require the recording of the situation that prompted the disclosure and a list of the individuals to whom the disclosure was made. This record should be maintained in the education file of the student who was the subject of the health or safety concern. Upon request to inspect and review records, that student should be able to access this documentation.

An educational agency or institution must record the following information when it discloses personally identifiable information from education records under the health or safety emergency exception in §99.31(a)(10) and §99.36:

i. The articulable and significant threat to the health or safety of a student or other individuals that formed the basis of the disclosure; and

ii. The parties to whom the agency or institution disclosed the information.

§99.32(a)(5)

Military Recruiters and the Solomon Amendment

While not included in the list of exceptions in §99.31, an area of uncertainty for many institutions has to do with military recruiters and their access to personally identifiable information from education records. The Solomon Amendment is the legislation that facilitates access to education records by military recruiters and was an important amendment to both FERPA and other education provisions.

Civil Rights and Military Recruitment

After the conclusion of the Vietnam War, staffing of the United States Armed Forces was left largely to volunteers and storefront recruiting strategies. While the nation was at peace, such a passive stance on military recruitment was not only reasonable but adequate. With the increase in global conflicts and the escalation of military armament toward the end of the 20th century, however, the government realized that more aggressive recruitment strategies would be necessary to maintain military strength at a level that would engender political and national comfort.

Influenced by the graduate recruiting efforts of big business and commercial employers, military recruiters took the initiative to create a visible presence on college campuses throughout the nation. Participating in college career fairs and other events to promote visibility, the military recruiters sought access to young people to promote military service and the vocational benefits of military service to the nation. But their efforts were not always welcome and met, in some cases, with marked resistance.

The Civil Rights Movement, exploding as it did during the Kennedy administration, grew and spread into many other areas of American society. During the 1980s, sexual orientation became an extremely volatile issue. The decade witnessed a spike in incidences of discrimination as well as of hate crimes. FERPA added gender to the list of items not recommended as directory information, attempting to curb the availability of data that could lead to hate crimes. Progressive employers, both private and governmental, extended their policies of nondiscrimination to include sexual orientation. But the military was not one of these entities.

If discovered, service men and women could be dishonorably discharged based upon the mere suspicion of homosexual tendencies or desires. Further, a dishonorable discharge would disqualify the service person for benefits from the Veterans Administration. But a loss of benefits was not the only danger. With an increase in hate crimes in general American society, the military was not without its own heinous incidents.

On October 27, 1992, Third Class Petty Officer Allen R. Schindler, Jr. was brutally murdered because he was gay by a fellow shipmate. The murder caused an international sensation because of its brutality. In a public toilet in Japan, Schindler was savagely beaten until his corpse was beyond recognition. Schindler's family members were only able to identify the body by the tattoos they recognized on Schindler's arms.

The controversy about gay people in the military arena grew to such magnitude that in 1993, President Bill Clinton proposed a policy of "Don't Ask, Don't Tell" where the military was involved. When passed into law as PL 103–60 (10 USC §654), the policy was seen as the epitome of discrimination against gay and other individuals whose identities created discomfort for the military's staunchly conservative personnel. Crafted by General Colin Powell, the policy was announced by President Clinton, who directly cited the Schindler murder of the previous year.

In *The Pentagon's New Policy Guidelines on Homosexuals in the Military* (1993), the government argued that sexual orientation of itself did not bar an individual from serving in the military. It was only homosexual conduct

---

Allen R. Schindler, Jr.

Despite being gay, Allen R. Schindler, Jr. enthusiastically joined the U.S. Navy fresh out of high school and became a Radioman Petty Officer Third Class. He served on the U.S.S. Midway, and had its emblem tattooed on his arm before being transferred to the U.S.S. Belleau Wood in 1991.

Aboard the Belleau Wood, Allen confided to family that he was often targeted because he was gay. In 1992, the Belleau Wood was en route from its home port in San Diego to Japan. On a stopover in Pearl Harbor, Allen playfully broadcast a message to the Pacific Fleet that translated "Too cute to be straight." For his prank, Allen was called before a public hearing and although placed on on leave, he was restricted to his ship.

On October 27, 1992, while on shore in Sasebo, Nagasaki, Allen was followed into a public restroom by Airman Apprentice Terry M. Helvey. Helvey worked in the weather department aboard the Belleau Wood and confessed a deep hatred for gay people. In the restroom, Helvey attacked and brutally stomped Allen to death. A shore patrolman reported that Allen's head was crushed, his face disfigured, his ribs broken, and his penis cut. The Japanese police reported no less than four fatal injuries, to which the pathologist added that every organ in Allen's body had been destroyed. Allen was just 22 years old.

The Navy was accused of trying to cover up the incident. But Helvey was convicted of murder, demoted, and sentenced to life imprisonment at the U.S. Disciplinary Barracks. He showed no remorse for his actions, claiming that he would "do it again" and that Allen "deserved it."

Charles Vins, Helvey's drinking buddy and accomplice, plea bargained his involvement in the crime and served only 78 days before being released and discharged.

In 1997, Lifetime Television produced a film entitled *Any Mother's Son: The Doris Hajdys Story*, chronicling Allen's story and the aftermath of his death from his mother's perspective.

that would not be tolerated—which, in itself, was not an entirely new policy. Service people who were discovered in what the military referred to as "sodomy"—certain oral or anal acts—were dishonorably discharged and denied benefits due from their military service.

The first such discharge is often attributed to Frederick Gotthold Enslin, a soldier who was separated from the military, on the approval of General George Washington, for "sodomy and perjury." Between 1942 and 1947, the *blue discharge* was the name given to dishonorable discharges based upon the discovery or suspicion of a nonheterosexual orientation. In the midst of the draft during the Vietnam conflict, suspicion was often voiced over individuals who claimed to be gay in order to avoid military service.

The Don't Ask, Don't Tell Policy specifically prohibited service people from disclosing or talking about their homosexual or bisexual orientation. At the same time, the legislation also barred military superiors from inquiring or investigating the sexual orientation of a service person. Suspicion involving the alleged commission of homosexual acts, however, could still be grounds for an investigation by the military.

In reaction to the Clinton policy, employers and institutions that had adopted nondiscrimination policies that included sexual orientation turned a cold shoulder to the armed forces—and to any other entity that did not publicly espouse its own policies of nondiscrimination. Businesses, institutions, and some governmental entities enacted policies to prevent

Blue Discharge

The blue discharge, or "blue ticket," derived its name from the blue paper upon which the orders were printed. Created in 1916, the process was a consolidation of two discharge processes already in existence—the administrative discharge and the unclassified discharge. During World War I, the blue discharge was used primarily to dismiss recruits who had joined the military while being underage.

The attachment of the blue discharge to homosexuals occurred during World War II. A 1944 directive instructed the army that homosexuals should be committed to a military hospital, examined by psychiatrists, and dishonorably discharged. The dishonorable discharge meant ineligibility for veteran benefits.

The discriminatory assault on homosexuals produced numerous discharges, with a report of up to 68,000 such separations by 1946. Some officials labored to overturn the negative impact on benefits of the dishonorable discharge, including William C. Menninger, director of the Psychiatry Consultants Division of the Surgeon General of the U.S. Army and Senator Bennett Champ Clark, the democrat from Missouri.

The blue discharge has also been used in military history to discriminate against African Americans and other black service people.

conducting business or even establishing relationships with entities that did not enact their own policies of nondiscrimination.

The responsibility for championing civil rights was taken seriously at many institutions of higher education. And this position put education at odds with the military because of the military's stance on homosexual service people. At the campus level, military recruiters were either denied access to student populations or forced to move their recruiting stations off campus. The practice was initially overlooked when the institution involved was a religious school or another institution with a demonstrated history of pacifism. But law schools began to resist the presence of military recruiters on their campuses, charging that the Don't Ask, Don't Tell Policy violated the First Amendment of the U.S. Constitution.

In the midst of the controversy, the American Association of Law Schools (AALS), with a membership of 166 of the nation's 188 accredited law schools, changed its bylaws to require member institutions to include nondiscrimination clauses regarding sexual orientation in their policies and to cease doing business with those who did not. Military recruiting was effectively banned.

Then came the Solomon Amendment.

Higher Education Standards for Military Recruitment Activity

First introduced in 1994 by U.S. Representative Gerald B.H. Solomon, the Solomon Amendment (10 USC §983) was enacted the following year as part of the National Defense Authorization Act. Like FERPA, the Solomon Amendment was structured as a spending statute, intended to deny Department of Defense funding to institutions that refused to provide access to military recruiters or that barred ROTC programs from the campus.

The amendment was specifically aimed at the postsecondary environment, where government funding was extensive and where young people were most open to the potential of military careers. K–12 would not become an arena for military recruiters until the No Child Left Behind (NCLB) legislation of President George W. Bush's administration, in the wake of 9/11 and the USA PATRIOT Act. (See the No Child Left Behind sidebar on page 66 and the sidebar on the Fairness for Military Recruiters Act at the end of this section.)

While government funding and support was extensive in higher education, law schools were not major recipients of Department of Defense funds or contracts. So, the tension between school and the military continued to fester until the Omnibus Appropriations Act of 1997 introduced changes

Gerald Brooks Hunt Solomon

Although born in Florida in 1930, Gerald B.H. Solomon established his career in and served the state of New York for many years as a Republican. He was elected to the New York Assembly in 1972 and served in the U.S. House of Representatives between 1979 and 1999.

Although Solomon served in the U.S. Marine Corps for only two years, 1951–1952, he was a strong supporter of the U.S. armed forces. He supported legislation to ban flag-burning and to strengthen the Selective Service System and sponsored the creation of the U.S. Department of Veteran Affairs. At one point, he led a group of former Marines who objected to the site chosen for the U.S. Air Force Memorial because it was too close to the site of the U.S. Marine Corps War Memorial.

Solomon died in 2001 and was buried in a Saratoga cemetery, which was renamed in his honor.

---

to the Solomon Amendment. The threat of the loss of federal funding was extended to include monies from the Departments of Labor, Health and Human Services, and Education. Into this expansion of the definition of "at-risk" monies was thrown government financial aid resources.

The Solomon Amendment continued to evolve as the tension and struggles continued. Unhappy with the potential loss of financial aid, Representative Barney Frank proposed the Frank-Campbell Amendment of 1999, eliminating financial aid monies from the at-risk funding of the Solomon Amendment spending statute. Multi-school campuses continued to be sources of discontent, however, as portions of the campus cooperated while others repulsed military recruiters altogether.

Finally, in 1999, the Solomon Amendment was significantly revised. The spending statute was directed toward institutions as single entities, threatening the loss of federal funds if even a portion of the institution did not cooperate with military recruiters. Like FERPA, the Solomon Amendment was revised to apply to the entire institution and all of its units, parts, or schools. And although financial aid had been eliminated from the at-risk funds by the Frank-Campbell Amendment, the recodification of Solomon added funding from the Department of Transportation to the at-risk mix.

A number of lawsuits were initiated in response to the continued revisions to Solomon, the most important of which was *Rumsfeld v. FAIR* in 2004. FAIR, or the Forum of Academic and Institutional Rights, was an association of some 30 law schools and faculty. In the law suit, FAIR contested that the latest rendition of the Solomon Amendment was unconstitutional, insisting that the amendment violated the First Amendment to the Constitution and thus could not be enforced.

While FAIR won its initial day in court, the Third Circuit Court of Appeals later ruled that schools could not ban the military from access to their campuses. Summarizing a unanimous ruling on the case by the U.S. Supreme Court in 2005, Chief John Roberts insisted that the Solomon Amendment did not violate the rights of schools or institutions. The presence of military recruiters on campus could not be taken as an approval of military doctrines or practices any more than the inclusion of other types of recruiters could be seen as an affirmation of their private philosophies or strategies.

> *A military recruiter's mere presence on campus does not violate a*
> *law school's right to associate, regardless of how repugnant the*
> *law school considers the recruiter's message.*
> —*Chief Justice Jon Roberts on Rumsfeld v FAIR*

Requirements under the Solomon Amendment

Under the Solomon Amendment, institutions must permit access to military recruiters from the five major branches of the armed services—the Army, the Navy, the Marine Corps, the Air Force, and the Coast Guard— once each academic term, whether quarter or semester.

Moreover, the Solomon Amendment allows military recruiters to request certain recruiting information from institutions about students. Most of the recruiting information data is considered directory information under FERPA or data that would normally be collected by the institution. But even if an institution has not designated certain data as directory information, the Solomon legislation amends FERPA to permit institutions to comply with such requests from military recruiters if the information is available.

Institutions must provide the information in whatever format they can do so and may charge military recruiters for the service—provided the institution also charges a fee to other entities that may seek and obtain similar

---

ARMED SERVICES—BRANCHES AND ELIGIBLE UNITS

Air Force: Air Force, Air Force Reserve, Air Force National Guard
Army: Army, Army Reserve, Army National Guard
Coast Guard: Coast Guard, Coast Guard Reserve
Marine Corps: Marine Corps, Marine Corps Reserve
Navy: Navy, Navy Reserve

recruiting information from the institution. The military recruiter should be treated no different than other business or commercial recruiters.

Recruitment Information Solomon Amendment	Directory Information FERPA
Name	Name
Address	Address
Telephone number	Telephone number
	E-mail address
	Student user ID
Age and date of birth	Date of birth
Place of birth	Place of birth
Level of education	Dates of attendance
	Enrollment status
Academic major	Major field of study
Degrees received	Degrees and awards received
	Photographs
Educational institution of most recent enrollment	Most recent previous school attended
	Participation in officially recognized activities and sports
	Height and weight of athletes

It is important to realize that while the Solomon Amendment requires cooperation with military recruiters and their requests for information, institutions are not required to provide information that they do not already collect or maintain. If a certain piece of information is not collected or maintained by the institution, the school need only provide a statement of explanation regarding why the data cannot be provided.

Because the Solomon Amendment is a spending statute like FERPA, institutions receiving federal funding must comply with the Solomon Amendment. With regards to the disclosure of information from education records, there is no conflict between FERPA and Solomon, provided the information requested by military recruiters is the recruiting information specified under the Solomon Amendment legislation.

Continuing Controversy for K–12

While military recruitment was addressed by the Solomon Amendment for higher education and the NCLB for K–12, controversy continues in

The Fairness for Military Recruiters Act

On February 12, 2009, U.S. Congressman Duncan D. Hunter, a member of the U.S. Armed Services Committee, introduced new legislation to ensure fair access to student information for military recruiters. HR 1026, or the Fairness for Military Recruiters Act, was introduced as an amendment to the Elementary and Secondary Education Act (ESEA) of 1965. The focus of the new legislation is the information about high school students covered by the No Child Left Behind (NCLB) Act.

NCLB already allows parents to withhold disclosure of their child's information to military recruiters, but suspicion has arisen about school officials withholding information on their own. Hunter's legislation seeks to ensure that military recruiters have the same access under NCLB as they have to post-secondary students under the Solomon Amendment. While stressing that parents maintain privacy controls for the individual who is under 18 years of age, the legislation goes on to require a written parental request for any withholding authorizations.

Hunter, the Republican representative for the 52nd District in California (North and Eastern San Diego County), is a veteran of the U.S. Marines. He served in both Iraq and Afghanistan.

regards to cooperation with military recruiters on the part of schools and other institutions. In the wake of the Afghanistan and Iraq conflicts that erupted during the Bush Administration, resistance has expanded beyond civil rights concerns to international justice and ethics. Citizens are once again questioning their rights and the constitutionality of being forced to welcome military recruiters on the campus.

Similar to the developing tension under the evolution of the Solomon Amendment, the K–12 sector has expressed its own bitter reactions to the requirements of NCLB and the subsequent amendments to NCLB. In February 2009, however, Congressman Duncan Hunter introduced new legislation that seeks to provide *fairness* for the treatment of military recruiters by K–12 administrators. While underscoring provisions already in NCLB, the Fairness for Military Recruiters Act sets a requirement for written parental authorization to substantiate the withholding of student information from military recruiters.

Chapter 6

Strategies for FERPA Compliance

Compliance with any set of regulations is tricky when the approach is fragmented and based upon inconsistent interpretation and application. Too often, institutional departments are isolated and left to define the impact of new rules and requirements upon their individual activities without any overarching guidance or restatement of the mission, vision, and values of the institution. Such a method, while useful for the immediate need, may result in conflicting policy, procedure, and practice, not to mention confusion and frustration on the part of students, staff, and parents. A strategy that appreciates the big picture, while adapting local needs and obligation, is often the more successful undertaking.

Consequently, the first step in developing a strategy for compliance with FERPA is a reconnection with the institutional mission and its meaning, as expressed through vision and values. Knowing what is important to the institution and its constituents will assist in framing the manner in which decisions about the application of FERPA are codified for the local campus community.

FERPA is a statute on privacy and is not meant to define higher education administration policy. It is not meant to impede or hinder pedagogy or educational business. As a privacy statute, FERPA protects the privacy of education records and the rights of parents and eligible students in relation to those education records. Keeping this in mind is essential to facilitating the process of defining a FERPA compliance strategy or auditing your current strategies for compliance with the regulations.

> The Office may require an educational agency or institution to submit reports, information on policies and procedures, annual notifications, training materials, and other information necessary to carry out its enforcement responsibilities...
>
> *§99.62*

Fortunately, the discussion about the investigatory practices of the Family Policy Compliance Office (FPCO) in the 2008 Amendments provides a cohesive framework from which to develop a strategy or conduct a self-assessment for compliance. The list of items in §99.62 unequivocally highlights the areas where the FPCO would focus an investigation to determine if a violation of the regulations has occurred. These areas are:

- Policies and procedures
- Annual notifications
- Training materials
- Reports
- Other necessary information

While the last two items are intentionally nonspecific, the first three represent standard operating processes for any business entity. Policy and procedure, the publication of disclosures, and the availability of staff training are all necessary components for businesses and institutions to protect and defend themselves against any manner of allegation—whether that be in formal courts of law or in the realm of public opinion and the media.

This chapter examines compliance with the FERPA requirements from the operational and business documentation perspective. What are the components that lead to compliance with the regulations? And, from the self-audit perspective, what areas should an institution examine to determine and assess its own FERPA compliance?

The Annual Notification

The annual notification is the first requirement of the regulations (see Chapter Three) and the one that, because of its nature and intent, summarizes the institution's commitment to compliance with FERPA. It functions in much the same way as a federal truth in lending statement, which banks

---

In response to an FPCO investigation, institutions may be required to submit:

- Reports
- Information on policies and procedures
- **Annual notifications**
- Training materials
- Other necessary information

and other financial institutions are required to provide to their account holders on an annual basis.

The concept of the annual notification was discussed in detail at the beginning of Chapter Three, the section on the guaranteed rights under FERPA. In this section, our discussion focuses on the annual notification as a compliance issue for the institution.

Disclosure of Rights and Practice

The annual notification is the institution's annual disclosure of rights and summarizes how the bearer of those rights may exercise or take advantage of them. Some institutions merge this notification with a policy statement on how and when information is disclosed from education records. But policies tend to be longer pieces of business documentation that include the determination of business values and needs, operating practice, and strategic planning contingencies. It should be emphasized that the annual notification is intended to be a notice, a reminder to students in attendance that they have rights under FERPA at the institution. In this sense, the annual notification may be an extract from a longer policy on student records but may not document the complete policy.

In §99.7, the regulations detail what components should make up the annual notification. But there are also recommendations and requirements throughout the regulations that affect what might be added to this initial list of disclosures in the annual notification. Basically, that list of components for the annual notification includes the following:

- The four primary guarantees made to parents and eligible students under FERPA

- Certain definitions that affect local practice and compliance with the regulations in the areas of access and disclosure of information

- Disclosure of practices that, while permitted, are not required but have, nevertheless, become commonplace or necessary at the institution

---

FERPA guarantees eligible students the following rights.

- The right to inspect and review education records
- The right to seek to amend education records
- The right to have some control over the disclosure of information from education records
- The right to file a complaint for an alleged violation of these FERPA rights

The first component grouping, given in §99.7(a)(2) is the statement of rights under FERPA. These are the four primary guarantees that were discussed in Chapter Three. The regulations, in other words, instruct institutions to announce and guarantee to parents and eligible students the basic rights that comprise FERPA.

To avoid misinterpretation or misunderstanding, the FERPA rights should be stated in the same way and using the same language as they appear in the regulations. The opportunity for local customization comes in the next section, §99.7(a)(3), which instructs institutions to provide in the annual notification the procedures for exercising those rights.

> The notice must include all of the following:
>
> i. The procedure for exercising the right to inspect and review education records.
>
> ii. The procedure for requesting amendment of records under §99.20.
>
> iii. If the educational agency or institution has a policy of disclosing education records under §99.31(a)(1), a specification of criteria for determining who constitutes a school official and what constitutes legitimate educational interest.
>
> *§99.7(a)(3)*

Policy and procedure are discussed later in this chapter, but a number of considerations are worth examining in the context of the annual notification. Primary amongst these is a consideration of the implications of keeping student records in multiple locations on campus.

With the proliferation of technology, the ability to create and maintain records is a capability that has been welcomed across campuses, both large and small. No longer is the registrar's office the only locus of student records. Wherever records are created and maintained at the institution, as long as those records are education records, compliance with FERPA is required. So, along with that records-creation capability comes the responsibility for compliance with FERPA.

> If an educational agency or institution receives funds under one or more of the programs covered by this section, the regulations in this part apply to the recipient as a whole, including each of its components (such as a department within a university).
>
> *§99.1(d)*

The problem is that practice may differ from one office to the next with regard to how records are maintained and how changes are processed to those records. Each and every procedure need not be contained in the annual notification, but the eligible student should at least be made aware that records exist across the campus and that access to those records for inspection and review should be requested individually from each recordkeeper. It may also be helpful to indicate that inspection and review applies only to education records and that exceptions do exist under the regulations (§99.3).

Special conditions that affect the exercise of a right may be disclosed in the annual notification. For instance, if a campus has outsourced its records management functions, it may be beneficial to disclose how storage and retrieval procedures impact the availability of records. If requests need to be made in writing, or if appointments need to be arranged for inspection and review, these requirements may be disclosed in the annual notification. FERPA and individual state laws regarding the production of records specify time frame expectations for the availability of those records. Once a request is submitted, the opportunity for inspection and review should be provided within that time frame. Any extenuating circumstances or the need for longer periods of time to assemble records should be communicated to the requesting party immediately.

The second component grouping is made up of definitions that are related to how the institution provides access to and discloses information from education records. In essence, the privacy rights under FERPA are made only to parents and eligible students. Disclosure to anyone else, to any third party, is an exception and must meet the requirements detailed in §99.31. In some cases, these exceptions may become ongoing practice or procedure. Where an exception becomes a practice, then that practice needs to be disclosed in the annual notification.

Among the exceptions that may become practice for the purposes of disclosure in the annual notification are the following.

- Disclosures to other school officials who have been determined to have a legitimate educational interest (§99.31(a)(1))
- Disclosures to other school systems or institutions where the individual seeks to, intends to, or has enrolled (§99.31(a)(2))
- Disclosures to state and local authorities that may further disclose information from education records on behalf of the institution (§99.31(a)(3))
- Disclosures in connection with financial aid (§99.31(a)(4))
- Disclosures to state and local authorities in connection with reporting to the juvenile justice system (§99.31(a)(5))

- Disclosures to organizations conducting studies (§99.31(a)(6))
- Disclosures to accreditation bodies (§99.31(a)(7))
- Disclosure to the parents of dependent students (§99.31(a)(8))
- Disclosures to comply with subpoenas and court orders (§99.31(a)(9))
- Disclosures in connection with a health or safety emergency (§99.31(a)(10) or where an articulable and significant risk is determined (§99.36)
- Disclosures in connection with crimes of violence and nonforcible sex offenses (§99.31(a)(14))
- Disclosures to parents of students under the age of 21 who are determined to have violated regulations governing the use or possession of alcohol or other controlled substances (§99.31(a)(15))
- Disclosures concerning sex offenders (§99.31(a)(16))

Acknowledgment of these kinds of disclosures in the annual notification need not include detailed procedures since the purpose is simply to notify students that the institution may make these kinds of disclosures.

In order to conduct any business successfully, a certain amount of information may need to be shared or made available to individuals and departments within the organization. The regulations, therefore, emphasize disclosures to *education* (or school) *officials*, and since the condition for disclosure to education officials is a *legitimate education interest*, both terms must be defined in the annual notification. Neither term, you will recall, is defined in the regulations. Rather, each institution is required to determine for itself how the two terms should be defined to meet the needs of its unique campus community. (Discussion of the definitions of education officials and legitimate educational interest, among other terms, is included in Chapter Two.)

A model notification is available on the home page of the Family Policy Compliance Office (at www.ed.gov/policy/gen/guid/fpco/index.html.

Publication of the Annual Notification

Other than stipulating that the annual notification should be made on a yearly basis, the FERPA regulations defer to the institution the determination of the method for notifying students in attendance. The qualifications on the annual notification requirement are:

- The notification needs to be made every year.
- The method of notification must be "reasonably likely" to inform eligible students in attendance of their rights.
- The notice must "effectively" notify students who are disabled of their rights under these regulations.

- (For K-12) The notice must effectively notify parents whose first or primary language is not English.

An educational agency or institution may provide this notice by any means that are reasonably likely to inform the parents or eligible students of their rights.

1. An educational agency or institution shall effectively notify parents or eligible students who are disabled.

2. An agency or institution of elementary or secondary education shall effectively notify parents who have a primary or home language other than English.

   §99.7(b)

In the mindset of the late 20th century, when everything was paper-based, institutions tended to place the annual notification in publications such as the catalog, the schedule of classes, student handbooks, guidebooks, and even in the student newspaper. Certainly, the greater the visibility of the annual notification, the more likely it was to inform students of their rights. Fortunately, the requirement is solely to inform students *in attendance* since the rights are guaranteed only to students currently in attendance.

With the trend toward electronic media at the beginning of the 21st century, the most likely and appropriate place for the annual notification is quickly becoming the campus website or within student access systems themselves. After all, the FERPA requirement is to "reasonably" inform eligible students of their rights. Institutions that require students to utilize campus systems for enrollment and business transactions, verification of the accuracy of records, and other campus communications may well argue that publication of the annual notification in this medium meets the qualification of reasonable and likely notice.

At some point, all publications may become electronic, but for the time being, it seems prudent to supplement electronic libraries with the traditional publications that likely are the first places that students and parents seek evidence of campus policy.

The second caveat expressed in the regulations is that notification be "effectively" available to certain types of students. The regulations mention the disabled student for postsecondary education, and, in the case of K–12 students, parents whose first language is not English.

Reasonable accommodations under the Americans with Disabilities Act (ADA) drive the first qualification, which requires the availability of the annual notification in formats that are accessible to the disabled, including the sight and hearing impaired. For K–12, the language consideration is an appropriate caution inspired from the No Child Left Behind (NCLB) Act.

The Historical Record

Discussions of the publication of the annual notification usually focus on concerns about reaching students in attendance. But another consideration that should be taken into account is that of the historical record. What if a question arises about your disclosure of FERPA rights two, ten, or more years ago? Having a policy that stipulates where your annual notification is published is certainly a starting point, but what about proof?

For the institution of higher education, the historical record is generally considered to be the catalog. The catalog documents the academic programs of the institution and often details courses and their descriptions, program and admission requirements, policies and procedures, and other historical information. The catalog is the marketing piece for prospective applicants and functions as an integral dossier promoting institutional advancement and funding qualification. It is the institution's official record of identity and achievement.

A good practice would be to include the annual notification in your catalog as a way of preserving a historical record of the institution's compliance with this FERPA requirement. This placement would be in addition to any other venues in which the annual notification may be contained. Because of its permanence as an archival record, inclusion in the catalog ensures proof positive of the institution's compliance with FERPA for generations to come.

Compliance with the Annual Notification Requirement

The annual notification requirement is the starting point for any review or self-audit for compliance with FERPA. In fact, the annual notification is often the best platform from which to construct FERPA training strategies for the campus. It is, after all, the annual notification which summarizes campus commitment to the regulations and provides a summary detail for students regarding the exercise of their rights.

While the campus registrar may be the most likely official to craft the institution's annual notification and define the process of its distribution, the FPCO website offers guidance to institutions struggling with some of the components of the disclosure.

Compliance Checklist: Annual Notification	
Publication	Where is your annual notification published? Do students in attendance know where to find it?
Time frame	Is the annual notification published annually?
Availability	Is the annual notification available to all students in attendance at the institution, including for those students with special needs and requirements?
Completeness	Are all of the required elements included in the annual notification?
Review	Is the annual notification reviewed and updated on a regular basis to ensure compliance with amendments and official guidance on FERPA?

Policy and Procedure

An important area of interest for any investigation, whether by the FPCO or by a court of law, is that of the institution's policies and procedures. Polices and procedures are documentation of the governing philosophy and performance structure of an organization, the operational manual of its existence as a commercial or public entity. Policies and procedures provide a foundation for why certain practices are perpetuated and why specific actions are taken. They guide the organization's response to situations that may be market-driven or the result of unexpected catastrophes.

In §99.62, the FERPA regulations declare that in response to an investigation by the Department of Education, institutions may be required to submit "information on policies and procedures." Curiously, this requirement is not expressed to cite policies and procedures directly but rather *information about* those policies and procedures. This is, no doubt, because policies and procedures can be quite extensive and encompass more areas than simply education records and student privacy. However, this is not to say that policies

In response to an FPCO investigation, institutions may be required to submit

- Reports
- **Information on policies and procedures**
- Annual notifications
- Training materials
- Other necessary information

and procedures may not provide a vital defense in support of an institution's position or response to any alleged violation of the regulations.

It is not the purpose of this volume to comprehensively address the records management concerns of policies and procedures. But since the FERPA regulations single out "information on policies and procedures" as a requirement in the process of investigating an alleged violation, it would be beneficial to focus on records management as it relates to an institution's compliance with FERPA.

Documentary Evidence

The terms *records* and *documentation* tend to invoke an initial image of something concrete—paper, in other words. When FERPA introduces the term *record*, it takes great pains to explain that records exist in a variety of media beyond paper forms, correspondence, and transcripts. The same is true of the term *record* where records management is concerned. What is important about the concept of a record is that a record attests to something. A record provides documentary evidence of people, actions, and things.

Where policy and procedure is concerned, this documentary evidence substantiates practice, guides decision making, and provides historical testimony. In that sense, there are certain characteristics that are necessarily a part of effective policy and procedure.

- *Written.* Policies and procedures demand the authority of the printed word. They must be formalized so as to accurately reflect the established position of the institution.
- *Accessible.* Policies and procedures must be available and easily accessible to staff and managers throughout the department, organization, or institution. You cannot expect people to follow rules unless they are aware of those rules, can consult them when the need arises, and can act on them. This last qualification further stipulates that policies and procedures must be written in a way that can be easily understood by the individuals who must follow them or put them into practice.
- *Current.* Policies and procedures must be kept current, incorporating new practices and requirements that result from new technologies, changes in legislation, and constituent demands.
- *Specific.* While some policies and procedures can address universal or global concerns for an organization, most must be specific enough to direct operations in a particular area or activity.
- *Evidentiary.* An organization must be able to produce its policies and procedures if necessary to defend itself in a court of law, in response to any legal investigation, or as an answer to the demand of students and other constituents.

Many of these characteristics seem obvious, but in a fast-paced business environment, the obvious is often overlooked. For example, there is a tendency to become overly legalistic in the language of policy. While such formality may be appreciated by attorneys, managers must remember that for policy and procedure to be effectively enforced, it must be understood by those who must follow the rules and by those who are affected by that policy.

Specificity is an important characteristic and in response to a FERPA investigation, it is specific policy and procedure that may be at issue. Some of the areas that would be of interest in a FERPA investigation are:

Annual Notification. This specific FERPA requirement is already addressed separately in this chapter.

Disclosure of Information from Student Records. How does the institution disclose information from education records? Disclosures include not only those in response to student requests but also requests from third parties. How does the institution determine whether disclosures—and what kind of disclosures—are appropriate? What other kinds of disclosures are appropriate to the specific campus community—to campus police, for example?

Amendment of Records. How do students request amendments to their records? How are the provisions for hearings and statements of determination (§99.20–99.22) carried out at the campus?

Disciplinary Processes. How is the disciplinary process adjudicated at the campus? Who is involved in a disciplinary proceeding? Where are decisions recorded and how are disciplinary records maintained? What impact, if any, do disciplinary matters have on the transcript?

Outsourcing and Contracting. What is the process for utilizing third parties for services that involve the disclosure of non-directory information from student records? Among the considerations here are the use of written agreements, FERPA training for the third-party service providers, and commitments for the recordation and transmission of authorized further disclosures, if warranted (§99.32–99.33).

Deceased Students. What is the institution's position on the disclosure of information from the education records of a deceased student? FERPA makes no requirements, but the question is not a rare one.

Records Retention. What are the institution's permanent and nonpermanent records? How long are nonpermanent records maintained? What is the process for and documentation of destruction of records?

Privacy Rights of the Deceased

Whether or not the dead have any rights often depends on who you ask. In many legal circles, the assertion is that the dead have no rights. And the charge seems to bear up since the Privacy Act of 1974 and legislative history overlook the issue. In the medical and law enforcement arena, the decedent ceases to be an individual and becomes property where custody rights become effective.

The U.S. Department of Defense (DoD) uses an assessment test posed by disclosure provisions in the Freedom of Information Act (FOIA). The FOIA permits government agencies to withhold disclosures if the disclosure would otherwise pose an invasion of privacy regarding personnel, medical, and law enforcement records.

In a 1998 Defense Board Privacy Opinion regarding deceased person's rights, published at www. defenselink.mil/privacy/opinions/op0002.htm, the DoD arrived at the following determination.

> Demise of a record subject (ending Privacy Act protection which permits disclosure only when required by the FOIA) does not mean the privacy protective features of the FOIA no longer apply. Public interest in disclosure must be balanced against the degree of invasion of personal privacy. An agency need not automatically, in all cases, "disclose inherently private information as soon as the individual dies, especially when the public's interest in the information is minimal." [*Kiraly v. Federal Bureau of Investigation*, 728 F 2d 273, 277 (6th Cir. 1984).]

The DoD concluded that since decedent records may have implications for the privacy of other individuals, great care should be exercised in determining what kind of information, if any, can be disclosed about a decedent.

And finally, there are other policies that may cover issues beyond FERPA but are certainly relevant to FERPA compliance.

Changes to and Appeals on Grades. How do students request a grade change or appeal a grade assigned in a course? Students cannot challenge a grade under FERPA, so the institution must make other provisions for dealing with disagreements about student performance and evaluation.

Access to Records. What is the procedure for accessing records that are not governed by FERPA requirements? Does admissions have a policy and procedure in place for applicant records? Is there a campus procedure for responding to requests regarding the records of deceased students? Who can access records? What recordation requirements apply, if any? How are original records filed and how is access to original documents controlled (removal from storage sites)?

Appeals. In nearly every area, there must be a process and/or a final decision maker identified to deal with situations that challenge the established procedure.

RECOMMENDED POLICY: RECORDS OF DECEASED STUDENTS

1. The privacy rights of deceased students are administered by (the institution), which affirms the continued privacy of education records, while recognizing the rights of court-appointed executors of the deceased student's estate.

2. Disclosures from the records of deceased students require the following documentation.

   - Written request detailing the specific records requested and the purpose for which the records are requested

   - Copy of the deceased student's death certificate

   - Documentation regarding the requesting party's right to the information being sought

3. Acceptable documentation for proof of the requesting party's right to access information includes, but is not limited to, the following.

   - Court or legal documentation of executor appointment or estate administrator

   - Copy of obituary, indicating surviving heirs and/or relationship of the requesting party

   - Formal request from the media or research organization specifying requested information and intended purpose(s) for use of the information

4. The institution reserves the right to review all requests for access to the records of deceased students and to make a final determination on the merit of the request and/or the appropriateness of the disclosure.

Access Agreements. Are staff—including student workers—adequately informed about the confidentiality of records, the applicable regulations, and the potential for disciplinary action, up to and including dismissal, for unauthorized disclosures? Agreements should exist and be maintained either in the department that "owns" the record or in the human resources office.

Technology Protocols. How are records backed-up and archived? In the event of system performance failures, how are information and entire databases reconstructed?

Contingency Planning and Business Recovery. What protocols are in place to address natural and human-initiated disasters and the business recovery process after a disaster? Access to student records, current registration data, class rosters, local addresses, and emergency contact information should be vital components for an immediate accounting of survivors following the disaster. Business recovery plans should include the continuity of educational activities and the ability to reconstruct education records.

Student Records Contingency Planning

Emergency and contingency planning that focuses on education records must incorporate both short- and long-term needs. Following the disaster, the health and safety of students must be of prime importance. Current registration data, location information, and emergency contact names are all important. As the business recovery commences, the reconstruction of student records takes precedence.

Depending upon local needs, emergency preparedness may incorporate a variety of strategies.

- Back-up systems and data may be stored and/or duplicated at sister institutions in another area of the country.

- Off-site storage of back-up data tapes and system information can be stored with professional archival or emergency storage companies. These firms often utilize temperature-controlled containment and storage facilities located in geologically stable environments to ensure reliable availability for business continuity in the event of a disaster.

- For short-term accountability assessment, downloads of student lists, location and emergency contact information, and registration schedules can be made to a laptop computer or notebook that can be easily taken by appropriate personnel during an evacuation.

Records Management Resources

A number of resources are available to institutions for the development, codification, and implementation of a successful records management strategy.

On campus, records management offices and campus archivists may be instrumental in taking the lead to establish broad campus policies, but individual offices need to establish their own policies and procedures that govern their specific areas of operation and business needs. After all, the needs of the registrar, admissions, financial aid, information technology, student health, and student life are unique in their activities as well as in the regulatory umbrellas under which they operate.

The literature on records management is vast, including volumes and white papers written to address the needs of specific industries. Numerous books and articles address areas of records management in all manner of media, including electronic, imaging, digital, and other formats or platforms.

One of the most helpful resources available to individual managers, offices, and institutions is ARMA International, an organization that effectively sets the standard for records management strategies in the United States and internationally. Membership in ARMA International includes

ARMA International

A not-for-profit professional association, ARMA International is the source authority for records and information management, both paper and electronic. The association's membership is comprised of records management professionals from a variety of industries, including government, law, health care, finance, and education. In addition to the United States and Canada, members come from at least 30 other countries.

Founded in 1955, the association was originally known as the Association of Records Managers and Administrators (ARMA). With the advances in communications and technology in the late 20th century, the field of records management experienced global expansion and generated an explosion of new business concerns and responsibilities. ARMA, therefore, became ARMA International.

In addition to its involvement with legislation and professional development, ARMA International provides resources to its members on all aspects of records management.

The association's website is www.arma.org.

records managers, archivists, information technology professionals, and records management programmers in various technologies and fields of operation. The fact that nations beyond the United States and Canada participate in the organization ensures some consistency in operations on a global basis as well as contributes to a broader awareness of issues and developing concerns for all of the represented professions.

For higher education, the American Association of Collegiate Registrars and Admissions Officers (AACRAO) has taken the lead and published recommendations for the retention of records at postsecondary institutions. AACRAO's recommendations encompass various types of forms and records created and maintained throughout the campus. The AACRAO guide provides an excellent model for establishing a local records retention policy and procedure.

Because this is an area of great concern to registrars and student affairs officials, a transcript guide offers recommendations on the type of information that should, according to AACRAO, be part of the historical, academic record of a student. Key considerations in regard to the transcript are academic relevance and chronological historicity.

AACRAO also publishes a number of other guides and manuals that address policy, procedure, and best practice in higher education processes.

	Compliance Checklist: Policies and Procedures
Publication	• Where are your policies and procedures officially published. • Are policies and procedures available to managers and staff in an easily accessible and understandable format?
Timeframe	Is policy development part of strategic planning and operational review protocols to ensure that polices and procedures are available to staff and business units as they are needed?
Availability	• Are policies and procedures available to managers and staff in an easily accessible and understandable manner. • Are policies and procedures formatted in such a way as to permit printing of individual policies and procedures for training and disclosure purposes?
Completeness	Are there any areas of business practice that are not codified through institutional policy and procedure? Beware of processes that expose staff and the institution to potential legal and public relations risk.
Review	Are policies and procedures evaluated on a regular basis to ensure applicability to changing practice and business requirements?

Training Materials

In response to an FPCO investigation, institutions may be required to submit

- Reports
- Information on policies and procedures
- Annual notifications
- **Training materials**
- Other necessary information

Included in the §99.62 list of items that the FPCO may request to review in the event of an investigation of an alleged FERPA violation is the institution's training materials.

> The Office may require an educational agency or institution to submit reports, information on policies and procedures, annual notifications, training materials, and other information necessary to carry out its enforcement responsibilities...
>
> *§99.62*

When proposed in the March 24, 2008, edition of the *Federal Register*, the reasons given were hardly elucidating.

> *The [proposed] regulations are needed to clarify the kinds of information that may be required should the Office seek to determine whether a violation constitutes a policy or practice of the agency or institution. [Page 15591]*

And the December 9, 2008, issue of the *Federal Register* included no responses to the original proposal.

The inclusion of training materials in the list of investigatory items is not a surprise. In the aftermath of the Virginia Tech tragedy, federal investigators determined that there was a significant lack of understanding on the part of campus staff in regard to FERPA. Education officials were unsure about what they could communicate, even to each other. This fear of violating FERPA was the reason for silence on the part of education officials who might have raised concern about the emotional and psychological state of the student before the explosion of violence that claimed so many staff and faculty lives.

Legislating Training

Wikipedia begins its entry on training with the following definition:

> *The term training refers to the acquisition of knowledge, skills, and competencies as a result of the teaching of vocational or practical skills and knowledge that relate to specific useful competencies.*

Unfortunately, training as a value in organizations is not often given the priority it should have. For many managers, allowing for training means having to deal with periods of short staffing, not to mention the costs associated with the professional development programs themselves. And human resources professionals know only too well that in budget-cutting periods, training is often the first initiative to go.

Yet, training is an important part of workforce development and the leadership development of individual employees. As processes change in business and industry, staff members need to be educated and their skills sets upgraded to keep their performance relevant to the current state of the business environment. This strategy of continuing education or lifelong learning specifically includes knowledge, skills, and competencies—distinct components of individual development that are all equally necessary to ensure success and fulfillment.

The last decade of the 20th century witnessed a vast array of programs and initiatives focused on engendering and inspiring ongoing personal and organizational renewal. The benchmarks for quality service became equated with empowerment and the ability to get things done efficiently and effectively. Because a knowledgeable workforce is essential to success, the focus on training and adequately equipping professionals to perform in their assigned arenas has made its way even into legislation.

In 2007, the Federal Trade Commission (FTC), the National Credit Union Administration (NCUA), and a number of other federal banking agencies collaborated on a proposed amendment to the Fair and Accurate Credit Transactions (FACT) Act of 2003. Known as the Identity Theft Red Flags and Address Discrepancies Rules, or Red Flags Rules, the legislation was passed and set to go into effect on November 1, 2008. The implementation date was twice delayed by the FTC, first to May 1, 2009, and then to August 1, 2009.

The Red Flags Rule is concerned primarily with the accounts of financial institutions and creditors who offer clients "covered accounts." This is where the legislation affects postsecondary institutions since its student accounts and other financial services may qualify under the legislation.

FACT refers to a *creditor* as an entity that defers payment for services through a *covered account*, which is an account relationship that includes multiple payments or transactions. Institutions are creditors when students have an option of paying for tuition and services over a period of time or through a series of payments. Also qualifying are those institutional card services that allow students, faculty, and staff to deposit funds that can be used at campus retail establishments, such as the bookstore, food outlets, and copy centers, or for other campus services. Appropriate amounts are deducted from the

---

Implications of the Red Flags Rule

To halt the incidence of identity theft in the financial industry, the Federal Trade Commission (FTC), the National Credit Union Administration (NCUA), and other federal agencies proposed the Red Flags Rule as an amendment to 2003's Fair and Accurate Credit Transactions (FACT) Act. The rule contains a number of requirements revolving around the establishment of identity theft prevention programs at financial institutions and institutions acting as financial entities. Written program materials, the designation of a program moderator, and protocols for identity theft detection and response are among the provisions of the rule.

The rule also gives the FTC enforcement authority. Violations of the rule carry civil penalties of up to $2,500 per violation. The FTC may also issue cease and desist orders in applicable situations.

The emergence of the Red Flags Rule and its applicability to financial accounting affects student accounting, financial aid, and other financial services provided to students, staff, and faculty on campus. But the codification of endeavors to curb identity theft in financial transactions may also have implications for identity theft activity in other institutional recordkeeping endeavors—specifically, fraudulent transcripts and the processing of certain changes to personally identifiable information (such as address changes).

While there is no applicability of the Red Flags Rule to nonfinancial activities, a precedent has been set for institutional responsibility and proactive strategies to combat identity theft.

card each time the cardholder makes a purchase or initiates a transaction. Additional funds can be added to the card balance at any time.

The purpose of the Red Flags Rule is to identify and to force creditors to react quickly at the first instance or detection of any signs or intimations of potential identity theft. A *red flag*, in the legislation, is "a pattern, practice, or specific activity that indicates the possible existence of identity theft."

Among other things, the Red Flags Rule requires a creditor to identify red flags in its operations and to develop protocols for responding to those red flags. The rule is so stringent that it requires the institution to develop its identity theft prevention program, document the program in written form, and formally seek concurrence of the highest levels of institutional authority. Not only must a program manager or key point person be named to oversee the program, but relevant staff must undergo training to ensure that they are able to detect and respond to potential red flag activity whenever it should occur.

The training requirement is one of the first instances of such a provision in legislation. Usually, the passage of a bill, like a new policy in an organization, carries the implication that people need to be educated on what is changed or what is being introduced. With the Red Flags Rule, however, there is no assumption, because the training requirement is stipulated as a matter of compliance.

Although FERPA is not as explicit, the concern for training of all campus staff exists and has been evident by the outreach efforts of the Family Policy Compliance Office (FPCO) and its regular training efforts throughout the nation. In each of its presentations, the FPCO has insisted that training needs to be carried back to other campus staff, ensuring that awareness and responsibility are campuswide.

RED FLAGS

Federal banking regulators have identified at least 26 red flags or indicators of potential identity theft activity. Generally, these red flags involve financial accounts and include the following.

Address discrepancies

Name discrepancies—identification, insurance information

Presentation of suspicious documentation

Inconsistencies with data and information already on file

Unusual use or suspicious activity on a covered account

Unusual or suspicious activity reported by consumers, law enforcement, and others

Who Needs to be Trained?

The first question that comes to the minds of managers is a practical one: who needs to be trained on FERPA? And unfortunately, the immediate objection is familiar one: isn't FERPA more of a concern for the registrar and for other student records offices? The response should be an emphatic and decided "No!"

Who needs to be trained on FERPA?	
Academic advisors	Faculty
Academic department personnel	Financial aid advisors
Admissions recruiters and officers	Hospitality directors and tour guides
Advancement staff	Housing directors and staff
Advisors to student groups	Information technology
Advisors to student publications	Librarians
Alumni offices	Ombuds counselors and staff
Archivists	Outside service providers
Athletic coaches and staff	Parent relations staff
Bursars	Parents
Campus activities coordinators	Recreational services staff
Campus counsel	Records managers
Campus life staff	Registrar and registrar staff
Campus telephone operators	Residence assistants
Campus representatives	Secretaries and receptionists
Campus safety officers and personnel	Student accountants
Career center advisors and staff	Student affairs
Chancellors and vice chancellors	Student committee members
Collections and financial accounting staff	Student health providers
Computer training staff	Students in attendance
Curators and student showcase staff	Student workers
Deans	Study abroad staff
Department managers and support staff	Teaching assistants
Disability service officers	Theater and performance directors

Everyone on campus who deals with student information, who has access and custody of student information, and who has occasion to disclose information from student records needs to be aware of the personal and institutional responsibilities under FERPA. This population includes a wide range of education officials. Each institution needs to determine for itself who would be included in this group—indeed, where the risk of unauthorized disclosure may exist. And making that determination, the institution needs to ensure that training and training resources are available for this population.

The list of campus personnel who may or may not require FERPA training is general and not exhaustive. Whether or not training is relevant for each of these individuals depends upon the job responsibilities assigned to each position or class of employees at each institution or campus.

When determining who needs training, every aspect of the individual's job responsibilities must be examined to determine where the potential for unauthorized disclosures of information may occur. Many times, the potential for *unintentional* disclosure is overlooked.

- Think about social situations where faculty and campus administrators may be brought together with parents and other sponsors or guardians. A natural opening to any conversation might well be about the academic performance of individual students.
- What about post-game events that include parents, coaches, and the media?
- What about the aftermath of an event that draws attention to students and situations at your campus? Are protocols in place to put reporters and other media representatives in touch with the campus officials who know what can and cannot be disclosed?

While FERPA training strategies begin with the registrar and other recordkeepers of student information, that is only the beginning.

Training Resources

In the revision to §99.62, the importance of campus-wide training and compliance is indirectly referenced. Should an investigation be opened into a potential violation of FERPA at a campus, the FPCO will need to determine the level of awareness and expertise of the education officials involved in the alleged violation. The level of training afforded local campus officials is important in determining whether a potential violation is the result of ignorance, misunderstanding, or deliberate practice, however uninformed. Therefore, training materials may be required to substantiate or explain the circumstances contributing to the alleged violation.

FERPA TRAINING RESOURCES—ON CAMPUS

- Registrar or director of student records
- Dean/vice chancellor of student affairs
- Campus counsel
- Records management office/division

Knowing that training materials might be requested by the FPCO as part of an investigation is a key benefit of the 2008 Amendments. On the one hand, the importance of developing and maintaining FERPA training strategies on the campus is underscored. On the other hand, campuses must be ready to produce documentation demonstrating how education officials and staff are educated in their FERPA responsibilities. These materials need not be individually developed at the campus, but they must exist as proof of campus efforts to ready staff for their responsibilities.

Publications, videos, and other materials may be maintained in a central library or made available on training websites. At the very least, managers should have ready access to FERPA reference materials, whether it be the library of information compiled on the Department of Education website (www.ed.gov) or other commercially available materials.

A number of training resources and strategies are available to institutions. These include:

- In-person training seminars and programs
- Electronic media programs—audio and/or over the web
- Publications and newsletters
- Prerecorded media programs

In-person training programs are usually the most effective because they allow participants to interact with the presenter and to ask questions specific to their individual workplace concerns. Resources for in-person presentations may even be available on campus. The registrar is a good place to start. Campus counsel is another resource, although because of their schedules, campus attorneys may not always be readily available for training or for consultation with general staff.

If the institution must seek external resources, presentations can be customized to the individual campus operations and procedures. The FPCO

FERPA TRAINING RESOURCES—IN-PERSON PRESENTATIONS

American Association of Collegiate Registrars and Admissions Officers (AACRAO)
(www.aacrao.org) Annual meeting and higher education programs scheduled throughout the year. State and regional associations, part of the national AACRAO organization, hold their own annual meetings and professional development events.

Cliff Ramirez & Associates
(www.pdrenterprises.net) Consultation and customized on-site FERPA training.

U.S. Department of Education, Family Policy Compliance Office (FPCO)
(www.ed.gov) The FPCO is the office in the U.S. Department of Education charged with interpreting, adjudicating, and enforcing FERPA. The FPCO presents training events for K–12 and for higher education throughout the year. Programs are arranged through individual school districts, local colleges and universities, and AACRAO.

has conducted general training to both higher education and K–12. Local professionals have also contributed their expertise through professional development events and conferences. To be sure, there is a growing number of FERPA experts—including yours truly—throughout the country.

Where in-person or on-site programs are not possible, participation in audio conferences and webinars offers an opportunity to train a large group relatively quickly and inexpensively. A number of major conference providers that cater to K–12 and higher education present programs on FERPA and the application of FERPA in various and specific areas of education operations. While training for larger groups is facilitated in this way, the ability to ask questions or to engage in a conversation specific to the participant's campus is often short-circuited by the distance learning format.

Publications may be difficult to find unless you know where to look. A number of quality providers quickly come to mind.

AACRAO Publications. The American Association of Collegiate Registrars and Admissions Officers (www.aacrao.org) periodically publishes a *FERPA Guide* and its *AACRAO Transcript* newsletter is a good source of timely information regarding FERPA and other higher education concerns.

CLHE Publications. From the legislative perspective, the Council on Law in Higher Education (www.clhe.org) is a valuable resource for information regarding all regulations and proposed legislative action

---

FERPA TRAINING RESOURCES—MEDIA PRESENTATIONS

Academic Impressions

(www.academicimpressions.com) Webinars on a variety of topics for education; audiotapes of previous conference broadcasts available for purchase.

ELI Research—Audio Solutionz

(www.audiosolutionz.com) Audio conferences; audiotapes of previous audio conference broadcasts available for purchase.

LRP Conferences

(www.lrpconferences.com) Audio conferences; audiotapes of previous audio conference broadcasts available for purchase.

Progressive Business Publications

(www.pbconferences.com and www.higheredhero.com) Audio conferences; audiotapes of previous audio conference broadcasts available for purchase.

---

from Capitol Hill that affect higher education. The CLHE has produced book-length resources, such as *Privacy in the 21st Century* and online newsletters, such as *The Regulatory Advisor*.

Wiley/Jossey-Bass. Publications and newsletters provide extensive and timely information on FERPA and other higher education strategies and operations. Jossey-Bass (www.josseybass.com) is an imprint of John Wiley and Sons., Inc. (www.wiley.com) and the publisher of this volume and other valuable resources. *The FERPA Answer Book for Higher Education Professionals* provides legal and operational assistance regarding FERPA. *The Successful Registrar* and *The Enrollment Management Newsletter*, both recently acquired from LRP Publications, keep higher education professionals current on legislation, trends, and change.

LRP Publications. A number of FERPA titles are included in the online catalog of LRP Publications (www.lrp.com). *Managing the Privacy of Student Records* includes both a textbook for in-class or individual study and a manual for facilitators who lead FERPA training sessions. *Managing the Privacy of Student Records* was created to provide higher education institutions with an off-the-shelf FERPA workshop that could be easily tailored to local campus needs. A number of FERPA training videos are also available from LRP.

FERPA PUBLICATIONS FROM CLIFFORD A. RAMIREZ

Available through LRP Publications

Managing the Privacy of Student Records: A Textbook of FERPA Basics, 2002. This is the workbook for the *Managing the Privacy of Student Records* workshop that can be used in class or as an individual, interactive study aid. Essentials from the workshop are conveyed in a fast-moving presentation that is comprehensive and a quick read.

Managing the Privacy of Student Records: The Leader's Guide, 2002. This is the facilitator's teaching manual, providing instruction and background information for conducting the *Managing the Privacy of Student Records* workshop at your campus. Includes additional handouts and scenarios for discussion.

The FERPA Transition: Helping Parents Adjust to Higher Education Records Laws, 2004. A guide for education officials in interpreting and explaining FERPA to parents and other campus clients and constituents. Includes a summary exposition of legislation that has amended FERPA since its initial passage.

FERPA: What You Can and Can't Release, 2004. FERPA basics are presented in this training video that can be used as a refresher for staff meetings and professional development events.

Records Management in Higher Education: Ensuring Organization, Efficiency, and Legal Compliance, 2006. Written with records management expert Linda Arquieta-Herrera. A records management manual for higher education recordkeepers and managers.

Available from Jossey-Bass

The FERPA Answer Book for Higher Education Professionals, 2009. Updated and revised with attorney Aileen Gelpi. A legal question and answer book on issues and concerns that revolve around FERPA and FERPA compliance. Includes a subscription for ongoing updates and revisions to the manual.

Progressive Business Publications. In addition to audio conferences, Progress Business Publications (www.pbp.com) offers newsletters and other resources. For K–12, *Legal Update for Teachers* is a monthly newsletter specifically targeted to teachers, principals, and other administrators in elementary and secondary education.

The Chronicle of Higher Education. The premier news-reporting agency on education, the *Chronicle of Higher Education* (chronicle.com) provides a wealth of information on various concerns for faculty, staff, and the public.

Insider Higher Ed. For online reference, Insider Higher Ed (www.insidehighered.com) focuses on higher education concerns from numerous perspectives such as legislation, policy, and culture.

Compliance Checklist: Training	
Timeliness	How often are training and reminders about training provided to staff? Reminders should be made at least once a year.
Resources and Awareness	• Do campus faculty and staff know where to direct questions regarding FERPA? • Have you created FERPA training materials or a library of training materials that are available to staff throughout your campus? • Do you publicize FERPA training opportunities at your campus?
Tracking	• How do you track staff and faculty participation in FERPA training? • Are staff and faculty provided with training or training reminders at least once a year?
Review	How do you evaluate the effectiveness of your FERPA training?

Reports and Other Documentation

The last component of items that an institution may be required to produce for the FPCO during an investigation of an alleged FERPA violation includes "reports...and other information necessary to carry out its enforcement responsibilities" (§99.62). In fact, prior to the 2008 Amendments, the regulations at §99.62 read simply as follows.

The Office may require an educational agency or institution to submit reports containing information necessary to resolve complaints under the Act and the regulations in this part.

The inclusion of the other three items—information on policies and procedures, annual notifications, and training materials—represents a more serious expansion of the FPCO's investigatory responsibilities and enforcement authority of the FERPA provisions.

When the regulations, in §99.62, refer to reports and other information that may be relevant to the investigation, the kind of documentation included here is extremely broad and may have relevance only to the specifics

---

In response to an FPCO investigation, institutions must submit

- **Reports**
- Information on policies and procedures
- Annual notifications
- Training materials
- **Other necessary information**

of the complaint. Records may need to be culled from various areas of the campus. Remember that FERPA applies to all components and offices of an institution (§99.1(d)).

The nature of the alleged violation will dictate the kind of records or additional information that may need to be provided to the FPCO. In the case of *Gonzaga v. Doe* (see the sidebar on page 25), the relevant information would have included documentation and specifics of the investigation that was clandestinely conducted by university officials behind John Doe's back. That this particular case ran its gamut through the courts of Washington State and even to the U.S. Supreme Court is indicative that all information necessary to a particular complaint may need to be produced and require extensive evaluation.

Documentation and records that are not voluntarily surrendered may be subject to the demands of a court subpoena. And, as with all requests for inspection and review, documents that have been requested for that purpose cannot be destroyed before the opportunity for inspection and review has been provided.

EXAMPLES OF REPORTS AND OTHER DOCUMENTATION

Catalogs

Confidential records, including assessments and evaluations

Correspondence, including both written and electronic

Data downloads and extracts

Departmental and institutional reports

Disciplinary records and disciplinary hearing documentation

Disclosure records

Education records

Faculty handbooks and other materials

Forms, blank and completed

Housing and campus life records

Meeting minutes and exhibits

Miscellaneous documentation and publications

Office files and records

Official reports compiled, published and unpublished

Program requirements

Publications, including both paper and electronic

Student directories

Student handbooks, guides, and program materials

Transcripts and transcript legends

In considering "reports...and other information," institutional officials should be reminded of the critical importance of their records management strategies and of the need for documented policy and procedure. As stated before, policies are part of the vital records of an institution. In a court of law, policies can be the documentary evidence that officially substantiates institutional action and practice.

Compliance Checklist: Reports and Other Documentation	
Availability	• Are institutional files maintained in a complete and organized manner?
	• Are documents, policies, and other reports easy to locate and reproduce if necessary?
Review	• Are your records management and records retention policies reviewed periodically to ensure they are up to date and consistent with institutional needs?
	• Are your records management and records retention policies reviewed periodically to ensure they are up to date and consistent with appropriate legislation and regulation?

Maintaining FERPA Compliance

Achieving FERPA compliance is only as good as an institution's strategy for maintaining its compliance with the regulations. In many ways, attaining a level of compliance is a quest that must occur each and every day of one's business operations. The nature of transactions change, after all. There are always new third-party entities with which to deal. And the types of requests for information may change from day to day.

Maintaining institutional compliance is an ongoing challenge that exists on two levels.

First of all, there is the daily response to business that compels education officials throughout the campus to exercise judgment and to perform their jobs in a manner that communicates the character of the institution while upholding the privacy rights of students defined under FERPA. Keeping staff and faculty well trained and reinforcing the tenets of responsibility are important to ensuring success in these daily operations.

But there is another level of compliance that needs some comment— and that is the area of compliance from periodic evaluation of processes and practice.

It is not difficult to become so immersed in the traffic of transactions that subtle and sometimes dangerous changes make their way into our practice and operations. The stimulus can be as harmless as a revision to stationery or as major as the implementation of new software that provides

HIGHER EDUCATION CONSULTING RESOURCES

American Association of Collegiate Registrars and Admissions Officers (AACRAO) Consulting (consulting.aacrao.org)
AACRAO Consulting provides support in a variety of operational areas in higher education.

ARMA International (www.arma.org)
ARMA International is an organization of records management specialists in a number of different fields, including business, government, law enforcement, education, and medicine.

Registrar and Enrollment Services Consulting for Colleges and Universities (RESCCU) (www.resccu.com)
Founded by Dr. Evelyn Babey in 2002, RESCCU provides enrollment management consulting and training both nationally and internationally.

greater data mining potential for groups of individuals across campus. In some cases, the anticipated impact may have been considered by a select few; in others, the impact is left until after the consequences of undertaking the changes become evident.

Regardless of circumstances and operational stance, one of the best practice recommendations from records managers is a periodic evaluation of practice to test compliance, effectiveness, and sustainability. And it is an exercise that should be accomplished on a number of levels throughout the organization. Managers often complete this kind of assessment in isolated retreats that contribute to annual strategic planning efforts. But the staff who are actually doing the work need to be given time to assess their processes to ensure that the principles of policy are still being carried out in procedure and practice.

Setting aside time on an annual basis to make this kind of critical assessment is important because it allows the organization to catch inconsistencies and potential areas of concern that might not otherwise be addressed until the occurrence of a major problem. When urgent crises strike, everyone goes into emergency mode, which may or may not address the symptoms that led to the emergency in the first place. By taking time to carefully assess and critically gauge operations, institutions can make the appropriate changes and ensure the allocation of resources to keep operations in compliance.

There is an old proverb that says, "An ounce of prevention is worth a pound of cure." In the case of legal and regulatory compliance, the benefits are obvious.

Compliance Checklist: Maintaining Compliance	
Timeframe	• Set aside time—at least on an annual basis—to conduct a comprehensive self-audit of FERPA compliance.

Completeness	• Ensure that self-audit activities are performed at all levels of the institution.
	• When conducting a self-audit for FERPA compliance, examine and review all of the following areas.
	  • Policies and procedures
	  • Annual notification
	  • Training strategies
	  • Response to changes in business needs
	  • Recent legislation

Documentation	• Record your annual review in minutes of appropriate meetings.

Afterthoughts

On the Rights of Postsecondary Students

CLEAR AND SIMPLE is the invariable expectation we have of any kind of training program in which we participate—and it has certainly been the singular goal of this volume. But while the presentation of the material has hopefully encouraged and affirmed for you a new level of expertise with the FERPA regulations, the matter of application still remains. One must subsequently endeavor to take the new knowledge or understanding and incorporate it into business practices back at the college or university. This is where many discover the most difficulty, because new learning may require confronting challenging practices and attitudes that may have become imbued in or aligned with institutional history and tradition.

How do you characterize your relationship with your students? And from that determination, how do you define the roles of your own education officials and the place of parents and other third parties in your campus community? The answers to these questions are important because coming to terms with these values has a direct influence on your success in implementing your FERPA compliance initiatives.

Pivotal to everything you do on the campus is how you view your students and how you determine and guarantee the rights to which they are entitled.

FERPA and other legislation provide the foundations for making a legal assessment, from which institutional relationships can take shape. Recognizing the student's passage from K–12 into the postsecondary environment, the declaration in §99.5(a) of the FERPA regulations unequivocally reassigns rights from parents to eligible students. Some FERPA trainers have even used this citation to assert that parents have no FERPA rights in the postsecondary environment.

> When a student becomes an eligible student, the rights accorded to, and consent required of, parents under this part, transfer from the parents to the student.
>
> *§99.5(a)*

Throughout this book, I have endeavored to demonstrate that the fabric of federal and state legislation affirms the rights of postsecondary students as adults in society. If college students are adults in the eyes of the law, then essentially, they possess the same rights as any other individual in the education community—the same inherent personal rights as faculty, staff, parents, and other individuals. Citizens are created equal, after all, and possess those certain "inalienable rights" that have become the subject of law and legislation—among these, those codified in FERPA, the right to privacy and the privacy of education records.

But what are the implications of this declaration? FERPA certainly spells out rights in relation to education records and the disclosure or availability of information from those education records. In other areas, the policies and procedures of our catalogs detail the contractual agreements of the consumer relationship between the student and the institution. Where else does the characterization of these rights impact?

> *Intelligence is the ability to see implication.*
> —ST. THOMAS AQUINAS

The most important implication, especially where citizen rights are concerned, is that there can be no in loco parentis stance where the postsecondary environment is concerned. Whenever in loco parentis is raised, it is usually done so in the context of discipline and behavior. Society, as discussed in Chapter Three, was unwilling to interfere in the parental right to discipline children for many centuries, even when that right was exercised by delegated representatives, such as by a school. But circumstances and the privacy dialogue of the 20th century changed all of that.

Nevertheless, lingering in our education system are archaic attitudes toward letters of recommendation. Despite the provisions outlined in §99.12 of the FERPA regulations, there are still schools and faculty that treat the process without acknowledging the privacy rights of the student. Under the guise of confidentiality, these somehow privileged letters, composed by an individual with some in-depth familiarity with the subject in question, are supposed to provide classified information about a student's academic performance and civic character. Some even insist on the authority of faculty and schools to coerce students into giving up their rights of access to these letters. Can we force fellow citizens to give up rights?

In light of the late 20th century focus on mentoring and leadership development, the concealment of valuable feedback and responsible guidance to the student strikes a curious and politically undemocratic note.

One would expect composers of letters of recommendation to use these valuable teaching moments to counsel and guide students regarding their choices for the future, their continued academic development, and their continued growth as men and women.

> *If we value independence, if we are disturbed by the growing*
> *conformity of knowledge, of values, of attitudes, which our present*
> *system induces, then we may wish to set up conditions of learning*
> *which make for uniqueness, for self-direction, and for self-initiated*
> *learning.*
>
> —CARL ROGERS

In 1997, I was working at UCLA and had been elected president of the UCLA Administrators and Supervisors Association (ASA). ASA was an organization created by staff to provide for their own continuing educational opportunities at the campus. One of my ASA colleagues was Linnaea Mallette, an inspiring and energetic woman who worked in the Office of Contracts and Grants. Despite a hearing disability, Linnaea had become a successful professional speaker and was an oft-requested presenter on behalf of disability awareness. That year, Linnaea wanted to do something to help staff members who were kept back in their jobs by an inability or fear of speaking in public. She developed and created the Bruin Toastmasters, to which ASA added its support.

The purpose of the Bruin Toastmasters, of course, was to provide a safe training space for staff members to build their self-confidence and to develop presentation skills. It was not long, however, before a male student who, having heard about the Bruin Toastmasters, approached the group with a request to join its regular meetings.

I spoke with the student about his interest in the employee group at the end of his first Toastmasters meeting. The young man was a senior, scheduled to graduate in a few months. He confessed that after attending the career fairs on campus, he realized that he did not have the adequate skills or the social confidence to enter the job market. He had the academic knowledge but not the ability to successfully present himself to a prospective employer.

Desperate about his perceived lack of readiness for the working world, the student shared his concern with his father. Perhaps the student would have been better off at a smaller school, where he could receive the individual attention he needed. But the boy's father brushed the complaint aside, insisting that the UCLA degree would nevertheless look good on his resume. Still apprehensive, the young man sought out his own avenues to build his social finesse—which is what brought him to the Bruin Toastmasters.

An educational system isn't worth a great deal if it teaches young people how to make a living but doesn't teach them how to make a life.

—UNKNOWN

Education and systems of education have not been without their critics or pundits who attempt to put institutionalized education in its place. Mark Twain once confessed: "I have never let my schooling interfere with my education."

Apart from the pedagogy of the classroom, which is generally concerned with the attainment of a diploma or of a degree, one has to consider the environment or community of education. Here, the whole of the environment must revolve around the education of the student—pragmatically as well as intellectually. The various components of the institution are not without their educational usefulness. Financial aid and student accounting should be teaching students how to handle their finances and not just be concerned with collecting payments or setting up financial disbursements. Campus life and housing offices are responsible for the social indoctrination of the student who may, for the first time in her life, be away from home or adapting to a community of nonfamily members. And academic counselors should be facilitating student development in the areas of perseverance and commitment to the programs of their individual majors and courses of study.

In a similar way, registrar's offices and other recordkeeping entities must be involved in teaching students to manage the privacy of their personal information. Disclosures to parents—or anyone, for that matter—should not be taken lightly. And parents must be brought into this realization, cooperating with the totality of an educational endeavor that attempts to mold a young person for life. The postsecondary community should be that: an opportunity for development on an adult level and not merely a perpetuation of the K–12 environment.

While we aim to educate staff regarding FERPA and student privacy, our outreach and recruiting efforts should make it clear to parents what the higher education environment is all about. The vestiges of middle and high school are gone. Now, the student must act with responsibility, self-directedness, and maturity. How the student establishes his character in the postsecondary environment is an indication of how well the young person will perform in later life—as a professional, as a citizen, and as an adult.

Social critics have not had much confidence in our institutions—education included. "History is a race between education and catastrophe," quipped H.G. Wells. To which Carl Rogers adds, "The only person who is educated is the one who has learned how to learn and change." Perhaps, despite the laurels of esteemed institutional names in education, the process itself has not kept up with the demands of the rest of society. In some ways, 19th century approaches are still preserved and defended as "tried and proven."

> *In the measurement world, you set a goal and strive for it. In the*
> *universe of possibility, you set the context and let life unfold.*
> —BENJAMIN ZANDER AND ROSAMUND STONE ZANDER,
> *THE ART OF POSSIBILITY:*
> *TRANSFORMING P ROFESSIONAL AND PERSONAL LIFE*

Futurists throughout the 20th century envisioned societies where education and even the nurturing process happen away from the general society, overseen by the state or by other officially designated experts. That is the reality in Aldous Huxley's *Brave New World*. But what would be taught? Would it not be a conformism to a present set of ideals that, in many respects, inhibits an individual's prospect for the future?

One of the most captivating depictions of the impact of education and conditioning occurs in the work of Arthur C. Clarke, the science fiction writer, inventor, and futurist who gave us *2001: A Space Odyssey*. In his early novel *Against the Fall of Night* (1953), later expanded as *The City and the Stars* (1956), Clarke presents a world where the educational system has conditioned young people to limit themselves to the known world, to refrain from dreaming, to experience only what has been captured for them to experience (in virtual games much as are now being developed), and to never ask questions. Yet, it is in the asking of questions that discoveries are made and the experience of humanity broadened.

Clarke was a great futurist, suggesting the use of satellites and other technological advancements long before civilization had the wherewithal to create them. In his 1997 novel, *3001: The Final Odyssey*, Clarke presents a world where education takes an entirely different place in society. In 3001, books have disappeared. Knowledge resides in a databank that is available to all human beings. Individuals are equipped with a telepathic ability to communicate with the collective, social database. Whatever knowledge is required can be downloaded upon request, leaving one to question the place of experience—one of the last, great differentiators of individual performance for employers.

Until we live in a world like Clarke's *3001*, the education process must continue to evolve with the demands that our society places on it. From the human rights perspective, that means an education community encouraging students—and parents—to help the young person develop into the able and equipped citizen demanded by contemporary needs.

> *Imagination is more important than knowledge. Knowledge is limited. Imagination encircles the world.*
>
> —ALBERT EINSTEIN

I applauded the efforts of the UCLA student who wanted to be a part of our Bruin Toastmasters group. But my conversation with the student made me wonder about how many other students go through college or university with only the attainment of a degree as their goal. Already human resource circles have begun to look at competencies, and not just facts on a resume, as a method of recruiting and selecting individuals with the greatest potential. All too often, as many employers are discovering, a degree on paper and demonstrated performance and achievement can bear little or no relation.

One of our Franklin Covey *7 Habits of Highly Effective People* strategies is to encourage college students—and all human beings—to develop their own personal leadership, to define their goals and to shape their lives around the attainment of those goals. This kind of character development, which places personal fulfillment before material or financial success, is often lacking in our educational systems. Even when presented as time management, this kind of training has sadly been dismissed from curricula as too religious or too spiritual, and not skills-based enough.

Even where staff and professional development are concerned, our thinking has advanced only slightly since the manufacturing boom of earlier centuries. We forget that the word "education" comes from the Latin phrase *e ducare,* meaning "to lead forth." Education is leading an individual into a new experience and awareness of self and of the world in which the individual lives.

Education, and not just higher education, needs to reassess itself and redefine itself for the 21st century. This is not just a challenge for education but for every sector of our society. Evaluation is a process that should happen with regularity in every human endeavor. And sometimes, the challenge to think anew, to try other methods, to turn in a different direction comes from the unlikeliest of sources. If only educators, at all levels, have the courage to test the systems in which we have all become comfortable and content!

From my days at Antioch University, I am reminded of a wonderful quote from one of the greatest American educators of all time—Horace Mann. After Antioch's founding in 1852, Mann was designated its first president and taught political economy, moral philosophy, and natural theology at the college. In one of his commencement speeches, Mann summed up the challenge for all men and women alike: "Be ashamed to die," he cried, "until you have won some victory for humanity!"

No meeting or commencement could take place at Antioch without some reference to the work and inspiration of its first president. Whenever he was quoted, it was often these singular words which have become the signature motto for the university. And whenever they are invoked, Mann's words are framed so as to address not only graduating students, but staff, faculty, and the attending community alike.

Clearly and simply, the challenge remains.

Be ashamed to die until you have won some victory for humanity!
—HORACE MANN

Appendix I

34 CFR § 99—

Family Educational Rights and Privacy Act

Section Contents

§ 99.21 Under what conditions does a parent or eligible student have the right to a hearing?

§ 99.22 What minimum requirements exist for the conduct of a hearing?

Subpart D—May an Educational Agency or Institution Disclose Personally Identifiable Information from Education Records?

§ 99.30 Under what conditions is prior consent required to disclose information?

§ 99.31 Under what conditions is prior consent not required to disclose information?

§ 99.32 What recordkeeping requirements exist concerning requests and disclosures?

§ 99.33 What limitations apply to the redisclosure of information?

§ 99.34 What conditions apply to disclosure of information to other educational agencies or institutions?

§ 99.35 What conditions apply to disclosure of information for Federal or State program purposes?

§ 99.36 What conditions apply to disclosure of information in health and safety emergencies?

§ 99.37 What conditions apply to disclosing directory information?

§ 99.38 What conditions apply to disclosure of information as permitted by State statute adopted after November 19, 1974, concerning the juvenile justice system?

§ 99.39 What definitions apply to the nonconsensual disclosure of records by postsecondary educational institutions in connection with disciplinary proceedings concerning crimes of violence or non-forcible sex offenses?

Subpart E—What Are the Enforcement Procedures?

§ 99.60 What functions has the Secretary delegated to the Office and to the Office of Administrative Law Judges?

§ 99.61 What responsibility does an educational agency or institution have concerning conflict with State or local laws?

§ 99.62 What information must an educational agency or institution submit to the Office?

§ 99.63 Where are complaints filed?

§ 99.64 What is the investigation procedure?

§ 99.65 What is the content of the notice of investigation issued by the Office?

§ 99.66 What are the responsibilities of the Office in the enforcement process?

§ 99.67 How does the Secretary enforce decisions?

Appendix A to Part 99—Crimes of Violence Definitions
Authority: 20 U.S.C. 1232g, unless otherwise noted.
Source: 53 FR 11943, Apr. 11, 1988, unless otherwise noted.

Subpart A—General

§ 99.1 To Which Educational Agencies or Institutions Do These Regulations Apply?

(a) Except as otherwise noted in §99.10, this part applies to an educational agency or institution to which funds have been made available under any program administered by the Secretary, if—

(1) The educational institution provides educational services or instruction, or both, to students; or

(2) The educational agency is authorized to direct and control public elementary or secondary, or postsecondary educational institutions.

(b) This part does not apply to an educational agency or institution solely because students attending that agency or institution receive non-monetary benefits under a program referenced in paragraph (a) of this section, if no funds under that program are made available to the agency or institution.

(c) The Secretary considers funds to be made available to an educational agency or institution of funds under one or more of the programs referenced in paragraph (a) of this section—

(1) Are provided to the agency or institution by grant, cooperative agreement, contract, subgrant, or subcontract; or

(2) Are provided to students attending the agency or institution and the funds may be paid to the agency or institution by those students for educational purposes, such as under the Pell Grant Program and the

Guaranteed Student Loan Program (titles IV-A-1 and IV-B, respectively, of the Higher Education Act of 1965, as amended).

(d) If an educational agency or institution receives funds under one or more of the programs covered by this section, the regulations in this part apply to the recipient as a whole, including each of its components (such as a department within a university).

(*Authority:* 20 U.S.C. 1232g)

[53 FR 11943, Apr. 11, 1988, as amended at 61 FR 59295, Nov. 21, 1996; 65 FR 41852, July 6, 2000]

§ 99.2 What Is the Purpose of These Regulations?

The purpose of this part is to set out requirements for the protection of privacy of parents and students under section 444 of the General Education Provisions Act, as amended.

(*Authority:* 20 U.S.C. 1232g)

Note to §99.2: 34 CFR 300.610 through 300.626 contain requirements regarding the confidentiality of information relating to children with disabilities who receive evaluations, services or other benefits under Part B of the Individuals with Disabilities Education Act (IDEA). 34 CFR 303.402 and 303.460 identify the confidentiality of information requirements regarding children and infants and toddlers with disabilities and their families who receive evaluations, services, or other benefits under Part C of IDEA. 34 CFR 300.610 through 300.627 contain the confidentiality of information requirements that apply to personally identifiable data, information, and records collected or maintained pursuant to Part B of the IDEA.

[53 FR 11943, Apr. 11, 1988, as amended at 61 FR 59295, Nov. 21, 1996; 73 FR 74851, Dec. 9, 2008]

§ 99.3 What Definitions Apply to These Regulations?

The following definitions apply to this part:

Act means the Family Educational Rights and Privacy Act of 1974, as amended, enacted as section 444 of the General Education Provisions Act.

(*Authority:* 20 U.S.C. 1232g)

Attendance includes, but is not limited to—

(a) Attendance in person or by paper correspondence, videoconference, satellite, Internet, or other electronic information and telecommunications technologies for students who are not physically present in the classroom; and

(b) The period during which a person is working under a work-study program.

(*Authority:* 20 U.S.C. 1232g)

Biometric record, as used in the definition of *personally identifiable information*, means a record of one or more measurable biological or behavioral characteristics that can be used for automated recognition of an individual. Examples include fingerprints; retina and iris patterns; voiceprints; DNA sequence; facial characteristics; and handwriting.

(*Authority:* 20 U.S.C. 1232g)

Dates of attendance.

(a) The term means the period of time during which a student attends or attended an educational agency or institution. Examples of dates of attendance include an academic year, a spring semester, or a first quarter.

(b) The term does not include specific daily records of a student's attendance at an educational agency or institution.

(*Authority:* 20 U.S.C. 1232g(a)(5)(A))

Directory information means information contained in an education record of a student that would not generally be considered harmful or an invasion of privacy if disclosed.

(a) Directory information includes, but is not limited to, the student's name; address; telephone listing; electronic mail address; photograph; date and place of birth; major field of study; grade level; enrollment status (e.g., undergraduate or graduate, full-time or part-time); dates of attendance; participation in officially recognized activities and sports; weight and height of members of athletic teams; degrees, honors and awards received; and the most recent educational agency or institution attended.

(b) Directory information does not include a student's—

(1) Social security number; or

(2) Student identification (ID) number, except as provided in paragraph (c) of this section.

(c) Directory information includes a student ID number, user ID, or other unique personal identifier used by the student for purposes of accessing or communicating in electronic systems, but only if the identifier cannot be used to gain access to education records except when used in conjunction with one or more factors that authenticate the user's identity, such as a personal identification number (PIN), password, or other factor known or possessed only by the authorized user.

(*Authority:* 20 U.S.C. 1232g(a)(5)(A))

Disciplinary action or proceeding means the investigation, adjudication, or imposition of sanctions by an educational agency or institution with respect to an infraction or violation of the internal rules of conduct applicable to students of the agency or institution.

Disclosure means to permit access to or the release, transfer, or other communication of personally identifiable information contained in education records by any means, including oral, written, or electronic means, to any party except the party identified as the party that provided or created the record.
(*Authority:* 20 U.S.C. 1232g(b)(1) and (b)(2))

Educational agency or institution means any public or private agency or institution to which this part applies under §99.1(a).
(*Authority:* 20 U.S.C. 1232g(a)(3))

Education records.

(a) The term means those records that are:

    (1) Directly related to a student; and

    (2) Maintained by an educational agency or institution or by a party acting for the agency or institution.

(b) The term does not include:

    (1) Records that are kept in the sole possession of the maker, are used only as a personal memory aid, and are not accessible or revealed to any other person except a temporary substitute for the maker of the record.

    (2) Records of the law enforcement unit of an educational agency or institution, subject to the provisions of §99.8.

    (3) (i) Records relating to an individual who is employed by an educational agency or institution, that:

        (A) Are made and maintained in the normal course of business;

        (B) Relate exclusively to the individual in that individual's capacity as an employee; and

        (C) Are not available for use for any other purpose.

     (ii) Records relating to an individual in attendance at the agency or institution who is employed as a result of his or her status as a student are education records and not excepted under paragraph (b)(3)(i) of this definition.

    (4) Records on a student who is 18 years of age or older, or is attending an institution of postsecondary education, that are:

     (i) Made or maintained by a physician, psychiatrist, psychologist, or other recognized professional or paraprofessional acting in his or her professional capacity or assisting in a paraprofessional capacity;

(ii) Made, maintained, or used only in connection with treatment of the student; and

(iii) Disclosed only to individuals providing the treatment. For the purpose of this definition, "treatment" does not include remedial educational activities or activities that are part of the program of instruction at the agency or institution; and

(5) Records created or received by an educational agency or institution after an individual is no longer a student in attendance and that are not directly related to the individual's attendance as a student.
   (*Authority:* 20 U.S.C. 1232g(a)(4))

(6) Grades on peer-graded papers before they are collected and recorded by a teacher.

Eligible student means a student who has reached 18 years of age or is attending an institution of postsecondary education.
(*Authority:* 20 U.S.C. 1232g(d))

Institution of postsecondary education means an institution that provides education to students beyond the secondary school level; "secondary school level" means the educational level (not beyond grade 12) at which secondary education is provided as determined under State law.
(*Authority:* 20 U.S.C. 1232g(d))

Parent means a parent of a student and includes a natural parent, a guardian, or an individual acting as a parent in the absence of a parent or a guardian.
(*Authority:* 20 U.S.C. 1232g)

Party means an individual, agency, institution, or organization.
(*Authority:* 20 U.S.C. 1232g(b)(4)(A))

Personally Identifiable Information
The term includes, but is not limited to—
(a) The student's name;
(b) The name of the student's parent or other family members;
(c) The address of the student or student's family;
(d) A personal identifier, such as the student's social security number, student number, or biometric record;
(e) Other indirect identifiers, such as the student's date of birth, place of birth, and mother's maiden name;

(f) Other information that, alone or in combination, is linked or link-able to a specific student that would allow a reasonable person in the school community, who does not have personal knowledge of the relevant circumstances, to identify the student with reasonable certainty; or

(g) Information requested by a person who the educational agency or institution reasonably believes knows the identity of the student to whom the education record relates.

(*Authority:* 20 U.S.C. 1232g)

Record means any information recorded in any way, including, but not limited to, handwriting, print, computer media, video or audio tape, film, microfilm, and microfiche.

(*Authority:* 20 U.S.C. 1232g)

Secretary means the Secretary of the U.S. Department of Education or an official or employee of the Department of Education acting for the Secretary under a delegation of authority.

(*Authority:* 20 U.S.C. 1232g)

Student, except as otherwise specifically provided in this part, means any individual who is or has been in attendance at an educational agency or institution and regarding whom the agency or institution maintains education records.

(*Authority:* 20 U.S.C. 1232g(a)(6))

[53 FR 11943, Apr. 11, 1988, as amended at 60 FR 3468, Jan. 17, 1995; 61 FR 59295, Nov. 21, 1996; 65 FR 41852, July 6, 2000; 73 FR 74851, Dec. 9, 2008]

§ 99.4 What Are the Rights of Parents?

An educational agency or institution shall give full rights under the Act to either parent, unless the agency or institution has been provided with evidence that there is a court order, State statute, or legally binding document relating to such matters as divorce, separation, or custody that specifically revokes these rights.

(*Authority:* 20 U.S.C. 1232g)

§ 99.5 What Are the Rights of Students?

(a) (1) When a student becomes an eligible student, the rights accorded to, and consent required of, parents under this part transfer from the parents to the student.

(2) Nothing in this section prevents an educational agency or institution from disclosing education records, or personally

identifiable information from education records, to a parent without the prior written consent of an eligible student if the disclosure meets the conditions in §99.31(a)(8), §99.31(a)(10), §99.31(a)(15), or any other provision in §99.31(a).

(b) The Act and this part do not prevent educational agencies or institutions from giving students rights in addition to those given to parents.

(c) An individual who is or has been a student at an educational institution and who applies for admission at another component of that institution does not have rights under this part with respect to records maintained by that other component, including records maintained in connection with the student's application for admission, unless the student is accepted and attends that other component of the institution.

(*Authority:* 20 U.S.C. 1232g(d))

[53 FR 11943, Apr. 11, 1988, as amended at 58 FR 3188, Jan. 7, 1993; 65 FR 41853, July 6, 2000; 73 FR 74852, Dec. 9, 2008]

§ 99.6 [Reserved]

§ 99.7 What Must an Educational Agency or Institution Include in its Annual Notification?

(a) (1) Each educational agency or institution shall annually notify parents of students currently in attendance, or eligible students currently in attendance, of their rights under the Act and this part.

(2) The notice must inform parents or eligible students that they have the right to—

(i) Inspect and review the student's education records;

(ii) Seek amendment of the student's education records that the parent or eligible student believes to be inaccurate, misleading, or otherwise in violation of the student's privacy rights;

(iii) Consent to disclosures of personally identifiable information contained in the student's education records, except to the extent that the Act and §99.31 authorize disclosure without consent; and

(iv) File with the Department a complaint under §§99.63 and 99.64 concerning alleged failures by the educational agency or institution to comply with the requirements of the Act and this part.

(3) The notice must include all of the following:

(i) The procedure for exercising the right to inspect and review education records.

(ii) The procedure for requesting amendment of records under §99.20.

(iii) If the educational agency or institution has a policy of disclosing education records under §99.31(a)(1), a specification of criteria for determining who constitutes a school official and what constitutes a legitimate educational interest.

(b) An educational agency or institution may provide this notice by any means that are reasonably likely to inform the parents or eligible students of their rights.

(1) An educational agency or institution shall effectively notify parents or eligible students who are disabled.

(2) An agency or institution of elementary or secondary education shall effectively notify parents who have a primary or home language other than English.

(Approved by the Office of Management and Budget under control number 1880–0508)

(*Authority:* 20 U.S.C. 1232g (e) and (f))

[61 FR 59295, Nov. 21, 1996]

§ 99.8 What Provisions Apply to Records of a Law Enforcement Unit?

(a) (1) *Law enforcement unit* means any individual, office, department, division, or other component of an educational agency or institution, such as a unit of commissioned police officers or non-commissioned security guards, that is officially authorized or designated by that agency or institution to—

(i) Enforce any local, State, or Federal law, or refer to appropriate authorities a matter for enforcement of any local, State, or Federal law against any individual or organization other than the agency or institution itself; or

(ii) Maintain the physical security and safety of the agency or institution.

(2) A component of an educational agency or institution does not lose its status as a *law enforcement unit* if it also performs other, non-law enforcement functions for the agency or institution, including investigation of incidents or conduct that constitutes or leads to a disciplinary action or proceedings against the student.

(b) (1) Records of a law enforcement unit means those records, files, documents, and other materials that are—

(i) Created by a law enforcement unit;

(ii) Created for a law enforcement purpose; and

(iii) Maintained by the law enforcement unit.

(2) Records of a law enforcement unit does not mean—

(i) Records created by a law enforcement unit for a law enforcement purpose that are maintained by a component of the educational agency or institution other than the law enforcement unit; or

(ii) Records created and maintained by a law enforcement unit exclusively for a non-law enforcement purpose, such as a disciplinary action or proceeding conducted by the educational agency or institution.

(c) (1) Nothing in the Act prohibits an educational agency or institution from contacting its law enforcement unit, orally or in writing, for the purpose of asking that unit to investigate a possible violation of, or to enforce, any local, State, or Federal law.

(2) Education records, and personally identifiable information contained in education records, do not lose their status as education records and remain subject to the Act, including the disclosure provisions of §99.30, while in the possession of the law enforcement unit.

(d) The Act neither requires nor prohibits the disclosure by an educational agency or institution of its law enforcement unit records.

(*Authority:* 20 U.S.C. 1232g(a)(4)(B)(ii))

[60 FR 3469, Jan. 17, 1995]

Subpart B—What Are the Rights of Inspection and Review of Education Records?

§ 99.10 What Rights Exist for a Parent or Eligible Student to Inspect and Review Education Records?

(a) Except as limited under §99.12, a parent or eligible student must be given the opportunity to inspect and review the student's education records. This provision applies to—

(1) Any educational agency or institution; and

(2) Any State educational agency (SEA) and its components.

   (i) For the purposes of subpart B of this part, an SEA and its components constitute an educational agency or institution.

   (ii) An SEA and its components are subject to subpart B of this part if the SEA maintains education records on students who are or have been in attendance at any school of an educational agency or institution subject to the Act and this part.

(b) The educational agency or institution, or SEA or its component, shall comply with a request for access to records within a reasonable period of time, but not more than 45 days after it has received the request.

(c) The educational agency or institution, or SEA or its component shall respond to reasonable requests for explanations and interpretations of the records.

(d) If circumstances effectively prevent the parent or eligible student from exercising the right to inspect and review the student's education records, the educational agency or institution, or SEA or its component, shall—

(1) Provide the parent or eligible student with a copy of the records requested; or

(2) Make other arrangements for the parent or eligible student to inspect and review the requested records.

(e) The educational agency or institution, or SEA or its component shall not destroy any education records if there is an outstanding request to inspect and review the records under this section.

(f) While an education agency or institution is not required to give an eligible student access to treatment records under paragraph (b)(4) of the definition of *Education records* in §99.3, the student may have those records reviewed by a physician or other appropriate professional of the student's choice.

(*Authority:* 20 U.S.C. 1232g(a)(1) (A) and (B))

[53 FR 11943, Apr. 11, 1988, as amended at 61 FR 59296, Nov. 21, 1996]

§ 99.11 May an Educational Agency or Institution Charge a Fee for Copies of Education Records?

(a) Unless the imposition of a fee effectively prevents a parent or eligible student from exercising the right to inspect and review the student's education records, an educational agency or institution may charge a fee for a copy of an education record which is made for the parent or eligible student.

(b) An educational agency or institution may not charge a fee to search for or to retrieve the education records of a student.

(*Authority:* 20 U.S.C. 1232g(a)(1))

§ 99.12 What Limitations Exist on the Right to Inspect and Review Records?

(a) If the education records of a student contain information on more than one student, the parent or eligible student may inspect and review or be informed of only the specific information about that student.

(b) A postsecondary institution does not have to permit a student to inspect and review education records that are:

(1) Financial records, including any information those records contain, of his or her parents;

(2) Confidential letters and confidential statements of recommendation placed in the education records of the student before January 1, 1975, as long as the statements are used only for the purposes for which they were specifically intended; and

(3) Confidential letters and confidential statements of recommendation placed in the student's education records after January 1, 1975, if:

  (i) The student has waived his or her right to inspect and review those letters and statements; and

  (ii) Those letters and statements are related to the student's:

    (A) Admission to an educational institution;

    (B) Application for employment; or

    (C) Receipt of an honor or honorary recognition.

(c) (1) A waiver under paragraph (b)(3)(i) of this section is valid only if:

    (i) The educational agency or institution does not require the waiver as a condition for admission to or receipt of a service or benefit from the agency or institution; and

    (ii) The waiver is made in writing and signed by the student, regardless of age.

(2) If a student has waived his or her rights under paragraph (b)(3)(i) of this section, the educational institution shall:

(i) Give the student, on request, the names of the individuals who provided the letters and statements of recommendation; and

(ii) Use the letters and statements of recommendation only for the purpose for which they were intended.

(3)   (i) A waiver under paragraph (b)(3)(i) of this section may be revoked with respect to any actions occurring after the revocation.

(ii) A revocation under paragraph (c)(3)(i) of this section must be in writing.

(*Authority:* 20 U.S.C. 1232g(a)(1) (A), (B), (C), and (D))

[53 FR 11943, Apr. 11, 1988, as amended at 61 FR 59296, Nov. 21, 1996]

Subpart C—What Are the Procedures for Amending Education Records?

§ 99.20 How Can a Parent or Eligible Student Request Amendment of the Student's Education Records?

(a) If a parent or eligible student believes the education records relating to the student contain information that is inaccurate, misleading, or in violation of the student's rights of privacy, he or she may ask the educational agency or institution to amend the record.

(b) The educational agency or institution shall decide whether to amend the record as requested within a reasonable time after the agency or institution receives the request.

(c) If the educational agency or institution decides not to amend the record as requested, it shall inform the parent or eligible student of its decision and of his or her right to a hearing under §99.21.

(*Authority:* 20 U.S.C. 1232g(a)(2))

[53 FR 11943, Apr. 11, 1988; 53 FR 19368, May 27, 1988, as amended at 61 FR 59296, Nov. 21, 1996]

§ 99.21 Under What Conditions Does a Parent or Eligible Student Have the Right to a Hearing?

(a) An educational agency or institution shall give a parent or eligible student, on request, an opportunity for a hearing to challenge the content of the student's education records on the grounds that the information contained in the education records is inaccurate, misleading, or in violation of the privacy rights of the student.

(b) (1) If, as a result of the hearing, the educational agency or institution decides that the information is inaccurate, misleading, or otherwise in violation of the privacy rights of the student, it shall:

(i) Amend the record accordingly; and

(ii) Inform the parent or eligible student of the amendment in writing.

(2) If, as a result of the hearing, the educational agency or institution decides that the information in the education record is not inaccurate, misleading, or otherwise in violation of the privacy rights of the student, it shall inform the parent or eligible student of the right to place a statement in the record commenting on the contested information in the record or stating why he or she disagrees with the decision of the agency or institution, or both.

(c) If an educational agency or institution places a statement in the education records of a student under paragraph (b)(2) of this section, the agency or institution shall:

(1) Maintain the statement with the contested part of the record for as long as the record is maintained; and

(2) Disclose the statement whenever it discloses the portion of the record to which the statement relates.

(*Authority:* 20 U.S.C. 1232g(a)(2))
[53 FR 11943, Apr. 11, 1988, as amended at 61 FR 59296, Nov. 21, 1996]

§ 99.22 What Minimum Requirements Exist for the Conduct of a Hearing?

The hearing required by §99.21 must meet, at a minimum, the following requirements:

(a) The educational agency or institution shall hold the hearing within a reasonable time after it has received the request for the hearing from the parent or eligible student.

(b) The educational agency or institution shall give the parent or eligible student notice of the date, time, and place, reasonably in advance of the hearing.

(c) The hearing may be conducted by any individual, including an official of the educational agency or institution, who does not have a direct interest in the outcome of the hearing.

(d) The educational agency or institution shall give the parent or eligible student a full and fair opportunity to present evidence relevant to the issues raised under §99.21. The parent or eligible student may, at their own expense, be assisted or represented by one or more individuals of his or her own choice, including an attorney.

(e) The educational agency or institution shall make its decision in writing within a reasonable period of time after the hearing.

(f) The decision must be based solely on the evidence presented at the hearing, and must include a summary of the evidence and the reasons for the decision.

(*Authority:* 20 U.S.C. 1232g(a)(2))

Subpart D—May an Educational Agency or Institution Disclose Personally Identifiable Information from Education Records?

§ 99.30 Under What Conditions Is Prior Consent Required to Disclose Information?

(a) The parent or eligible student shall provide a signed and dated written consent before an educational agency or institution discloses personally identifiable information from the student's education records, except as provided in §99.31.

(b) The written consent must:

    (1) Specify the records that may be disclosed;

    (2) State the purpose of the disclosure; and

    (3) Identify the party or class of parties to whom the disclosure may be made.

(c) When a disclosure is made under paragraph (a) of this section:

    (1) If a parent or eligible student so requests, the educational agency or institution shall provide him or her with a copy of the records disclosed; and

    (2) If the parent of a student who is not an eligible student so requests, the agency or institution shall provide the student with a copy of the records disclosed.

(d) "Signed and dated written consent" under this part may include a record and signature in electronic form that—

    (1) Identifies and authenticates a particular person as the source of the electronic consent; and

(2) Indicates such person's approval of the information contained in the electronic consent.

(*Authority:* 20 U.S.C. 1232g (b)(1) and (b)(2)(A))

[53 FR 11943, Apr. 11, 1988, as amended at 58 FR 3189, Jan. 7, 1993; 69 FR 21671, Apr. 21, 2004]

§ 99.31 Under What Conditions Is Prior Consent Not Required to Disclose Information?

(a) An educational agency or institution may disclose personally identifiable information from an education record of a student without the consent required by §99.30 if the disclosure meets one or more of the following conditions:

(1) (i) (A) The disclosure is to other school officials, including teachers, within the agency or institution whom the agency or institution has determined to have legitimate educational interests.

(B) A contractor, consultant, volunteer, or other party to whom an agency or institution has outsourced institutional services or functions may be considered a school official under this paragraph provided that the outside party—

(*1*) Performs an institutional service or function for which the agency or institution would otherwise use employees;

(*2*) Is under the direct control of the agency or institution with respect to the use and maintenance of education records; and

(*3*) Is subject to the requirements of §99.33(a) governing the use and redisclosure of personally identifiable information from education records.

(ii) An educational agency or institution must use reasonable methods to ensure that school officials obtain access to only those education records in which they have legitimate educational interests. An educational agency or institution that does not use physical or technological access controls must ensure that its administrative policy for controlling access to education records is effective and that it remains in compliance with the legitimate educational interest requirement in paragraph (a)(1)(i)(A) of this section.

(2) The disclosure is, subject to the requirements of §99.34, to officials of another school, school system, or institution of postsecondary education where the student seeks or intends to enroll, or where the student

is already enrolled so long as the disclosure is for purposes related to the student's enrollment or transfer.

Note: Section 4155(b) of the No Child Left Behind Act of 2001, 20 U.S.C. 7165(b), requires each State to assure the Secretary of Education that it has a procedure in place to facilitate the transfer of disciplinary records with respect to a suspension or expulsion of a student by a local educational agency to any private or public elementary or secondary school in which the student is subsequently enrolled or seeks, intends, or is instructed to enroll.

(3) The disclosure is, subject to the requirements of §99.35, to authorized representatives of—

   (i) The Comptroller General of the United States;

   (ii) The Attorney General of the United States;

   (iii) The Secretary; or

   (iv) State and local educational authorities.

(4) (i) The disclosure is in connection with financial aid for which the student has applied or which the student has received, if the information is necessary for such purposes as to:

   (A) Determine eligibility for the aid;

   (B) Determine the amount of the aid;

   (C) Determine the conditions for the aid; or

   (D) Enforce the terms and conditions of the aid.

   (ii) As used in paragraph (a)(4)(i) of this section, *financial aid* means a payment of funds provided to an individual (or a payment in kind of tangible or intangible property to the individual) that is conditioned on the individual's attendance at an educational agency or institution.

(*Authority:* 20 U.S.C. 1232g(b)(1)(D))

(5) (i) The disclosure is to State and local officials or authorities to whom this information is specifically—

   (A) Allowed to be reported or disclosed pursuant to State statute adopted before November 19, 1974, if the allowed reporting or disclosure concerns the juvenile justice system and the system's ability to effectively serve the student whose records are released; or

   (B) Allowed to be reported or disclosed pursuant to State statute adopted after November 19, 1974, subject to the requirements of §99.38.

(ii) Paragraph (a)(5)(i) of this section does not prevent a State from further limiting the number or type of State or local officials to whom disclosures may be made under that paragraph.

(6) (i) The disclosure is to organizations conducting studies for, or on behalf of, educational agencies or institutions to:

(A) Develop, validate, or administer predictive tests;

(B) Administer student aid programs; or

(C) Improve instruction.

(ii) An educational agency or institution may disclose information under paragraph (a)(6)(i) of this section only if—

(A) The study is conducted in a manner that does not permit personal identification of parents and students by individuals other than representatives of the organization that have legitimate interests in the information;

(B) The information is destroyed when no longer needed for the purposes for which the study was conducted; and

(C) The educational agency or institution enters into a written agreement with the organization that—

(1) Specifies the purpose, scope, and duration of the study or studies and the information to be disclosed;

(2) Requires the organization to use personally identifiable information from education records only to meet the purpose or purposes of the study as stated in the written agreement;

(3) Requires the organization to conduct the study in a manner that does not permit personal identification of parents and students, as defined in this part, by anyone other than representatives of the organization with legitimate interests;

and

(4) Requires the organization to destroy or return to the educational agency or institution all personally identifiable information when the information is no longer needed for the purposes for which the study was conducted and specifies the time period in which the information must be returned or destroyed.

(iii) An educational agency or institution is not required to initiate a study or agree with or endorse the conclusions or results of the study.

(iv) If this Office determines that a third party outside the educational agency or institution to whom information is disclosed under this paragraph (a)(6) violates paragraph (a)(6)(ii)(B) of this section, the educational agency or institution may not allow that third party access to personally identifiable information from education records for at least five years.

(v) For the purposes of paragraph (a)(6) of this section, the term *organization* includes, but is not limited to, Federal, State, and local agencies, and independent organizations.

(7) The disclosure is to accrediting organizations to carry out their accrediting functions.

(8) The disclosure is to parents, as defined in §99.3, of a dependent student, as defined in section 152 of the Internal Revenue Code of 1986.

(9) (i) The disclosure is to comply with a judicial order or lawfully issued subpoena.

(ii) The educational agency or institution may disclose information under paragraph (a)(9)(i) of this section only if the agency or institution makes a reasonable effort to notify the parent or eligible student of the order or subpoena in advance of compliance, so that the parent or eligible student may seek protective action, unless the disclosure is in compliance with—

(A) A Federal grand jury subpoena and the court has ordered that the existence or the contents of the subpoena or the information furnished in response to the subpoena not be disclosed;

(B) Any other subpoena issued for a law enforcement purpose and the court or other issuing agency has ordered that the existence or the contents of the subpoena or the information furnished in response to the subpoena not be disclosed; or

(C) An *ex parte* court order obtained by the United States Attorney General (or designee not lower than an Assistant Attorney General) concerning investigations or prosecutions of an offense listed in 18 U.S.C. 2332b(g)(5)(B) or an act of domestic or international terrorism as defined in 18 U.S.C. 2331.

(iii) (A) If an educational agency or institution initiates legal action against a parent or student, the educational agency or institution may disclose to the court, without a court order or subpoena, the education records of the student that are relevant for the educational agency or institution to proceed with the legal action as plaintiff.

(B) If a parent or eligible student initiates legal action against an educational agency or institution, the educational agency or institution may disclose to the court, without a court order or subpoena, the student's education records that are relevant for the educational agency or institution to defend itself.

(10)   The disclosure is in connection with a health or safety emergency, under the conditions described in §99.36.

(11)   The disclosure is information the educational agency or institution has designated as "directory information," under the conditions described in §99.37.

(12)   The disclosure is to the parent of a student who is not an eligible student or to the student.

(13)   The disclosure, subject to the requirements in §99.39, is to a victim of an alleged perpetrator of a crime of violence or a non-forcible sex offense. The disclosure may only include the final results of the disciplinary proceeding conducted by the institution of postsecondary education with respect to that alleged crime or offense. The institution may disclose the final results of the disciplinary proceeding, regardless of whether the institution concluded a violation was committed.

(14)   (i) The disclosure, subject to the requirements in §99.39, is in connection with a disciplinary proceeding at an institution of postsecondary education. The institution must not disclose the final results of the disciplinary proceeding unless it determines that—

(A) The student is an alleged perpetrator of a crime of violence or non-forcible sex offense; and

(B) With respect to the allegation made against him or her, the student has committed a violation of the institution's rules or policies.

(ii) The institution may not disclose the name of any other student, including a victim or witness, without the prior written consent of the other student.

(iii) This section applies only to disciplinary proceedings in which the final results were reached on or after October 7, 1998.

(15)   (i) The disclosure is to a parent of a student at an institution of postsecondary education regarding the student's violation of any Federal, State, or local law, or of any rule or policy of the institution, governing the use or possession of alcohol or a controlled substance if—

(A) The institution determines that the student has committed a disciplinary violation with respect to that use or possession; and

(B) The student is under the age of 21 at the time of the disclosure to the parent.

(ii) Paragraph (a)(15) of this section does not supersede any provision of State law that prohibits an institution of postsecondary education from disclosing information.

(16) The disclosure concerns sex offenders and other individuals required to register under section 170101 of the Violent Crime Control and Law Enforcement Act of 1994, 42 U.S.C. 14071, and the information was provided to the educational agency or institution under 42 U.S.C. 14071 and applicable Federal guidelines.

(b) (1) *De-identified records and information.* An educational agency or institution, or a party that has received education records or information from education records under this part, may release the records or information without the consent required by §99.30 after the removal of all personally identifiable information provided that the educational agency or institution or other party has made a reasonable determination that a student's identity is not personally identifiable, whether through single or multiple releases, and taking into account other reasonably available information.

(2) An educational agency or institution, or a party that has received education records or information from education records under this part, may release de-identified student level data from education records for the purpose of education research by attaching a code to each record that may allow the recipient to match information received from the same source, provided that—

(i) An educational agency or institution or other party that releases de-identified data under paragraph (b)(2) of this section does not disclose any information about how it generates and assigns a record code, or that would allow a recipient to identify a student based on a record code;

(ii) The record code is used for no purpose other than identifying a de-identified record for purposes of education research and cannot be used to ascertain personally identifiable information about a student; and

(iii) The record code is not based on a student's social security number or other personal information.

(c) An educational agency or institution must use reasonable methods to identify and authenticate the identity of parents, students, school officials, and any other parties to whom the agency or institution discloses personally identifiable information from education records.

(d) Paragraphs (a) and (b) of this section do not require an educational agency or institution or any other party to disclose education records or information from education records to any party except for parties under paragraph (a)(12)of this section.

(*Authority:* 20 U.S.C. 1232g(a)(5)(A), (b), (h), (i), and (j)).

[53 FR 11943, Apr. 11, 1988; 53 FR 19368, May 27, 1988, as amended at 58 FR 3189, Jan. 7, 1993; 61 FR 59296, Nov. 21, 1996; 65 FR 41853, July 6, 2000; 73 FR 74852, Dec, 9, 2008; 74 FR 401, Jan. 6, 2009]

§ 99.32 What Recordkeeping Requirements Exist Concerning Requests and Disclosures?

(a) (1) An educational agency or institution must maintain a record of each request for access to and each disclosure of personally identifiable information from the education records of each student, as well as the names of State and local educational authorities and Federal officials and agencies listed in §99.31(a)(3) that may make further disclosures of personally identifiable information from the student's education records without consent under §99.33(b).

(2) The agency or institution shall maintain the record with the education records of the student as long as the records are maintained.

(3) For each request or disclosure the record must include:

(i)The parties who have requested or received personally identifiable information from the education records; and

(ii)The legitimate interests the parties had in requesting or obtaining the information.

(4) An educational agency or institution must obtain a copy of the record of further disclosures maintained under paragraph (b)(2) of this section and make it available in response to a parent's or eligible student's request to review the record required under paragraph (a)(1) of this section.

(5) An educational agency or institution must record the following information when it discloses personally identifiable information from education records under the health or safety emergency exception in §99.31(a)(10) and §99.36:

(i) The articulable and significant threat to the health or safety of a student or other individuals that formed the basis for the disclosure; and

(ii) The parties to whom the agency or institution disclosed the information.

(b) (1) Except as provided in paragraph (b)(2) of this section, if an educational agency or institution discloses personally identifiable information from education records with the understanding authorized under §99.33(b), the record of the disclosure required under this section must include:

   (i) The names of the additional parties to which the receiving party may disclose the information on behalf of the educational agency or institution; and

   (ii) The legitimate interests under §99.31 which each of the additional parties has in requesting or obtaining the information.

(2) (i) A State or local educational authority or Federal official or agency listed in §99.31(a)(3) that makes further disclosures of information from education records under §99.33(b) must record the names of the additional parties to which it discloses information on behalf of an educational agency or institution and their legitimate interests in the information under §99.31 if the information was received from:

   (A) An educational agency or institution that has not recorded the further disclosures under paragraph (b)(1) of this section; or

   (B) Another State or local educational authority or Federal official or agency listed in §99.31(a)(3).

   (ii) A State or local educational authority or Federal official or agency that records further disclosures of information under paragraph (b)(2)(i) of this section may maintain the record by the student's class, school, district, or other appropriate grouping rather than by the name of the student.

   (iii) Upon request of an educational agency or institution, a State or local educational authority or Federal official or agency listed in §99.31(a)(3) that maintains a record of further disclosures under paragraph (b)(2)(i) of this section must provide a copy of the record of further disclosures to the educational agency or institution within a reasonable period of time not to exceed 30 days.

(c) The following parties may inspect the record relating to each student:

(1) The parent or eligible student.

(2) The school official or his or her assistants who are responsible for the custody of the records.

(3) Those parties authorized in §99.31(a) (1) and (3) for the purposes of auditing the recordkeeping procedures of the educational agency or institution.

(d) Paragraph (a) of this section does not apply if the request was from, or the disclosure was to:

(1) The parent or eligible student;

(2) A school official under §99.31(a)(1);

(3) A party with written consent from the parent or eligible student;

(4) A party seeking directory information; or

(5) A party seeking or receiving records in accordance with §99.31(a)(9) (ii)(A) through (C).

(Approved by the Office of Management and Budget under control number 1880–0508)

(*Authority:* 20 U.S.C. 1232g(b)(1) and (b)(4)(A))

[53 FR 11943, Apr. 11, 1988, as amended at 61 FR 59297, Nov. 21, 1996; 73 FR 74853, Dec. 9, 2008]

§ 99.33 What Limitations Apply to the Redisclosure of Information?

(a) (1) An educational agency or institution may disclose personally identifiable information from an education record only on the condition that the party to whom the information is disclosed will not disclose the information to any other party without the prior consent of the parent or eligible student.

(2) The officers, employees, and agents of a party that receives information under paragraph (a)(1) of this section may use the information, but only for the purposes for which the disclosure was made.

(b) (1) Paragraph (a) of this section does not prevent an educational agency or institution from disclosing personally identifiable information with the understanding that the party receiving the information may make further disclosures of the information on behalf of the educational agency or institution if—

(i) The disclosures meet the requirements of §99.31; and

(ii) (A) The educational agency or institution has complied with the requirements of §99.32(b); or

(B) A State or local educational authority or Federal official or agency listed in §99.31(a)(3) has complied with the requirements of §99.32(b)(2).

(2) A party that receives a court order or lawfully issued subpoena and rediscloses personally identifiable information from education records on behalf of an educational agency or institution in response to that order or subpoena under §99.31(a)(9) must provide the notification required under §99.31(a)(9)(ii).

(c) Paragraph (a) of this section does not apply to disclosures under §§99.31(a)(8), (9), (11), (12), (14), (15), and (16), and to information that postsecondary institutions are required to disclose under the Jeanne Clery Disclosure of Campus Security Policy and Campus Crime Statistics Act, 20 U.S.C. 1092(f) (Clery Act), to the accuser and accused regarding the outcome of any campus disciplinary proceeding brought alleging a sexual offense.

(d) An educational agency or institution must inform a party to whom disclosure is made of the requirements of paragraph (a) of this section except for disclosures made under §§99.31(a)(8), (9), (11), (12), (14), (15), and (16), and to information that postsecondary institutions are required to disclose under the Clery Act to the accuser and accused regarding the outcome of any campus disciplinary proceeding brought alleging a sexual offense.

(e) If this Office determines that a third party outside the educational agency or institution improperly rediscloses personally identifiable information from education records in violation of this section, or fails to provide the notification required under paragraph (b)(2) of this section, the educational agency or institution may not allow that third party access to personally identifiable information from education records for at least five years.

(*Authority:* 20 U.S.C. 1232g(b)(4)(B))

[53 FR 11943, Apr. 11, 1988, as amended at 61 FR 59297, Nov. 21, 1996; 65 FR 41853, July 6, 2000; 73 FR 74853, Dec. 9, 2008]

§ 99.34 What Conditions Apply to Disclosure of Information to Other Educational Agencies or Institutions?

(a) An educational agency or institution that discloses an education record under §99.31(a)(2) shall:

(1) Make a reasonable attempt to notify the parent or eligible student at the last known address of the parent or eligible student, unless:

(i) The disclosure is initiated by the parent or eligible student; or

(ii) The annual notification of the agency or institution under §99.7 includes a notice that the agency or institution forwards education records to other agencies or institutions that have requested the records and in which the student seeks or intends to enroll or is already enrolled so long as the disclosure is for purposes related to the student's enrollment or transfer;

(2) Give the parent or eligible student, upon request, a copy of the record that was disclosed; and

(3) Give the parent or eligible student, upon request, an opportunity for a hearing under subpart C.

(b) An educational agency or institution may disclose an education record of a student in attendance to another educational agency or institution if:

(1) The student is enrolled in or receives services from the other agency or institution; and

(2) The disclosure meets the requirements of paragraph (a) of this section.

(*Authority:* 20 U.S.C. 1232g(b)(1)(B))

[53 FR 11943, Apr. 11, 1988, as amended at 61 FR 59297, Nov. 21, 1996; 73 FR 74854, Dec. 9, 2008]

§ 99.35 What Conditions Apply to Disclosure of Information for Federal or State Program Purposes?

(a) (1) Authorized representatives of the officials or agencies headed by officials listed in §99.31(a)(3) may have access to education records in connection with an audit or evaluation of Federal or State supported education programs, or for the enforcement of or compliance with Federal legal requirements that relate to those programs.

(2) Authority for an agency or official listed in §99.31(a)(3) to conduct an audit, evaluation, or compliance or enforcement activity is not conferred by the Act or this part and must be established under other Federal, State, or local authority.

(b) Information that is collected under paragraph (a) of this section must:

(1) Be protected in a manner that does not permit personal identification of individuals by anyone other than the officials or agencies headed by officials referred to in paragraph (a) of this section, except that those officials and agencies may make further disclosures of personally identifiable information from education records on behalf of the

educational agency or institution in accordance with the requirements of §99.33(b); and

(2) Be destroyed when no longer needed for the purposes listed in paragraph (a) of this section.

(c) Paragraph (b) of this section does not apply if:

(1) The parent or eligible student has given written consent for the disclosure under §99.30; or

(2) The collection of personally identifiable information is specifically authorized by Federal law.

(*Authority:* 20 U.S.C. 1232g(b)(3))

[53 FR 11943, Apr. 11, 1988, as amended at 73 FR 74854, Dec. 9, 2008]

§ 99.36 What Conditions Apply to Disclosure of Information in Health and Safety Emergencies?

(a) An educational agency or institution may disclose personally identifiable information from an education record to appropriate parties, including parents of an eligible student, in connection with an emergency if knowledge of the information is necessary to protect the health or safety of the student or other individuals.

(b) Nothing in this Act or this part shall prevent an educational agency or institution from—

(1) Including in the education records of a student appropriate information concerning disciplinary action taken against the student for conduct that posed a significant risk to the safety or well-being of that student, other students, or other members of the school community;

(2) Disclosing appropriate information maintained under paragraph (b)(1) of this section to teachers and school officials within the agency or institution who the agency or institution has determined have legitimate educational interests in the behavior of the student; or

(3) Disclosing appropriate information maintained under paragraph (b)(1) of this section to teachers and school officials in other schools who have been determined to have legitimate educational interests in the behavior of the student.

(c) In making a determination under paragraph (a) of this section, an educational agency or institution may take into account the totality of the circumstances pertaining to a threat to the health or safety of a student or other individuals. If the educational agency or institution determines that there is an articulable and significant threat to the health or safety of a student or other individuals, it may disclose information from education records to any person whose knowledge of the information is necessary to protect the health or safety of the student or other individuals. If, based on the information available at the time of the determination, there is a rational basis for the determination, the Department will not substitute its judgment for that of the educational agency or institution in evaluating the circumstances and making its determination.

(*Authority:* 20 U.S.C. 1232g (b)(1)(I) and (h))

[53 FR 11943, Apr. 11, 1988; 53 FR 19368, May 27, 1988, as amended at 61 FR 59297, Nov. 21, 1996; 73 FR 74854, Dec. 9, 2008]

§ 99.37 What Conditions Apply to Disclosing Directory Information?

(a) An educational agency or institution may disclose directory information if it has given public notice to parents of students in attendance and eligible students in attendance at the agency or institution of:

(1) The types of personally identifiable information that the agency or institution has designated as directory information;

(2) A parent's or eligible student's right to refuse to let the agency or institution designate any or all of those types of information about the student as directory information; and

(3) The period of time within which a parent or eligible student has to notify the agency or institution in writing that he or she does not want any or all of those types of information about the student designated as directory information.

(b) An educational agency or institution may disclose directory information about former students without complying with the notice and opt out conditions in paragraph (a) of this section. However, the agency or institution must continue to honor any valid request to opt out of the disclosure of directory information made while a student was in attendance unless the student rescinds the opt out request.

(c) A parent or eligible student may not use the right under paragraph (a)(2) of this section to opt out of directory information disclosures to prevent an educational agency or institution from disclosing or requiring a student to disclose the student's name, identifier, or institutional e-mail address in a class in which the student is enrolled.

(d) An educational agency or institution may not disclose or confirm directory information without meeting the written consent requirements in §99.30 if a student's social security number or other non-directory information is used alone or combined with other data elements to identify or help identify the student or the student's records.

(*Authority:* 20 U.S.C. 1232g(a)(5) (A) and (B))

[53 FR 11943, Apr. 11, 1988, as amended at 73 FR 74854, Dec. 9, 2008]

§ 99.38 What Conditions Apply to Disclosure of Information as Permitted by State Statute Adopted after November 19, 1974, Concerning the Juvenile Justice System?

(a) If reporting or disclosure allowed by State statute concerns the juvenile justice system and the system's ability to effectively serve, prior to adjudication, the student whose records are released, an educational agency or institution may disclose education records under §99.31(a)(5)(i)(B).

(b) The officials and authorities to whom the records are disclosed shall certify in writing to the educational agency or institution that the information will not be disclosed to any other party, except as provided under State law, without the prior written consent of the parent of the student.

(*Authority:* 20 U.S.C. 1232g(b)(1)(J))

[61 FR 59297, Nov. 21, 1996]

§ 99.39 What Definitions Apply to the Nonconsensual Disclosure of Records by Postsecondary Educational Institutions in Connection with Disciplinary Proceedings Concerning Crimes of Violence or Non-Forcible Sex Offenses?

As used in this part:

Alleged perpetrator of a crime of violence is a student who is alleged to have committed acts that would, if proven, constitute any of the following offenses or attempts to commit the following offenses that are defined in appendix A to this part:

Arson

Assault offenses

Burglary

Criminal homicide—manslaughter by negligence

Criminal homicide—murder and nonnegligent manslaughter

Destruction/damage/vandalism of property

Kidnapping/abduction

Robbery

Forcible sex offenses.

Alleged perpetrator of a nonforcible sex offense means a student who is alleged to have committed acts that, if proven, would constitute statutory rape or incest. These offenses are defined in appendix A to this part.

Final results means a decision or determination, made by an honor court or council, committee, commission, or other entity authorized to resolve disciplinary matters within the institution. The disclosure of final results must include only the name of the student, the violation committed, and any sanction imposed by the institution against the student.

Sanction imposed means a description of the disciplinary action taken by the institution, the date of its imposition, and its duration.

Violation committed means the institutional rules or code sections that were violated and any essential findings supporting the institution's conclusion that the violation was committed.

(*Authority:* 20 U.S.C. 1232g(b)(6))

[65 FR 41853, July 6, 2000]

Subpart E—What Are the Enforcement Procedures?

§ 99.60 What Functions Has the Secretary Delegated to the Office and to the Office of Administrative Law Judges?

(a) For the purposes of this subpart, *Office* means the Family Policy Compliance Office, U.S. Department of Education.

(b) The Secretary designates the Office to:

    (1) Investigate, process, and review complaints and violations under the Act and this part; and

    (2) Provide technical assistance to ensure compliance with the Act and this part.

(c) The Secretary designates the Office of Administrative Law Judges to act as the Review Board required under the Act to enforce the Act with respect to all applicable programs. The term *applicable program* is defined in section 400 of the General Education Provisions Act.

(*Authority:* 20 U.S.C. 1232g (f) and (g), 1234)

[53 FR 11943, Apr. 11, 1988, as amended at 58 FR 3189, Jan. 7, 1993]

§ 99.61 What Responsibility Does an Educational Agency or Institution Have Concerning Conflict with State or Local Laws?

If an educational agency or institution determines that it cannot comply with the Act or this part due to a conflict with State or local law, it shall notify the Office within 45 days, giving the text and citation of the conflicting law.

(*Authority:* 20 U.S.C. 1232g(f))

§ 99.62 What Information Must an Educational Agency or Institution Submit to the Office?

The Office may require an educational agency or institution to submit reports, information on policies and procedures, annual notifications, training materials, and other information necessary to carry out its enforcement responsibilities under the Act or this part.

(*Authority:* 20 U.S.C. 1232g(f) and (g))

[73 FR 74854, Dec. 9, 2008]

§ 99.63 Where Are Complaints Filed?

A parent or eligible student may file a written complaint with the Office regarding an alleged violation under the Act and this part. The Office's address is: Family Policy Compliance Office, U.S. Department of Education, 400 Maryland Avenue, SW., Washington, DC 20202.

(*Authority:* 20 U.S.C. 1232g(g))

[65 FR 41854, July 6, 2000, as amended at 73 FR 74854, Dec. 9, 2008]

§ 99.64 What Is the Investigation Procedure?

(a) A complaint must contain specific allegations of fact giving reasonable cause to believe that a violation of the Act or this part has occurred. A complaint does not have to allege that a violation is based on a policy or practice of the educational agency or institution.

(b) The Office investigates a timely complaint filed by a parent or eligible student, or conducts its own investigation when no complaint has been filed or a complaint has been withdrawn, to determine whether an educational agency or institution has failed to comply with a provision of the Act or this part. If the Office determines that an educational agency or institution has failed to comply with a provision of the Act or this part, it may also determine whether the failure to comply is based on a policy or practice of the agency or institution

(c) A timely complaint is defined as an allegation of a violation of the Act that is submitted to the Office within 180 days of the date of the alleged violation or of the date that the complainant knew or reasonably should have known of the alleged violation.

(d) The Office may extend the time limit in this section for good cause shown.

(*Authority:* 20 U.S.C. 1232g(f))

[53 FR 11943, Apr. 11, 1988, as amended at 58 FR 3189, Jan. 7, 1993; 65 FR 41854, July 6, 2000; 73 FR 74854, Dec. 9, 2008]

§ 99.65 What Is the Content of the Notice of Investigation Issued by the Office?

(a) The Office notifies the complainant, if any, and the educational agency or institution in writing if it initiates an investigation under §99.64(b). The notice to the educational agency or institution—

(1) Includes the substance of the allegations against the educational agency or institution; and

(2) Directs the agency or institution to submit a written response and other relevant information, as set forth in §99.62, within a specified period of time, including information about its policies and practices regarding education records.

(b) The Office notifies the complainant if it does not initiate an investigation because the complaint fails to meet the requirements of §99.64.

(*Authority:* 20 U.S.C. 1232g(g))

[73 FR 74855, Dec. 9, 2008]

§ 99.66 What Are the Responsibilities of the Office in the Enforcement Process?

(a) The Office reviews a complaint, if any, information submitted by the educational agency or institution, and any other relevant information. The Office may permit the parties to submit further written or oral arguments or information.

(b) Following its investigation, the Office provides to the complainant, if any, and the educational agency or institution a written notice of its findings and the basis for its findings.

(c) If the Office finds that an educational agency or institution has not complied with a provision of the Act or this part, it may also find that the failure to comply was based on a policy or practice of the agency or institution. A notice of findings issued under paragraph (b) of this section to an educational agency or institution that has not complied with a provision of the Act or this part—

(1) Includes a statement of the specific steps that the agency or institution must take to comply; and

(2) Provides a reasonable period of time, given all of the circumstances of the case, during which the educational agency or institution may comply voluntarily.

(*Authority:* 20 U.S.C. 1232g(f))

[53 FR 11943, Apr. 11, 1988, as amended at 73 FR 74855, Dec. 9, 2008]

§ 99.67 How Does the Secretary Enforce Decisions?

(a) If an educational agency or institution does not comply during the period of time set under §99.66(c), the Secretary may take any legally available enforcement action in accordance with the Act, including, but not limited to, the following enforcement actions available in accordance with part E of the General Education Provisions Act—

(1) Withhold further payments under any applicable program;

(2) Issue a compliant to compel compliance through a cease-and-desist order; or

(3) Terminate eligibility to receive funding under any applicable program.

(b) If, after an investigation under §99.66, the Secretary finds that an educational agency or institution has complied voluntarily with the Act or this part, the Secretary provides the complainant and the agency or institution written notice of the decision and the basis for the decision.

(Note: 34 CFR part 78 contains the regulations of the Education Appeal Board)

(*Authority:* 20 U.S.C. 1232g(f); 20 U.S.C. 1234)

[53 FR 11943, Apr. 11, 1988; 53 FR 19368, May 27, 1988, as amended at 58 FR 3189, Jan. 7, 1993; 73 FR 74855, Dec. 9, 2008]

Appendix A to Part 99—Crimes of Violence Definitions

Arson

Any willful or malicious burning or attempt to burn, with or without intent to defraud, a dwelling house, public building, motor vehicle or aircraft, personal property of another, etc.

Assault Offenses

An unlawful attack by one person upon another.

Note: By definition there can be no "attempted" assaults, only "completed" assaults.

(a) *Aggravated Assault*. An unlawful attack by one person upon another for the purpose of inflicting severe or aggravated bodily injury. This type of assault usually is accompanied by the use of a weapon or by means likely to produce death or great bodily harm. (It is not necessary that injury result from an aggravated assault when a gun, knife, or other weapon is used which could and probably would result in serious injury if the crime were successfully completed.)

(b) *Simple Assault*. An unlawful physical attack by one person upon another where neither the offender displays a weapon, nor the victim suffers obvious severe or aggravated bodily injury involving apparent broken bones, loss of teeth, possible internal injury, severe laceration, or loss of consciousness.

(c) *Intimidation*. To unlawfully place another person in reasonable fear of bodily harm through the use of threatening words or other conduct, or both, but without displaying a weapon or subjecting the victim to actual physical attack.

Note: This offense includes stalking.

Burglary

The unlawful entry into a building or other structure with the intent to commit a felony or a theft.

Criminal Homicide—Manslaughter by Negligence

The killing of another person through gross negligence.

Criminal Homicide—Murder and Nonnegligent Manslaughter

The willful (nonnegligent) killing of one human being by another.

Destruction/Damage/Vandalism of Property

To willfully or maliciously destroy, damage, deface, or otherwise injure real or personal property without the consent of the owner or the person having custody or control of it.

Kidnapping/Abduction

The unlawful seizure, transportation, or detention of a person, or any combination of these actions, against his or her will, or of a minor without the consent of his or her custodial parent(s) or legal guardian.

Note: Kidnapping/Abduction includes hostage taking.

Robbery

The taking of, or attempting to take, anything of value under confrontational circumstances from the control, custody, or care of a person or persons by force or threat of force or violence or by putting the victim in fear.

Note: Carjackings are robbery offenses where a motor vehicle is taken through force or threat of force.

Sex Offenses, Forcible

Any sexual act directed against another person, forcibly or against that person's will, or both; or not forcibly or against the person's will where the victim is incapable of giving consent.

(a) *Forcible Rape* (Except "Statutory Rape"). The carnal knowledge of a person, forcibly or against that person's will, or both; or not forcibly or against the person's will where the victim is incapable of giving consent because of his or her temporary or permanent mental or physical incapacity (or because of his or her youth).

(b) *Forcible Sodomy.* Oral or anal sexual intercourse with another person, forcibly or against that person's will, or both; or not forcibly or against the person's will where the victim is incapable of giving consent because of his or her youth or because of his or her temporary or permanent mental or physical incapacity.

(c) *Sexual Assault With An Object.* To use an object or instrument to unlawfully penetrate, however slightly, the genital or anal opening of the body of another person, forcibly or against that person's will, or both; or not forcibly or against the person's will where the victim is incapable of giving consent because of his or her youth or because of his or her temporary or permanent mental or physical incapacity.

Note: An "object" or "instrument" is anything used by the offender other than the offender's genitalia. Examples are a finger, bottle, handgun, stick, etc.

(d) *Forcible Fondling*. The touching of the private body parts of another person for the purpose of sexual gratification, forcibly or against that person's will, or both; or not forcibly or against the person's will where the victim is incapable of giving consent because of his or her youth or because of his or her temporary or permanent mental or physical incapacity.

Note: Forcible Fondling includes "Indecent Liberties" and "Child Molesting."

Nonforcible Sex Offenses (Except "Prostitution Offenses")
Unlawful, nonforcible sexual intercourse.

(a) *Incest*. Nonforcible sexual intercourse between persons who are related to each other within the degrees wherein marriage is prohibited by law.

(b) *Statutory Rape*. Nonforcible sexual intercourse with a person who is under the statutory age of consent.

(*Authority:* 20 U.S.C. 1232g(b)(6) and 18 U.S.C. 16)
[65 FR 41854, July 6, 2000]
[US Code of Federal Regulations, March 2009]

Appendix II

20 USC §1232G

Title 20—Education

Chapter 31—General Provisions Concerning Education

Subchapter III—General Requirements and Conditions Concerning Operation and Administration of Education Programs: General Authority of Secretary

Part 4—Records; Privacy; Limitation on Withholding Federal Funds

Sec. 1232g. Family Educational and privacy rights

[Laws in effect as of January 3, 2007]

(a) Conditions for availability of funds to educational agencies or institutions; inspection and review of education records; specific information to be made available; procedure for access to education records; reasonableness of time for such access; hearings; written explanations by parents; definitions

(1) (A) No funds shall be made available under any applicable program to any educational agency or institution which has a policy of denying, or which effectively prevents, the parents of students who are or have been in attendance at a school of such agency or at such institution, as the case may be, the right to inspect and review the education records of their children. If any material or document in the education record of a student includes information on more than one student, the parents of one of such students shall have the right to inspect and review only such part of such material or document as relates to such student or to be informed of the specific information contained in such part of such material. Each educational agency or institution shall establish appropriate procedures for the granting of a request by parents for access to the education records of their children within a reasonable period of time, but in no case more than forty-five days after the request has been made.

(B) No funds under any applicable program shall be made available to any State educational agency (whether or not that agency is an educational agency or institution under this section) that has a policy of denying, or effectively prevents, the parents of students the right to inspect and review the education records maintained by the State educational agency on their children who are or have been in attendance at any school of an educational agency or institution that is subject to the provisions of this section.

(C) The first sentence of subparagraph (A) shall not operate to make available to students in institutions of postsecondary education the following materials:

(i) financial records of the parents of the student or any information contained therein;

(ii) confidential letters and statements of recommendation, which were placed in the education records prior to January 1, 1975, if such letters or statements are not used for purposes other than those for which they were specifically intended;

(iii) if the student has signed a waiver of the student's right of access under this subsection in accordance with subparagraph (D), confidential recommendations—

(I) respecting admission to any educational agency or institution,

(II) respecting an application for employment, and

(III) respecting the receipt of an honor or honorary recognition.

(D) A student or a person applying for admission may waive his right of access to confidential statements described in clause (iii) of subparagraph (C), except that such waiver shall apply to recommendations only if (i) the student is, upon request, notified of the names of all persons making confidential recommendations and (ii) such recommendations are used solely for the purpose for which they were specifically intended. Such waivers may not be required as a condition for admission to, receipt of financial aid from, or receipt of any other services or benefits from such agency or institution.

(2) No funds shall be made available under any applicable program to any educational agency or institution unless the parents of students who are or have been in attendance at a school of such agency or at such institution are provided an opportunity for a hearing by such agency or institution, in accordance with regulations of the Secretary, to challenge the content of such student's education records, in order to insure that the records are not inaccurate, misleading, or otherwise in violation of the privacy rights of students, and to provide an opportunity for the correction or deletion of any such inaccurate, misleading or otherwise inappropriate data contained therein and to insert into such records a written explanation of the parents respecting the content of such records.

(3) For the purposes of this section the term "educational agency or institution" means any public or private agency or institution which is the recipient of funds under any applicable program.

(4) (A) For the purposes of this section, the term "education records" means, except as may be provided otherwise in subparagraph (B), those records, files, documents, and other materials which—
(i) contain information directly related to a student; and
(ii) are maintained by an educational agency or institution or by a person acting for such agency or institution.
(B) The term "education records" does not include—
(i) records of instructional, supervisory, and administrative personnel and educational personnel ancillary thereto which are in the sole possession of the maker thereof and which are not accessible or revealed to any other person except a substitute;
(ii) records maintained by a law enforcement unit of the educational agency or institution that were created by that law enforcement unit for the purpose of law enforcement;
(iii) in the case of persons who are employed by an educational agency or institution but who are not in attendance at such agency or institution, records made and maintained in the normal course of business which relate exclusively to such person in that person's capacity as an employee and are not available for use for any other purpose; or
(iv) records on a student who is eighteen years of age or older, or is attending an institution of postsecondary education, which are made or maintained by a physician, psychiatrist, psychologist, or other recognized professional or paraprofessional acting in his professional or paraprofessional capacity, or assisting in that capacity, and which are made, maintained, or used only in connection with the provision of treatment to the student, and are not available to anyone other than persons providing such treatment, except that such records can be personally reviewed by a physician or other appropriate professional of the student's choice.

5) (A) For the purposes of this section the term "directory information" relating to a student includes the following: the student's name, address, telephone listing, date and place of birth, major field of study, participation in officially recognized activities and sports, weight and height of members of athletic teams, dates of attendance, degrees and awards received, and the most recent previous educational agency or institution attended by the student.

(B) Any educational agency or institution making public directory information shall give public notice of the categories of information which it has designated as such information with respect to each student attending the institution or agency and shall allow a reasonable period of time after such notice has been given for a parent to inform the institution or agency that any or all of the information designated should not be released without the parent's prior consent.

(6) For the purposes of this section, the term "student" includes any person with respect to whom an educational agency or institution maintains education records or personally identifiable information, but does not include a person who has not been in attendance at such agency or institution.

(b) Release of education records; parental consent requirement; exceptions; compliance with judicial orders and subpoenas; audit and evaluation of federally-supported education programs; recordkeeping

(1) No funds shall be made available under any applicable program to any educational agency or institution which has a policy or practice of permitting the release of education records (or personally identifiable information contained therein other than directory information, as defined in paragraph (5) of subsection (a) of this section) of students without the written consent of their parents to any individual, agency, or organization, other than to the following—

(A) other school officials, including teachers within the educational institution or local educational agency, who have been determined by such agency or institution to have legitimate educational interests, including the educational interests of the child for whom consent would otherwise be required;

(B) officials of other schools or school systems in which the student seeks or intends to enroll, upon condition that the student's parents be notified of the transfer, receive a copy of the record if desired, and have an opportunity for a hearing to challenge the content of the record;

(C) (i) authorized representatives of (I) the Comptroller General of the United States, (II) the Secretary, or (III) State educational authorities, under the conditions set forth in paragraph (3), or

(ii) authorized representatives of the Attorney General for law enforcement purposes under the same conditions as apply to the Secretary under paragraph (3);

(D) in connection with a student's application for, or receipt of, financial aid;

(E) State and local officials or authorities to whom such information is specifically allowed to be reported or disclosed pursuant to State statute adopted--

(i) before November 19, 1974, if the allowed reporting or disclosure concerns the juvenile justice system and such system's ability to effectively serve the student whose records are released, or

      (ii) after November 19, 1974, if—

          (I) the allowed reporting or disclosure concerns the juvenile justice system and such system's ability to effectively serve, prior to adjudication, the student whose records are released; and

          (II) the officials and authorities to whom such information is disclosed certify in writing to the educational agency or institution that the information will not be disclosed to any other party except as provided under State law without the prior written consent of the parent of the student.

(F) organizations conducting studies for, or on behalf of, educational agencies or institutions for the purpose of developing, validating, or administering predictive tests, administering student aid programs, and improving instruction, if such studies are conducted in such a manner as will not permit the personal identification of students and their parents by persons other than representatives of such organizations and such information will be destroyed when no longer needed for the purpose for which it is conducted;

(G) accrediting organizations in order to carry out their accrediting functions;

(H) parents of a dependent student of such parents, as defined in section 152 of title 26;

(I) subject to regulations of the Secretary, in connection with an emergency, appropriate persons if the knowledge of such information is necessary to protect the health or safety of the student or other persons; and

(J) (i) the entity or persons designated in a Federal grand jury subpoena, in which case the court shall order, for good cause shown, the educational agency or institution (and any officer, director, employee, agent, or attorney for such agency or institution) on which the subpoena is served, to not disclose to any person the existence or contents of the subpoena or any information furnished to the grand jury in response to the subpoena; and

      (ii) the entity or persons designated in any other subpoena issued for a law enforcement purpose, in which case the court or other issuing agency may order, for good cause shown, the educational agency or institution (and any officer, director, employee, agent, or attorney for such agency or institution) on which the subpoena is served, to not disclose to any person the existence or contents of the subpoena or any information furnished in response to the subpoena.

Nothing in subparagraph (E) of this paragraph shall prevent a State from further limiting the number or type of State or local officials who will continue to have access thereunder.

(2) No funds shall be made available under any applicable program to any educational agency or institution which has a policy or practice of releasing, or providing access to, any personally identifiable information in education records other than directory information, or as is permitted under paragraph (1) of this subsection, unless—

(A) there is written consent from the student's parents specifying records to be released, the reasons for such release, and to whom, and with a copy of the records to be released to the student's parents and the student if desired by the parents, or

(B) except as provided in paragraph (1)(J), such information is furnished in compliance with judicial order, or pursuant to any lawfully issued subpoena, upon condition that parents and the students are notified of all such orders or subpoenas in advance of the compliance therewith by the educational institution or agency.

(3) Nothing contained in this section shall preclude authorized representatives of (A) the Comptroller General of the United States, (B) the Secretary, or (C) State educational authorities from having access to student or other records which may be necessary in connection with the audit and evaluation of Federally-supported education programs, or in connection with the enforcement of the Federal legal requirements which relate to such programs: Provided, That except when collection of personally identifiable information is specifically authorized by Federal law, any data collected by such officials shall be protected in a manner which will not permit the personal identification of students and their parents by other than those officials, and such personally identifiable data shall be destroyed when no longer needed for such audit, evaluation, and enforcement of Federal legal requirements.

(4) (A) Each educational agency or institution shall maintain a record, kept with the education records of each student, which will indicate all individuals (other than those specified in paragraph (1)(A) of this subsection), agencies, or organizations which have requested or obtained access to a student's education records maintained by such educational agency or institution, and which will indicate specifically the legitimate interest that each such person, agency, or organization has in obtaining this information. Such record of access shall be available only to parents, to the school official and his assistants who are responsible for the custody of such records, and to persons or organizations authorized in, and under the conditions of,

clauses (A) and (C) of paragraph (1) as a means of auditing the operation of the system.

 (B) With respect to this subsection, personal information shall only be transferred to a third party on the condition that such party will not permit any other party to have access to such information without the written consent of the parents of the student. If a third party outside the educational agency or institution permits access to information in violation of paragraph (2)(A), or fails to destroy information in violation of paragraph (1)(F), the educational agency or institution shall be prohibited from permitting access to information from education records to that third party for a period of not less than five years.

(5) Nothing in this section shall be construed to prohibit State and local educational officials from having access to student or other records which may be necessary in connection with the audit and evaluation of any federally or State supported education program or in connection with the enforcement of the Federal legal requirements which relate to any such program, subject to the conditions specified in the proviso in paragraph (3).

(6) (A) Nothing in this section shall be construed to prohibit an institution of postsecondary education from disclosing, to an alleged victim of any crime of violence (as that term is defined in section 16 of title 18), or a nonforcible sex offense, the final results of any disciplinary proceeding conducted by such institution against the alleged perpetrator of such crime or offense with respect to such crime or offense.

 (B) Nothing in this section shall be construed to prohibit an institution of postsecondary education from disclosing the final results of any disciplinary proceeding conducted by such institution against a student who is an alleged perpetrator of any crime of violence (as that term is defined in section 16 of title 18), or a nonforcible sex offense, if the institution determines as a result of that disciplinary proceeding that the student committed a violation of the institution's rules or policies with respect to such crime or offense.

 (C) For the purpose of this paragraph, the final results of any disciplinary proceeding—

  (i) shall include only the name of the student, the violation committed, and any sanction imposed by the institution on that student; and

  (ii) may include the name of any other student, such as a victim or witness, only with the written consent of that other student.

(7) (A) Nothing in this section may be construed to prohibit an educational institution from disclosing information provided to the institution

under section 14071 of title 42 concerning registered sex offenders who are required to register under such section.

(B) The Secretary shall take appropriate steps to notify educational institutions that disclosure of information described in subparagraph (A) is permitted.

(c) Surveys or data-gathering activities; regulations

Not later than 240 days after October 20, 1994, the Secretary shall adopt appropriate regulations or procedures, or identify existing regulations or procedures, which protect the rights of privacy of students and their families in connection with any surveys or data-gathering activities conducted, assisted, or authorized by the Secretary or an administrative head of an education agency. Regulations established under this subsection shall include provisions controlling the use, dissemination, and protection of such data. No survey or data-gathering activities shall be conducted by the Secretary, or an administrative head of an education agency under an applicable program, unless such activities are authorized by law.

(d) Students' rather than parents' permission or consent

For the purposes of this section, whenever a student has attained eighteen years of age, or is attending an institution of postsecondary education, the permission or consent required of and the rights accorded to the parents of the student shall thereafter only be required of and accorded to the student.

(e) Informing parents or students of rights under this section

No funds shall be made available under any applicable program to any educational agency or institution unless such agency or institution effectively informs the parents of students, or the students, if they are eighteen years of age or older, or are attending an institution of postsecondary education, of the rights accorded them by this section.

(f) Enforcement; termination of assistance

The Secretary shall take appropriate actions to enforce this section and to deal with violations of this section, in accordance with this chapter, except that action to terminate assistance may be taken only if the Secretary finds there has been a failure to comply with this section, and he has determined that compliance cannot be secured by voluntary means.

(g) Office and review board; creation; functions

The Secretary shall establish or designate an office and review board within the Department for the purpose of investigating, processing, reviewing, and adjudicating violations of this section and complaints which may be filed concerning alleged violations of this section. Except for the conduct of hearings, none of the functions of the Secretary under this section shall be carried out in any of the regional offices of such Department.

(h) Disciplinary records; disclosure

Nothing in this section shall prohibit an educational agency or institution from—

(1) including appropriate information in the education record of any student concerning disciplinary action taken against such student for conduct that posed a significant risk to the safety or well-being of that student, other students, or other members of the school community; or

(2) disclosing such information to teachers and school officials, including teachers and school officials in other schools, who have legitimate educational interests in the behavior of the student.

(i) Drug and alcohol violation disclosures

(1) In general

Nothing in this Act or the Higher Education Act of 1965 [20 U.S.C. 1001 et seq.] shall be construed to prohibit an institution of higher education from disclosing, to a parent or legal guardian of a student, information regarding any violation of any Federal, State, or local law, or of any rule or policy of the institution, governing the use or possession of alcohol or a controlled substance, regardless of whether that information is contained in the student's education records, if—

(A) the student is under the age of 21; and

(B) the institution determines that the student has committed a disciplinary violation with respect to such use or possession.

(2) State law regarding disclosure

Nothing in paragraph (1) shall be construed to supersede any provision of State law that prohibits an institution of higher education from making the disclosure described in subsection (a) of this section.

(j) Investigation and prosecution of terrorism

(1) In general

Notwithstanding subsections (a) through (i) of this section or any provision of State law, the Attorney General (or any Federal officer or employee, in a position not lower than an Assistant Attorney General, designated by the Attorney General) may submit a written application to a court of competent jurisdiction for an ex parte order requiring an educational agency or institution to permit the Attorney General (or his designee) to—

(A) collect education records in the possession of the educational agency or institution that are relevant to an authorized investigation or prosecution of an offense listed in section 2332b(g)(5)(B) of title 18, or an act of domestic or international terrorism as defined in section 2331 of that title; and

(B) for official purposes related to the investigation or prosecution of an offense described in paragraph (1)(A), retain, disseminate, and use (including as evidence at trial or in other administrative or judicial proceedings) such records, consistent with such guidelines as the Attorney General, after consultation with the Secretary, shall issue to protect confidentiality.

(2) Application and approval

(A) In general. An application under paragraph (1) shall certify that there are specific and articulable facts giving reason to believe that the education records are likely to contain information described in paragraph (1)(A).

(B) The court shall issue an order described in paragraph (1) if the court finds that the application for the order includes the certification described in subparagraph (A).

(3) Protection of educational agency or institution

An educational agency or institution that, in good faith, produces education records in accordance with an order issued under this subsection shall not be liable to any person for that production.

(4) Record-keeping

Subsection (b)(4) of this section does not apply to education records subject to a court order under this subsection.

(Pub. L. 90-247, title IV, Sec. 444, formerly Sec. 438, as added Pub. L. 93-380, title V, Sec. 513(a), Aug. 21, 1974, 88 Stat. 571; amended Pub. L. 93-568, Sec. 2(a), Dec. 31, 1974, 88 Stat. 1858; Pub. L. 96-46, Sec. 4(c), Aug. 6, 1979, 93 Stat. 342; Pub. L. 101-542, title II, Sec. 203, Nov. 8, 1990, 104 Stat. 2385; Pub. L. 102-325, title XV, Sec. 1555(a), July 23, 1992, 106 Stat. 840; renumbered Sec. 444 and amended Pub. L. 103-382, title II, Secs. 212(b)(1), 249, 261(h), Oct. 20, 1994, 108 Stat. 3913, 3924, 3928; Pub. L. 105-244, title IX, Secs. 951, 952, Oct. 7, 1998, 112 Stat. 1835, 1836; Pub. L. 106-386, div. B, title VI, Sec. 1601(d), Oct. 28, 2000, 114 Stat. 1538; Pub. L. 107-56, title V, Sec. 507, Oct. 26, 2001, 115 Stat. 367; Pub. L. 107-110, title X, Sec. 1062(3), Jan. 8, 2002, 115 Stat. 2088.)

Appendix II 20 USC §1232G

Bibliography and Resources

Legislation and Government Publications

U.S. Code of Federal Regulations. Family Educational Rights and Privacy Act (FERPA), 34 CFR §99. Washington D.C.: U.S. Government Printing Office.

U.S. Office of the Federal Register. *The Federal Register,* Part II: Department of Education, 34 CFR Part 99. Washington D.C.: National Archives and Records Administration, Tuesday, December 9, 2008.

U.S. Office of the Federal Register. *The Federal Register,* Part II: Department of Education, 34 CFR Part 99. Washington D.C.: National Archives and Records Administration, Monday, March 24, 2008.

U.S. Office of the Federal Register. *The Federal Register,* Department of the Treasury, Office of the Comptroller of the Currency, 12 CFR Part 41; Federal Reserve System, 12 CFR Part 222; Federal Deposit Insurance Corporation, 12 CFR Parts 334 and 364; Department of the Treasury, Office of Thrift Supervision, 12 CFR 571; National Credit Union Administration, 12 CFR Part 717; Federal Trade Commission, 16 CFR 681. Identity Theft Red Flags and Address Discrepancies Under the Fair and Accurate Credit Transactions Act of 2003; Final Rule. Washington D.C.: National Archives and Records Administration, Friday, November 9, 2007.

U.S. Office of the Federal Register. *The Federal Register,* Part IV: Department of Education, 34 CFR Part 99. Washington D.C.: National Archives and Records Administration, Monday, July 28, 2003.

Publications

AACRAO's Retention of Records: Guide for Retention and Disposal of Student Records. Washington, DC: American Association of Collegiate Registrars and Admissions Officers, 2000.

Arquieta-Herrera, Linda, and Ramirez, Clifford A., *Records Management in Higher Education: Ensuring Organization, Efficiency, and Legal Compliance.* Horsham, PA: LRP Publications, 2006.

Bakst, Daren, and Burgess, Sylvia, editors. *Privacy in the 21st Century: An Annual Review and Compendium for Higher Education Leaders.* Palm Beach Gardens, FL: Council on Law in Higher Education, 2004.

Gelpi, Aileen, and Ramirez, Clifford A., editors, *The FERPA Answer Book for Higher Education Professionals.* San Francisco: Jossey-Bass, 2009.

Hicks, Dennis J., Baker, Eliot G., Hawkey, Earl, Myers, Brad A., and Weese, Faith A., editors. *AACRAO 2006 FERPA Guide.* Washington, DC: American Association of Collegiate Registrars and Admissions Officers, 2006.

Lauren, Barbara, editor. *The Registrar's Guide: Evolving Best Practices in Records and Registration.* Washington, DC: American Association of Collegiate Registrars and Admissions Officers, 2006.

Ramirez, Clifford A., *The FERPA Transition: Helping Parents Adjust to Higher Education Records Laws.* Horsham, PA: LRP Publications, 2004.

Ramirez, Clifford A., *Managing the Privacy of Student Records: A Textbook of FERPA Basics.* Horsham, PA: LRP Publications, 2002.

Ramirez, Clifford A., *Managing the Privacy of Student Records: The Leader's Guide.* Horsham, PA: LRP Publications, 2002.

West's Encyclopedia of American Law. Rochester, NY: West Publishing Company, Thomson West, 1998.

Newsletters, Pamphlets, and Disclosures

Balancing Student Privacy and School Safety: A Guide to the Family Educational Rights and Privacy Act for Colleges and Universities. Washington, DC: U.S. Department of Education, Family Policy Compliance Office, October 2007.

Epstein, Joel. *Prevention Updates: The Higher Education Amendments.* Newton, MA: The Higher Education Center for Alcohol and Other Drug Prevention, June 1999.

Experian and Hudson Cook LLP. *The Red Flags Rule: An Experian White Paper.* Experian Information Solutions, Inc., 2008.

Feder, Jody, *The Family Educational Rights and Privacy Act: A Legal Overview.* CRS Report for Congress, RS 222341. Congressional Research Service, Washington D.C.: The U.S. Library of Congress, November 2005.

Joint Guidance on the Application of the Family Educational Rights and Privacy Act (FERPA) and the Health Insurance Portability and Accountability Act of 1996

(HIPAA) to Student Health Records. Washington, DC: U.S. Department of Health and Human Services and the U.S. Department of Education, November 2008.

Student and Exchange Visitor Information System: General Summary Quarterly Review for the Quarter Ending September 30, 2008. Washington, DC:U.S. Immigration & Customs Enforcement, October 7, 2008.

Summary of the HIPPA Privacy Rule. U.S. Department of Health & Human Services, Office of Civil Rights, OCR Privacy Brief, HIPAA Compliance Assistance, 2003.

Wheeler, Elizabeth A., *Legal Update for Teachers.* Malvern, PA: Center for Education & Employment Law, Progressive Business Publications, February 2009.

Web Publications

en.wikipedia.org/wiki/USA_PATRIOT_Act"U.S.A PATRIOT Act." Wikipedia, The Free Encyclopedia.

epic.org/privacy/1974act/The Privacy Act of 1974. Electronic Privacy Information Center, August 26, 2003

epic.org/privacy/student/Student Privacy. Electronic Privacy Information Center (EPIC), November 30, 2005.

epic.org/privacy/terrorism/usapatriot/The U.S.A. PATRIOT Act. Electronic Privacy Information Center, November 17, 2005.

exchanges.state.gov/jexchanges/sevis.html. The Student and Exchange Visitor Information System (SEVIS), U.S. Department of State.

www.9–11commission.gov. National Commission on Terrorist Attacks Upon the United States, National Archives, 2004.

www.answers.com/topic/section-1983–1"Section 1983." Law Encyclopedia, West's Encyclopedia of American Law, The Gale Group, 1998.

www.auschwitz.dk/Allen.htm. Allen Schindler Memorial, The Holocaust, Crimes, Heroes, and Villains.

www.cato.org/pubs/wtpapers/991201paper.html. "Privacy and Human Rights: Comparing the United States to Europe." Singleton Solveig, CATO White Papers. CATO Institute, 1999.

www.defenselink.mil/privacy/opinions/op002.htm. Defense Privacy Board Advisory Opinions: Privacy Rights and Deceased Persons. U.S. Department of Defense, September 23, 1998.

www.e2campus.com/jeanne_clery_act_story.htm. Jeanne Clery Act Story, e2Campus.

www.ed.gov/print/policy/gen/guid/fpco/ferpa/library/aacrao.html. Letter to AACRAO re SEVIS and Disclosures to DHS/ICE. Family Policy Compliance Office, U.S. Department of Education, August 27, 2004.

www.ftc.gov/bcp/edu/pubs/business/alerts/alt050.shtm. "New 'Red Flags Rule' Requirements for Financial Institutions and Creditors Will Help Fight Identity Theft." FTC Business Alert, Federal Trade Commission, January 15, 2009.

www.ftc.gov/opa/2009/04/redflagsrule.shtm. "FTC Will Grant Three-Month Delay of Enforcement of 'Red Flags' Rule Requiring Creditors and Financial Institutions to Adopt Identity Theft Prevention Programs." FTC Business Alert, Federal Trade Commission, April 30, 2009.www.hunter.house.gov/2009/02/hunter-introduces-the-fairness-for-miitary-recruiters-act"Hunter Introduces the Fairness for Military Recruiters Act," Congressman Duncan D. Hunter, U.S. House of Representatives, 2009.

www.insidehighered.com/layout/set/print/news/2008/12/09/ferpa. "Rules Seek to Clarify FERPA." Inside Higher Ed, December 9, 2008.

www.lawlink.nsw.gov.au/lawlink/lrc/ll_lrc.nsf/vwPrint1/LRC_cp01chp4. "Constitution Paper 1 (2007) – Invasion of Privacy: Privacy in the United States: 4. Privacy in the United States." Lawlink, 2007.

www.nacubo.org/x10808.xml?ss=pf. "FTC's Red Flags Rule Likely to Affect Colleges." National Association of College & University Business Officers, September 23, 2008.

www.privacyrights.org/ar/fairinfo.htm. "A Review of the Fair Information Principles: The Foundation of Privacy Public Policy." Privacy Rights Clearinghouse/UCAN. Privacy Rights Clearinghouse, 1997–2006.

www.rbs2.com/privacy.htm. "Privacy Law in the U.S.A." Ronald B. Standler, RBS2.com, 1996.

www.securitydirectornews.com/?p=article&id=sd200902NrYX30. "House Passes Bill for National Campus Security Center." Leischen Stelter, Security Director News, United Publications, February 2009.

www.securityoncampus.org/congress/cscpa/index.html. "Campus Sex Crimes Prevention Act." Security on Campus, 2005.

www.securityoncampus.org/lawyers/doegonzaga.html. John Doe v Gonzaga University, No. 69456–7. Security on Campus, May 2001.

www.ssa.gov/history/briefhistory3.html. "Historical Background and Development of Social Security." U.S. Social Security Administration, Social Security Online, March 2003.

www.September11News.com. September 11 News, The Archives of Global Change in the 21st Century.

www.whitehouse.gov/infocus/patriotact. U.S.A Patriot Act, White House, March 9, 2006.

Websites

911digitalarchive.org: 9/11: Digital Archive, Center for History and News Media.

bioguide.congress.gov: Biographical Directory of the U.S. Congress.

bulk.resource.org: Public.Resource.Org.

cspr.org: Computer Professionals for Social Responsibility.

law.jrank.org: Law Library – American Law & Legal Information, Net Industries.

maplight.org: Money and Politics: Illuminating the Connection.

supct.law.cornell.edu: Supreme Court of the United States, Cornell University Law School.

www.9–11–2001.org: 9/11.org.

www.aacrao.org: American Association of Collegiate Registrars and Admissions Officers

www.amw.com: America's Most Wanted.

www.answers.com: Answers.com Encyclopedia.

www.archive.org: U.S.A Government Documents.

www.cdt.org: Center for Democracy and Technology.

www.chronicle.com: The Chronicle of Higher Education.

www.clhe.org: Council on Law in Higher Education.

www.coe.int: Council of Europe. Paris, France.

www.cnn.com: CNN News.

www.definitions.uslegal.com: U.S. Legal Definitions.

www.dhs.gov: U.S. Department of Homeland Security.

www.dictionary.law.com: Law.Com Dictionary.

www.ed.gov: U.S. Department of Education.

www.edc.org/hec/: The Higher Education Center for Alcohol and Other Drug Prevention.

www.educationworld.com: Education World, Inc.

www.epic.org: Electronic Privacy Information Center.

www.fbi.gov: Federal Bureau of Investigation.

www.fra.org: Fleet Reserve Association.

www.ftc.gov: U.S. Federal Trade Commission.

www.govtrack.us: A Civic Project to Track Congress.

www.hb-rights.org: Hollis Brookline Rights.

www.hhs.gov: U.S. Department of Health and Human Services.

www.hipaa.org: Health Insurance Portability and Accountability Act.

www.ice.gov: U.S. Immigration and Customs Enforcement.

www.impliedconsent.org: Implied Consent.org.

www.insidehighered.com: Inside Higher Ed.

www.law.com: Law.com Law Dictionary, The People's Law Dictionary, London, UK.

www.lawcore.com: LawCore.

www.law.jrank.org: Law Library – American Law and Legal Information.

www.leclaw.com: 'Lectric Law Library.

www.thefreedictionary.com: The Free Legal Dictionary.

www.manhattanda.org: Office of the New York County District Attorney.

www.nacubo.org: National Association of College and University Business Officers.

www.nalp.org: National Association for Legal Career Professionals.

www.nndb.com: NNDB – Tracking the Entire World. Notable Names Database Weblog.

www.nycourts.gov/lawlibraries/glossary.shtml: Law Libraries, New York Unified Court System.

www.oiss.ca.gov: California Office of Information Security and Privacy Protection, State of California.

www.ojp.usdoj.gov: Office of Justice Programs, U.S. Department of Justice.

www.opencongress.org: Open Congress.org.

www.oyez.org: U.S. Supreme Court Media.

www.pacode.com: The Pennsylvania Code, State of Pennsylvania.

www.pbs.org: Public Broadcasting Service.

www.pcmag.com: PC Magazine.

www.privacyrights.org: Privacy Rights Clearinghouse.

www.privcom.gc.ca: Office of the Privacy Commissioner of Canada.

www.roa.org: Reserved Officers Association.

www.securit.com: Securit Information Security, Ontario, Canada.

www.securityfocus.com: SecurityFocus, Symantac Corporation, Calgary, Alberta, Canada.

www.securityoncampus.org: Security on Campus, Inc.

www.shredit.com: American Privacy Laws and Legislation – Shred It, Ontario, Canada.

www.spartacus.schoolnet.co.uk: Spartacus Educational, United Kingdom.

www.theregister.com: The Register, London, England.

www.ushmm.org: U.S. Holocaust Memorial Museum.

www.washingtonwatch.com: Washington Watch.com.

www.whitehouse.gov/omb/: U.S. Office of Management and Budget.

www.wikipedia.org: Wikipedia: The Free Encyclopedia.

www.wired.com: Wired.

Other Media

Ramirez, Clifford A. *FERPA: What You Can and Can't Release* (audiocassette), Horsham, PA: LRP Publications, 2004.

FERPA Fundamentals: What Higher Education Administrators Should Know (video). Horsham, PA: LRP Publications, 2004.

Index